In Our Own Voices

IN OUR OWN VOICES

Latino/a Renditions of Theology

Edited by
BENJAMÍN VALENTÍN

ORBIS BOOKS

Maryknoll, New York 10545

Founded in 1970, Orbis Books endeavors to publish works that enlighten the mind, nourish the spirit, and challenge the conscience. The publishing arm of the Maryknoll Fathers and Brothers, Orbis seeks to explore the global dimensions of the Christian faith and mission, to invite dialogue with diverse cultures and religious traditions, and to serve the cause of reconciliation and peace. The books published reflect the views of their authors and do not represent the official position of the Maryknoll Society. To learn more about Maryknoll and Orbis Books, please visit our website at www.maryknollsociety.org.

Published by Orbis Books, Maryknoll, New York 10545-0302.

Queries regarding rights and permissions should be addressed to: Orbis Books, P.O. Box 302, Maryknoll, New York 10545-0302.

Manufactured in the United States of America.

Library of Congress Cataloging-in-Publication Data

In our own voices : Latino/a renditions of theology / [edited by] Benjamin Valentin.
   p. cm.
  Includes bibliographical references and index.
  ISBN 978-1-57075-890-4 (pbk.)
  1. Hispanic American theology. I. Valentin, Benjamin.
  BT83.575.I5 2010
  230.089'68073—dc22
                               2010006839

Contents

Contributors

Roberto S. Goizueta is Margaret O'Brien Flatley Professor of Catholic Theology at Boston College, Boston, Massachusetts.

Michelle A. González is assistant professor of religious studies at University of Miami, Coral Gables, Florida.

Ada María Isasi-Díaz is professor of ethics and theology at Drew University Theological School, Madison, New Jersey.

Michael E. Lee is assistant professor of theology at Fordham University, Bronx, New York.

Carmen Nanko-Fernández is associate professor of pastoral ministry and director of the Ecumenical Doctor of Ministry program at Catholic Theological Union, Chicago, Illinois.

Harold J. Recinos is professor of church and society at Perkins School of Theology (Southern Methodist University), Dallas, Texas.

Luis N. Rivera-Pagán is emeritus professor of ecumenics at Princeton Theological Seminary, Princeton, New Jersey.

Jeanette Rodríguez is professor of theology and religious studies at Seattle University, Seattle, Washington.

Benjamín Valentín is professor of theology and culture and director of the Orlando E. Costas Lectureship in Latino/a Theology at Andover Newton Theological School, Newton Centre, Massachusetts.

Acknowledgments

I would like to thank all past, present, and future Latino/a theologians for contributing to the development of a discursive tradition worthy of recognition, engagement, and furtherance: a discursive tradition known as Latino/a theology. A hearty thanks is due to my beloved wife, Karina, not only for her unceasing support and understanding but also for help with manuscript preparation. As usual, I thank my colleagues and friends at Andover Newton Theological School for providing me with supportive space in which to work. And last but not least I thank Robert Ellsberg and all the folk at Orbis not only for their help in making this book a reality but also for their support of U.S. Latino/a theology and other forms and expressions of contextual and liberation theology throughout the years.

Introduction

Benjamín Valentín

In previous publications I have extolled the ingenuity and accomplishments of U.S. Hispanic/Latino(a) theology, and for very good reasons too.[1] We are after all talking about a theological tradition that has burst forth with all sorts of important interpretive innovations in the last thirty years or so. U.S. Hispanic/Latino(a) theology has heralded such influential theological innovations as the theorization of *mestizaje* (i.e., cultural hybridity) and popular religion; the portrayal of the historical Jesus as a Jewish *mestizo*—that is, as a kind of first-century "borderlands" Jew who stood at the margins of both Jewish and Gentile society; the exposition of a Chicano/a theology of liberation; the unveiling of the religious dimensions of art, literature, and other forms of creative Latino/a cultural expressions; the elaboration of a distinctive women's theology of liberation; the interpretation of biblical material through the lenses of prevalent Latino/a experiences; the promotion of postcolonial studies within biblical hermeneutics; the formulation of a distinctive Christian ethics based on Latino(a) notions of *dignidad*; the articulation of a liberating urban mission for the church or churches; the presentation of a Latino/a theological anthropology; the description of a liberationist Latino/a public theology; the suggestion of a new understanding of divine transcendence; and many other innovative developments.[2]

This is quite an impressive list of accomplishments, to say the least. It is also a list of achievement that has gradually drawn the attention of many within the theological and religious academy. This is an amazing feat in and of itself, given the dynamics of disrespect and neglect with which Latino/a scholars and Latinos/as in general have often had to contend in all sectors of our society. What's more, Latino/a theology has often been mistakenly identified, equated, or lumped together with the liberationist theologies that have emerged in Mexico and in the Spanish-speaking countries of the Caribbean Basin and of Central and South America. People who study, follow, or do theology have not always been discerning enough to realize that, though influenced in certain respects by the justice-seeking theological address that emerged in different parts of Latin

America, Latino/a theology is a distinct theological tradition that is bred and based in the United States. Followers of theology have not regularly realized, in other words, that this theological voice flows from the thought, writings, and activities of a heterogeneous group of theologians and religious scholars, composed of people who can trace their ancestry in some way or another to different parts of Spanish-speaking Latin America but yet call the United States their home. Despite these troubling patterns of neglect and oversight, however, Latino/a theology has managed to establish its own identity and to gain deserved notice along the way. And I dare say that this growing recognition is largely attributable to the impressive list of theological innovations just mentioned.

This list of thematic pursuits and innovative feats gives witness to a hale and hearty resourcefulness and originality in Latino/a theology. What it offers less evidence of, however, is an outright and persistent interest either in the study of classical theological themes, symbols, and doctrines, or in the analysis of our recent handling of them. It is reasonable to claim that the effort to interpret, to evaluate, and to reformulate the meanings of themes or doctrines such as God, Creation, human nature, human sin, Christ, the church, and eschatology, for instance, has received sparse consideration in the works of Latino/a theologians. To put it plainly, although some of this sort of theological work can be found within it, the archives of Latino/a theology are not exactly replete with this kind of formal, systematic, and reconstructive pursuit. I will note that to date the only representative illustration of a full-fledged Latino/a "systematic theology" one can point to is found in Justo Gonzalez's book *Mañana: Christian Theology from a Hispanic Perspective*. This book was published in 1990, and yet it is still the *only* thorough work in systematic theology written by a Latino or Latina author. And although one can find within the annals of Latino/a theology two anthologies that wander over the possible significance of certain Christian doctrines (i.e., *Teologia en Conjunto* [1997] and *Building Bridges, Doing Justice* [2009]), and a few single-authored books that look into individual doctrines in more length, these are neither plenteous nor, in some cases, thoroughgoing in their doctrinal analysis. Notable too is the fact that some doctrines or subject matters such as the doctrine of God, the different theories of atonement, eschatology, and the work of a Christian theology of religions have yet to be taken up in any substantive manner within Latino/a theology. And even in those cases where we have written much on a particular subject, such as in the case of the topic of Jesus Christ and the topic of theological anthropology, we Latino/a theologians have either not yet or not often taken the step to interpret, to scrutinize, or to extend the contours of our distinctive handling and rendering of it.

There may be some good reasons or at least understandable reasons for this general remissness. To begin with, U.S. Latino/a theology has had to focus on matters of methodology and the discovery of inbred theological sources in order to hit upon its discursive distinctiveness. It is understandable too that Latino/a theology would want to explore and bring into use new themes and motifs within the theological discussion. Indeed, it is even possible that some within the Latino/a theological community might deem the study of conventional themes or doctrines a limiting, boring, and outmoded enterprise in these late modern or postmodern times. Then again, it is also true that not all Latino/a theologians are trained as or identify themselves as systematic or constructive theologians. The truth is that only a handful of us respond to this particular calling, as others in our community identify with the vocation of the religious scholar/historiographer, or of the biblical interpreter, or of the church historian, or of the ethicist, or of some other area of specialization. All of these factors are real and sensible, and each can be said to bear a part in the sparseness and transience of doctrinal analysis found within Latino/a theology.

That being said, it is neither unreasonable nor unsound to put in a behest for a greater level of reflection on matters of doctrine or on the configurations of classical theological themes within Latino/a theology. As I see it, it is important that we take up this charge—that we take up the task of interpreting, scrutinizing, and reformulating the meanings of doctrines and theological terms—because the pursuit of theology not only calls for it but is even to a certain extent defined by it. Theology is certainly made up of many subdisciplines and can incorporate many reflective quests. Never to be forgotten among these tasks, however, is the task of interpreting, evaluating, and expounding upon the symbols, religious worldviews, and articles of faith that make up the Christian tradition. While these religious worldviews and propositions can be embodied in and expressed through texts and practices, they are also embodied in and set forth by way of symbolic constructs, core verbal depictions of life, meaningful themes, terms, and/or "doctrines" that require not only interpretation but also evaluation and emendation every now and again. This is all to say that we Latino/a theologians cannot evade the onus of a more systematic and reconstructive treatment of the basic symbols, themes, and doctrines of Christian theology. Besides, it is my belief both that there are enough of us to take on this particular charge on a more regular basis and that we Latino/a theologians can make a great contribution to the field of theology by way of the interpretation, evaluation, and reconstruction of the various Christian doctrines from a uniquely Latino/a point of view. To be clear, I don't want to give the impression that we haven't already been doing so, because plainly we have. Rather, I am simply suggesting that we can add to our theological ingenuity by exploring the possible meanings and applicability of the different Christian symbols, concepts, and doctrines more often and in a more methodical and intentional manner.

This volume seeks to contribute to the discussion of key theological concepts and doctrines within Latino/a theology specifically and in the field of theology more generally. Not concerned about any other subject matter or interest besides the treatment of Christian motifs and doctrines from a Latino/a point of view, it will attempt to cast light on some of the ways in which Latino/a theologians have either given thought to or can reconsider and reformulate the contours or meanings of key theological concepts. Six basic theological concepts, doctrines, or themes are dealt with in all: the concepts and/or doctrines of God, Creation, the nature of human *being*, Christ and/or Christology, the nature and present-day mission of the church or Christian churches, and eschatology.

The book opens with an essay written by Luis Rivera-Pagán, entitled "God the Liberator: Theology, History, and Politics." At first glance this piece strikes one as being a summary of the emergence and development of liberation theology—and a very good and thorough one at that. A deeper reading will reveal, however, that it offers even more than a perceptive recapitulation of the history of the liberation theology movement; it also calls attention to and extends an endorsement to liberation theology's novel way of thinking about God as "Liberator." God, Rivera-Pagán notes, is reconceived by the different theologies of liberation not as an immutable and impassible entelechy but, according to the biblical narratives, as a compassionate Eternal Spirit that hears and pays close attention to the cry of the oppressed and whose action in human history has the redemption of the downtrodden and excluded as its ultimate telos. This way of thinking about God is important in our times, he claims, as it makes provision for a view of God that transcends the limited depictions of religious fundamentalism and dogmatic secularism and offers a source of hope for many. Herein potentially lies Hispanic/Latino(a) liberation theology's main theoretical epistemological rupture and theological reconfiguration, Rivera-Pagán intimates: Instead of contriving arcane scholastic definitions of divine essence, it can think of and speak of God as Liberator.

The volume's second essay, entitled "La Tierra Theologies' Contribution to Creation Theologies," deals generally with the topic of Creation, and specifically with the conception of the earth as God's beautiful creation. In this article Jeanette Rodríguez articulates what she calls a theology of "La Tierra" (i.e., a theology of and for earth), and joins her perspective to the voices of indigenous elders, ecologists, and Hispanic/Latino(a) theologians to imagine new and hopeful ways to affirm the world at large. Her hope is to stimulate the blossoming of "La Tierra Theologies"—that is, theologies that affirm life, honor the earth, and promote the value of a holistic sensibility and a sustainable way of living.

The third essay also deals with the topic of Creation. Tendered by Carmen Nanko-Fernández and entitled "Creation: A Cosmo-politan Perspective," this essay employs a postcolonial lens in a critical analysis of select Latino/a theologians and their sources for theologizing on themes of creation. Nanko-Fernández's essay specifically examines the writings of Jeanette Rodríguez, Alejandro García-Rivera, and Virgilio Elizondo and focuses on their respective considerations of la tierra (the earth), cosmic fellowship among creatures, and mestizaje as new creation. Although appreciative of the theological works of these authors, Nanko-Fernández notes that they tender little attention to the role of the city as a locus for theological reflection, even though urban contexts are home to a majority of the Hispanic population and serve as a key theme in the work of several Latino/a biblical scholars. In face of this inattention, she both calls for and takes initial steps toward the elaboration of a postcolonial, urban hermeneutic in the development of creation theologies. Nanko-Fernández proposes that a "cosmo-politan" perspective offers a more nuanced retrieval of sources, posits a more integrated appreciation for the complexity of the relationship between cosmos and polis, and presents possibilities for new trajectories in Latino/a considerations of origins and ends.

With the fourth essay, "Who We Are: A Latino/a Constructive Anthropology," we move from the subject matter of Creation to the question of human nature and identity, or what is often referred to as the subject of theological anthropology. Written by Michelle González, this essay explores the distinctive emphases and hallmarks of Latino/a theological anthropology. After a brief overview of theological anthropology as it functions within systematic theology more generally, González throws light on four themes that appear frequently within the works of Latino/a theologians and that she believes form the basis for a unique Hispanic/Latino(a) rendering of the nature and purpose of humankind: these are mestizaje/mulatez or plurality and difference, community/family, interdependence/relatedness, and grace and culture.

The fifth and sixth essays of the book deal with the topic of Christology. My essay, "Who Do We Say He Was and Is? Jesus and Christology among Latino/a Theologians," takes the first stab at the subject of Latino/a Christology. The piece reviews the work of three Latino/a theologians who have contributed to the christological discussion: Virgilio Elizondo, Marina Herrera, and Luis Pedraja. This review includes not only an examination of the themes that appear in these works but also an evaluation of the importance and vulnerabilities of these works. The essay then proceeds to elucidate three patterns of christological thought in the writings of Elizondo, Herrera, and Pedraja. In this interpretive segment of the essay I suggest that the writings of these three Latino/a theologians display a gravitation toward a Christology from below, a high Christology, and a liberationist Christology. Michael Lee puts forth the second essay on Christology and the book's sixth essay overall, "A Way Forward for Latino/a Christology." This essay does Christology from the context of a growing divide between two accounts of the Latino/a experience in the United States. It suggests that while Latino/a Christology must continue to affirm and empower those Latinos/as who suffer unjustly, it must also assume a stance in relation to those segments of the Latino/a population that have achieved a measure of power and "success." Lee submits that Latino/a Christology can accomplish this dual task by complementing the rhetoric of empowerment with a rhetoric of kenosis.

The seventh and eighth essays of the book attend to the question of the nature and mission of the church—that is, to the subject of ecclesiology. The first of these two essays, entitled "The Church: A Latino Catholic Perspective," is put forward by Roberto S. Goizueta. Drawing on classic ecclesiological models, especially as articulated by Avery Dulles, this essay examines the key features of a Catholic perspective on the church. The essay analyzes the interrelationships among these six models of the church, and then proceeds to suggest that, when viewed from the perspective of contemporary U.S. Latino/a experience and the theologies emerging from that experience, a critical retrieval of these models would highlight particular aspects of the notion of the church that can be liberating and countercultural vis-à-vis both the larger church and society. Such a contextual ecclesiology will accord—and has accorded—special significance to certain images of the church such as: (1) communio; (2) sacrament; (3) people of God ("el pueblo de Dios"); (4) the crucified people ("pueblo crucificado"); and (5) a church of the borderlands. In the book's eighth essay, "Transforming Ecclesiology: Hip-Hop Matters," Harold J. Recinos explores the topic of the mainline Protestant Church's identity and mission from a unique angle—that is, from the standpoint of hip-hop culture. The wider society, he notes, often thinks that Latino youth in the barrio are lawless, reckless, meritless, and threatening. But these young people at the edges of society who are systematically disadvantaged by poverty, political marginalization, inadequate education, and discrimination have produced a hip-hop culture that describes how to live in a less crucifying world. His essay examines aspects of rap music produced by Latino rappers and shows how feelings of alienation and agency expressed through this expressive form call forth new ways of thinking about church and community.

The book's final essay, "Kin-dom of God: A Mujerista Proposal," touches on the subject of eschatology by way of an inquiry into the meaning of the biblical metaphor of the "kingdom of God." In this essay Ada María Isasi-Díaz looks briefly at what the metaphor "kingdom of God" has come to mean. She argues that the prevalent interpretation of this concept or metaphor in our day and age betrays the meaning and intention of this metaphor in the Gospels and has led to elitist, autocratic, and patriarchal conceptions that are simply oppressive. Isasi-Díaz proposes that the true meaning of the metaphor "kingdom of God" is best captured today by the notion of the "kin-dom of God" or "la familia de Dios/the family of God." She suggests that, given the importance of family in Latina/o culture, the notion of the "kin-dom of God" can have great resonance in Latina/o communities and can help to make the Gospel message a very concrete reality. The concept of "kin-dom of God" can have liberating implications beyond the Latina/o communities, however, as it can bring us to a revaluation of the ideals of fellowship, generosity, and equality.

That the essays in this book are different in tone and in form should already be obvious. Some of the essays are descriptive and interpretive in nature, while others are constructive and/or prescriptive. Some of the essays contain critical assessments either of Latino/a theological constructs or of wider theological trends, while others do not. And it should already be apparent that the essays enclosed divulge distinct approaches to their respective topics. This heterogeneity is not to be deemed a sign of incongruity or deviation, however. To begin with, variety is always to be expected in a multiauthored volume such as this. In addition, one could say that the multiformity communicated by this volume is to be embraced and celebrated, as it is a sign that Hispanic/Latino(a) theology has matured to the point that it includes a wide variety of perspectives, approaches, and tonalities. Furthermore, despite their diversity when it comes to approach, method, and style, it should not be ignored that the essays contained in this book join together in a number of ways. First, all of the essays in this volume inquire into the contours and meanings of classical Christian themes and doctrines. This shows that at some level they each deem the symbols, orienting ideas, concepts, and convictions of Christian theology as worthy subjects. Second, the essays in this volume unite in the belief that we Latino/a theologians have made and can continue to make a great contribution to the field of theology by way of the interpretation, evaluation, and reconstruction of the various Christian doctrines from a uniquely Latino/a point of view. Taken together, then, the essays collected here serve to call attention to some of the ways in which Latino/a theologians have been giving voice to theology and can continue to give voice to theology in a uniquely Latino/a way—that is, in a voice of our own.

Notes

1. For instance, see my essay "Strangers No More: An Introduction to, and an Interpretation of, U.S. Hispanic/Latino(a) Theology," in *The Ties That Bind: African American and Hispanic American/Latino(a) Theologies in Dialogue*, ed. Anthony B. Pinn and Benjamín Valentín (New York: Continuum International, 2001), and "Oye, Y Ahora Qué?/Say, Now What? Prospective Lines of Development for U.S. Hispanic/Latino(a) Theology," in *New Horizons in Hispanic/Latino(a) Theology*, ed. Benjamín Valentín (Cleveland, Ohio: Pilgrim Press, 2003).

2. For "some" examples of these themes, see especially the following authors and works: (1) on the interpretation and theological usage of *mestizaje*, Virgilio Elizondo, *Galilean Journey: The Mexican-American Promise* (Maryknoll, N.Y.: Orbis Books, 1983); and *The Future is Mestizo: Life Where Cultures Meet* (Bloomington, Ind.: Meyer-Stone Books, 1988); (2) on the theorizing of Latino/a popular religion, Orlando Espín, *The Faith of the People: Theological Reflections on Popular Catholicism* (Maryknoll, N.Y.: Orbis Books, 1997); Alex García-Rivera, *St. Martin de Porres: The "Little Stories" and the Semiotics of Culture* (Maryknoll, N.Y.: Orbis Books, 1995); and Jeanette Rodríguez, *Our Lady of Guadalupe: Faith and Empowerment among Mexican-American Women* (Austin: University of Texas Press, 1994); (3) on the portrayal of Jesus as a Jewish *mestizo*, Elizondo, *Galilean Journey*; (4) on the elaboration of a Chicano theology, Andrés G. Guerrero, *A Chicano Theology* (Maryknoll, N.Y.: Orbis Books, 1987); (5) on the valuation of aesthetics, Roberto Goizueta Jr., *Caminemos con Jesus: Toward a Hispanic/Latino Theology of Accompaniment* (Maryknoll, N.Y.: Orbis Books, 1995); Alex García-Rivera, *The Community of the Beautiful: A Theological Aesthetics* (Collegeville, Minn.: Liturgical Press, 1999); (6) on the elaboration of a *mujerista* theology, Ada María Isasi-Díaz, *En La Lucha/In the Struggle: A Hispanic Women's Liberation Theology* (Minneapolis: Fortress Press, 1993); and eadem, *Mujerista Theology: A Theology for the Twenty-first Century* (Maryknoll, N.Y.: Orbis Books, 1996); (7) on the reading of the Bible through Hispanic eyes, Justo L. González, *Santa Biblia: The Bible through Hispanic Eyes* (Nashville: Abingdon Press, 1996); (8) on postcolonial biblical hermeneutics, Fernando Segovia, *Decolonizing Biblical Studies: A View from the Margins* (Maryknoll, N.Y.: Orbis Books, 2000); (9) on Christian ethics from a Hispanic/Latino(a) perspective, Ismael García, *Dignidad: Ethics through Hispanic Eyes* (Nashville: Abingdon Press, 1997); (10) on an urban/barrio ecclesiology, Harold J. Recinos, *Hear the Cry: A Latino Pastor Challenges the Church* (Louisville: Westminster/John Knox Press, 1989); and idem,

Who Comes in the Name of the Lord? Jesus at the Margins (Nashville: Abingdon Press, 1997); (11) on a Latino/a theological anthropology, Miguel H. Díaz, *On Being Human: U.S. Hispanic and Rahnerian Perspectives* (Maryknoll, N.Y.: Orbis Books, 2001); and Michelle A. González, *Created in God's Image: An Introduction to Feminist Theological Anthropology* (Maryknoll, N.Y.: Orbis Books, 2007); (12) on the elaboration of a Latino/a liberationist public theology, Benjamín Valentín, *Mapping Public Theology: Beyond Culture, Identity, and Difference* (Harrisburg, Pa.: Trinity Press International, 2002); (13) and on the suggestion of new understandings of divine transcendence, Mayra Rivera, *The Touch of Transcendence: A Postcolonial Theology of God* (Louisville: Westminster John Knox Press, 2007).

1

God the Liberator

Theology, History, and Politics

Luis N. Rivera-Pagán

In memory of Marcella Althaus-Reid

The Bible . . . unlike the books of other ancient peoples, was . . . the
literature of a minor, remote people—and not the literature of its
rulers, but of its critics. The scribes and the prophets of Jerusalem
refused to accept the world as it was. They invented the literature of
political dissent and, with it, the literature of hope.
—Amos Elon, *Jerusalem: Battlegrounds of Memory*

The Bible is . . . an incendiary device: who knows what we'd make of
it, if we ever got our hands on it?
—Margaret Atwood, *The Handmaid's Tale*

A Theological *Enfant Terrible*

L iberation theology was the unforeseen *enfant terrible* in the academic
and ecclesial realms of theological production during the last decades of
the twentieth century. It brought to the conversation not only a new theme—
liberation—but also a new perspective on doing theology and a novel way of
referring to God's being and action in history. Its project to reconfigure the interplay between religious studies, history, and politics became a meaningful and
unavoidable topic of analysis and dialogue in the general theological discourse.
This has led many scholars to perceive in its emergence a drastic epistemological
rupture, a radical change in paradigm, a significant shift in both the ecclesial and
social role of theology.

Its origins are diverse, and not only native to theological and ecclesiastical horizons. One important source, neglected by some clerical accounts, was the complex constellation of liberation struggles during the sixties and early seventies. It was a time of social turmoil, when many things seemed out of joint: a strong antiwar movement protest, mainly directed against American military intervention in Vietnam and the global nuclear threat; a spread of decolonization movements all over the Third World; the feminist struggle against masculine patriarchy; a robust challenge to racial bigotry; the Stonewall rebellion (June 1969) against homophobia and gay discrimination; student protests in Paris, Prague, Mexico, and New York in opposition to repressive states of all stripes; guerilla insurgencies and social unrest in many Latin American nations. Many of these agents of social protest adopted the title of "liberation movement" as their public card of presentation. "Fronts of national liberation" flourished all over the Third World.[1]

Another significant factor was the development of a nondogmatic Marxism that read Marx's texts as an ethical critique on human oppression and as a projection of a utopian nonoppressive future, sort of a kingdom of freedom. This heterodox way of reading Marx, by authors such as the German philosopher Ernst Bloch, made possible something up to then considered unthinkable—a constructive and affirmative dialogue between theology and Marxism—at the margins of church and party hierarchies' rigid orthodoxies. Influential in this intellectual milieu was Bloch's 1968 *Atheismus im Christentum*,[2] whose hermeneutical performance diagnoses inside the biblical texts a struggle between the voices of the oppressors and those of the oppressed and provocatively asserts that whoever wants to be a good Marxist should constantly read the Bible (and vice versa, whoever wants to be a good Christian should have Marx as bedside reading).

Other iconoclast authors such as Herbert Marcuse and Franz Fanon were passionately read from Buenos Aires to Berlin, from Berkeley to Nairobi, with intentionalities not limited to academia.[3] Exiled from Brazil, Paulo Freire delivered scathing critiques of traditional educational systems and promoted a pedagogy for the liberation of the oppressed.[4] Martin Luther King, Jr., and Ernesto "Che" Guevara are probably the main emblematic icons and martyrs of those turbulent times. Paul Éluard's poem "Liberté," recited and sung in many languages, became its poetic hymn.

Within the churches important processes were taking place. Pope John XXIII summoned, to the surprise of many, the Second Vatican Council. Progressive Roman Catholic theologians consider Vatican II an important turning point in the modern history of their church.[5] According to their interpretation, the council had three main objectives:

1. To change the attitude of the Roman Catholic Church toward the modern post-Enlightenment intellectual world, from censure and condemnation to openness and dialogue. The Italian word *aggiornamento* became the watchword of the attempts to update the church.

2. To heal the fragmentation of Christianity by inserting the Roman Catholic Church in the emerging ecumenical movement. Delegates from Protestant and Orthodox churches were invited to observe the proceedings of the council. A series of bilateral and multilateral dialogues began between Rome and other Christian denominations.

3. To face with honesty and compassion the plight of a world suffering violence, oppression, and injustice. The council took place in a world sundered by national liberation struggles, civil wars, and the painful gap between the haves and the have-nots of the globe. The quest for peace and justice was conceived as an essential dimension of the being in the world of the church.

John XXIII's 1963 encyclical *Pacem in terris*, published in the context of that conciliar process, seemed to be another sign of renewal, from an attitude of anathema to a spirit of dialogue and solidarity. This ecclesiastical openness was accompanied by several theological projects that seemed to shape an alternative way of looking at social conflicts.[6] An attempt was made to configure a "political theology," as a way to design a creative dialogue with Marxism and post-Enlightenment secular ideologies.[7]

Latin American Liberation Theology

Vatican II was followed by regional synods of bishops. The most famous of them was the general meeting of Latin American Roman Catholic bishops that took place August 26 to September 6, 1968, at Medellín, Colombia. To the amazement of many observers, the Roman Catholic Church, which the radical intelligentsia in the continent had considered the ideological bulwark of prevailing social inequities, was promulgating, as a decisive pastoral challenge, solidarity with the poor and destitute.

If Vatican II opened the theological dialogue with modern rationality, Medellín was perceived as a prophetic convocation against poverty, inequality, and oppression. If Vatican II was concerned mainly with the gap between the church and secular modernity, Medellín, according to this reading, was more concerned with the scandal of social injustice on a Christian continent. In a crucial section of their final resolutions, the Latin American bishops linked the Christian faith with historical and social liberation.

The Latin American bishops cannot remain indifferent in the face of the tremendous social injustices existent in Latin America, which keeps the majority of our peoples in dismal poverty that in many cases becomes inhuman wretchedness. A deafening cry pours from the throats of millions of men and women asking their pastors for a liberation that reaches them from nowhere . . . Christ, our savior, not only

loved the poor . . . but also centered his mission in announcing liberation to the poor.[8]

Certainly, the Medellín conference was a meeting of bishops, not of theologians. But several Roman Catholic theologians perceived the final documents
and the general tone prevailing in the conference as allowing the possibility
of rethinking the theological enterprise from the perspective of the liberation
of the poor and downtrodden.[9] Prior to the Medellín meeting, in July 1968,
Gustavo Gutiérrez had given a lecture at Chimbote, Perú, significantly entitled
"Toward a Theology of Liberation,"[10] which coupled closely spiritual salvation
and human liberation. It proved to be a pioneer text for Latin American liberation theology. It also inaugurated Gutiérrez's more than five decades of fertile
theological production.

In 1971 Gutiérrez published the first edition of his most famous book, *Theology of Liberation*, a landmark in Latin American theological writing. His
triadic understanding of human liberation—liberation from social and economic oppression, history as a process of self-determined humanization, and
redemption from sinfulness—became classic.[11] That same year also was published Hugo Assmann's book *Opresión—Liberación: Desafío a los cristianos*.
Assmann placed the emerging liberation theology in the wider context of the
Third World: "The contextual starting point of a 'theology of liberation' is
the historical situation of domination experienced by the peoples of the Third
World."[12] Gutiérrez and Assmann were followed by a spate of other theologians
(Leonardo Boff, José Porfirio Miranda, Juan Luis Segundo, Jon Sobrino, Pablo
Richard, among others) whose writings were conceived as expressions of a new
intellectual understanding of the faith: liberation theology.[13]

Among the many texts that rocked the placid realm of theological production during those early years of Latin American liberation theology were José
Porfirio Miranda's *Marx y la Biblia*, an important contribution to a liberationist
hermeneutics, sort of a theological companion to Bloch's *Atheismus im Christentum*, and Juan Luis Segundo's *Liberación de la teología*, with its frontal challenge to traditional scholastic ways of doing theology.[14]

What could be considered to be the main tenets of this theological
movement?

1. The retrieval of the subversive memories inscribed in the sacred scriptures, hidden below layers of cultic regulations and doctrinal orthodoxies, but never totally effaced. A specific hermeneutical and exegetical
   concentration in the Exodus story as a paradigm of the liberating character of God's actions,[15] in the prophetic denunciations of injustice and
   oppression,[16] and in the confrontations of the historical Jesus against
   the Judean religious authorities and Roman political powers and his
   solidarity with the nobodies of Judea and Galilee.[17]

2. A historical understanding of Jesus' proclamation of God's kingdom.
   The kingdom is conceived as referring not to some otherworldly post-

mortem realm, but to the unceasing hope of a social configuration characterized by justice, solidarity, and freedom. Leonardo Boff and Jon Sobrino perceive Jesus as the Liberator, going back to the semantic roots of the term *redemption* (the deliverance of a captive or slave).[18]

3. The divine preferential option for the poor, the excluded, and the destitute of this world. The church has to become the church of the poor, sharing their sorrows, hopes, and struggles. Initially the accent was mainly socioeconomic, but it was gradually widened to include other categories of social exclusion (indigenous communities, racial and ethnic minorities, and women).[19]

4. Theology cannot be reduced to an intellectual understanding of the faith, but must also be a practical commitment for historical transformation. The category of praxis, partly borrowed from Paulo Freire's pedagogy of liberation, partly an adaptation of Marx's eleventh thesis on Feuerbach ("philosophers have hitherto only interpreted the world in various ways; the point is to change it"), acquired normative status. History, therefore, as the realm of the perennial struggle against oppressions and exclusions, emerged as the locus for Christian praxis.[20]

5. God is reconceived not as an immutable and impassible entelechy but, according to the biblical narratives, as a compassionate Eternal Spirit that hears and pays close attention to the cry of the oppressed and whose action in human history has the redemption of the downtrodden and excluded as its ultimate telos. Herein might be located liberation theology's main theoretical epistemological rupture and reconfiguration:[21] a novel way of thinking about God's being and action in history. Instead of contriving arcane scholastic definitions of divine essence, God is referred to as Liberator.

Latin American liberation theology strove to forge a new way of being the church in the world: the base ecclesial communities as the seeds for reconfiguring the church as "the people of God." These congregations were considered expressions of the church's solidarity with the poor and oppressed in their aspirations for liberation and human promotion. An impressive wealth of liturgical, musical, exegetical, homiletic, ethical, and literary resources was produced to promote social and human emancipation. Historical transformation was their key theme. Leonardo Boff even advocated a new genesis of the church.[22]

However, many in the hierarchical church, including some members of the Roman curia apex, viewed with marked distrust their potential disruptions of episcopal authority and moved to restrict their autonomy. Rome was also concerned about the consequences for dogmatic orthodoxy of this new theological perspective. A long protracted confrontation ensued that still goes on.

Political power matters. Since their colonial inception, an official linkage between the state and the Roman Catholic Church characterized Latin American nations. The royal patronage exercised by the Iberian crown entailed the acknowledgment by the church of the sovereignty and authority of the metropolitan state, but also the state's recognition of the Roman Catholic Church's primacy in religious affairs. It was sometimes the source of acute conflicts, whenever the ethical conscience of bishops, priests, missionaries, and theologians clashed with the severe exploitation of the native communities. Bartolomé de las Casas, to whose historical significance Gustavo Gutiérrez devoted a magnificent book,[23] is the most famous protagonist of such conflicts. Yet it was a convenient arrangement for both partners, for it conferred a sacred aura to the metropolitan sovereignty and conversely provided the church with state protection. The governments of the new states that emerged after the nineteenth century wars of independence promptly recognized the advantages of the royal patronage and tried to preserve it. This heritage forged a particular brand of Latin American Christendom closely linking the state and the Roman Catholic Church, a condition juridically inscribed in several national constitutions and Vatican concordats.

This official connection between church and state was venerable but also vulnerable. The prophetic and evangelical subversive memories inscribed in the Christian scriptures and traditions surfaced powerfully during the somber and violent times of Latin American military dictatorships (1964-1989) to shake the alliance between the political powers and church authorities. The most famous of the ensuing conflicts took place in the midst of the violent civil war in El Salvador, a place where nuns, priests, lay workers, and even the primate of the Roman Catholic Church, Archbishop Oscar Arnulfo Romero, were assassinated by the military or their right-wing allies.

Archbishop Romero tried to steer his church to become a defender of the poor and the persecuted. He recognized that the forbearance of the ruling clans was as limited as their economic interests were great. Two weeks before his assassination, in an interview to a Mexican newspaper, he foreshadowed his death and gave a theological and pastoral interpretation of his personal destiny.

> I have frequently been threatened with death . . . If God accepts the sacrifice of my life, then may my blood be the seed of liberty, and a sign of the hope that will soon become a reality . . . May my death, if it is accepted by God, be for the liberation of my people, and as a witness of hope in what is to come.[24]

His assassination convinced many church authorities that liberation theology was risking seriously the social well-being of the Roman Catholic Church and that a convenient long-standing church-state covenant was endangered by the radical political interventions of some members of the clergy. And they moved decisively to suppress it.

Ecclesiastical and social political considerations were not the only issues of concern for Vatican authorities. Doctrinal orthodoxy matters for the Roman Catholic Church. Under the prefecture of Cardinal Joseph Ratzinger, the Sacred Congregation for the Doctrine of the Faith strongly criticized what it considered liberation theology's ominous doctrinal deviations. On August 6, 1984, it issued, with the approval of Pope John Paul II, the admonishing "Instruction on Certain Aspects of the 'Theology of Liberation,'" followed by an admonition to Leonardo Boff, and another general critique, "Instruction on Christian Freedom and Liberation" (March 22, 1986). Liberation theology was indicted for borrowing improperly from Marxist thought, emphasizing historical and social liberation to the detriment of spiritual salvation, promoting class struggle instead of reconciliation, disdaining the church's social doctrine, and politicizing biblical hermeneutics, Christology, and the church. The goal of the authoritative reprimands was

> to draw attention . . . to the deviations and risks of deviation, damaging to the faith and to Christian living, that are brought by certain forms of liberation theology . . . the 'theologies of liberation' tend to misunderstand or to eliminate . . . the transcendence and gratuity of liberation in Jesus Christ, true God and true man . . . One needs to be on guard against the politicization of existence, which, misunderstanding the entire meaning of the kingdom of God and the transcendence of the person, begins to sacralize politics and betray the religion of the people in favor of the projects of revolution.[25]

Traditionally indictments like these were able to silence the accused theologians. Not this time. Prompt reactions by Gustavo Gutiérrez, Leonardo Boff, and Juan Luis Segundo were evident signs that Rome had lost the capability to repress the new theological movement.[26] A letter sent by John Paul II to the Brazilian bishops, dated April 9, 1986,[27] has been understood by several scholars as a truce of the growing dispute to avoid a sharp rupture in the Latin American church but also as a validation of the concept of social and political liberation as an important dimension of the church's pastoral mission. Several Roman Catholic theologians have sustained an effort to convince Rome that liberation theology is a valid and legitimate rethinking of the apostolic tradition that does not constitute a threat to the church's orthodoxy or integrity.[28] However, some influential sectors of the Roman curia still look askance at liberation theology, as evidenced by the Sacred Congregation for the Doctrine of the Faith's recent scathing critique of Jon Sobrino's Christology ("Notification on the Works of Father Jon Sobrino, SJ," 11/26/2006).[29]

Many Roman Catholic narratives disregard other sources that contributed to the birth of liberation theology. In the sixties, several Latin American Protestant churches were undergoing similar processes of rethinking the relationship between salvation, history as the sphere of divine-human encounter, and liberation.[30] In fact, the first extensive monograph that focused on historical and social liberation as the central hermeneutical key to conceptualize the Christian faith was the doctoral dissertation of Rubem Alves, a Brazilian Presbyterian. In May 1968, Alves defended successfully his dissertation at Princeton Theological Seminary. Its title was *Towards a Theology of Liberation*.[31] Alves wrote it under the direction of Richard Shaull, who for a good number of years had been working in theological education in Latin America, first in Colombia and later in Brazil, and who was crucial for the development of a liberationist theology in Protestant Latin American circles.[32] Shaull had also been instrumental in the 1970 English publication of Paulo Freire's *Pedagogy of the Oppressed*, a key text in the development of Latin American liberation theology.

Alves's dissertation is a powerful text, written in a splendid literary style. It was published as a book in 1969, two years before Gutiérrez's, but with a significant change in the title: *A Theology of Human Hope*. Apparently, the publishers believed that the concept of "hope," with its obvious connotations of the writings of Jürgen Moltmann, would be more commercially attractive or relevant than "liberation." Yet, despite the change of title, Alves conceptualizes the temporal dialectics proper to theological language in terms of a historical politics of liberation.

> The acts of remembering and hoping that determine the language of the community of faith, therefore, do not have any reality in themselves but in the engagement in the ongoing politics of liberation which is the situation and condition of theological intelligibility.[33]

Black Liberation Theology

But as it is wrong to locate the birth of liberation theology exclusively in Roman Catholic circles, it is also mistaken to situate it solely in Latin America. During the times of slavery and racial discrimination in the United States, black churches were communities of solidarity and hope for the enslaved peoples of African ancestry. Then and there the exodus story, the prophetic denunciations, and the story of the crucified but resurrected Jesus became the sung, preached, and hoped for sustaining bases for the narratives of the suffering black communities. Their bodies might be in bondage to their white masters, but their hearts and minds were nourished and comforted by the biblical stories of retribution and redemption.[34]

In continuity with that history, the African American churches became important protagonists in the civil rights movement for the elimination of racial discrimination in the United States. All over the U.S. South, black preachers became leaders in spreading the challenging message, and Gospel music acquired a more historically relevant twist. The speeches of Martin Luther King, Jr., are saturated with the cadences, intonations, and biblical images typical of African American preaching.[35] The lyrics of "We Shall Overcome," the emblematic hymn of the civil rights movement, is a variant of a prior hymn, "I'll Overcome Some Day," written in 1901 by Charles Albert Tindley, one of the founding fathers of African American Gospel music, and its melody is based on an even earlier defiant black song, the nineteenth-century spiritual "No More

Auction Block for Me," a subversive hymn revived in the twentieth century first by the powerful voice of Paul Robeson and later on by Bob Dylan.

> No more auction block for me
> No more, no more
> No more auction block for me
> Many thousands gone
>
> No more driver's lash for me
> No more, no more
> No more driver's lash for me
> Many thousands gone
>
> No more whip lash for me
> No more, no more
> No more pint of salt for me
> Many thousands gone.

In this social and ecclesiastical environment, some African American theologians began to rethink their intellectual role in the epic struggle of their people. Black liberation theology, rooted in the historical experience of slavery and racism, became an important partner in the theological table of dialogue, bringing to the conversation the issues of racial and ethnic discrimination. The foremost of the African American liberation theologians, though certainly not the only one, has been James Cone. In his 1969 book, *Black Theology and Black Power*, he still tentatively wrote: "the work of Christ is essentially a liberating work, directed toward and by the oppressed."[36] It was the foretaste of his 1970 groundbreaking text, *A Black Theology of Liberation*. Cone was not one to mince words in his radical transformation of theology.

> It is my contention that Christianity is essentially a religion of libera-tion. The function of theology is that of analyzing the meaning of that liberation for the oppressed so that they can know that their struggle for political, social, and economic justice is consistent with the gospel of Jesus Christ. Any theology that is indifferent to the theme of libera-tion is not Christian.
>
> In view of the biblical emphasis on liberation, it seems not only appropriate but necessary to define the Christian community as the community of the oppressed which joins Jesus Christ in his fight for the liberation of humankind.[37]

Black theology of liberation has become an important partner of theologi-cal discourse in the academic, ecclesiastical, and public social realms in all places where the African peoples have been subjected to dominion or control.[38] It has been able to dwell very creatively with the cultural and artistic traditions of their communities.[39]

Feminist Liberation Theology

Simultaneously to Latin American and African American theologians, feminist theologians were questioning radically the patriarchal and misogynistic traditions for so long prevailing in the history of Christianity. Certainly not all theologians would berate women as bitterly as Tertullian did in his treatise *On the Apparel of Women* ("And do you not know that you are [each] an Eve? The sentence of God on this sex of yours lives in this age: the guilt must of necessity live too. You are the devil's gateway: you are the unsealer of that [forbidden] tree: you are the first deserter of the divine law: you are she who persuaded him whom the devil was not valiant enough to attack. You destroyed so easily God's image, man. On account of your desert—that is, death—even the Son of God had to die"),[40] but it is hard to deny the historical importance of the Christian scriptures and traditions as ideological strongholds of patriarchy and female subordination. Key biblical texts, such as Genesis 3:16 ("To the woman [God] said: 'your husband shall rule over you'") and 1 Timothy 2:11-14 ("Let a woman learn in silence with full submission. I permit no woman to teach or to have authority over a man; she is to keep silent. For Adam was formed first, then Eve; and Adam was not deceived, but the woman was deceived and became a transgressor") have been constantly read theologically as implying a male priority in the order of creation and a female priority in the disorder of sin and philosophically as conveying an ontological masculine primacy.

Debates in most churches on the possibility of ordaining women led a good number of female theologians to question this misogynic tradition. Texts like Letty Russell's *Human Liberation in a Feminist Perspective: A Theology* (1974), Elisabeth Schüssler Fiorenza's *Feminist Theology as a Critical Theology of Liberation* (1975), and Phyllis Trible's *God and the Rhetoric of Sexuality* (1978), among many others, were bellwethers of a feminist liberation theology.[41] Possibly the most discussed academic feminist liberation theology for its comprehensive challenge to a system of patriarchal dominion for which she has coined the term *kyriarchy*, is Schüssler Fiorenza's 1983 tome *In Memory of Her*. She defines feminist theology as a "critical theology of liberation" that "seeks to develop . . . a historical-biblical hermeneutics of liberation."[42] Her ambitious project is to design a feminist way of looking at biblical and Early Christianity texts with the purpose of retrieving the silenced and repressed memory of the struggle between the early Christian practice of equality in discipleship and the Roman-Hellenistic cultural ethos of benevolent patriarchal dominion.

The originality and complexity of feminist theology's target of critique consists not only of the patriarchal ecclesiastical and theological traditions, but also the premises of masculine hegemony inscribed in the biblical texts themselves. The Bible is thus seen as a site of confrontation and contention between the egalitarian ethos of the early Jesus movement and the patriarchy of later New Testament texts. A feminist theology requires thus a hermeneutics of suspicion and imagination to unearth the polemics hidden in the sacred scriptures. The category of the "poor," foregrounded by the early Latin American theology, is not adequate to describe the inclusive character of the Jesus movement. To it must be added that of "the marginal" or "outcast," as a link between the "church of the poor" and the "church of women." The fundamental hermeneutical norm is therefore not the isolated sacred text but the history of women's struggle for liberation.

However, women of color immediately raised the objection that sex and gender should not be analyzed apart from issues of racial, ethnic, and cultural differences and discriminations. In the kaleidoscopic fragmentation of the human self and subjectivity typical of our postmodernist epoch, feminist liberation theology has engendered a black feminist theology, usually named womanist theology (Karen Baker-Fletcher, Katie Cannon, Emilie Townes, Renita Weems, Traci West, Delores Williams, among others), a Latin American feminist theology (Elsa Tamez, Ivone Gebara, Maria Clara Bingemer, among others), a Latina/Hispanic feminist theology (Ada María Isasi-Díaz, María Pilar Aquino, Michelle González, Daisy Machado, among others), and an Asian American feminist theology (Kwok Pui-Lan, Namsoon Kang, Wonhee Anne Joh, among others). Rooted in their own history of sorrows, struggles, and hopes, these various feminist theologies have disrupted significantly the theological endeavor, traditionally a masculine and androcentric academic realm.

The main point of contention in feminist theology relates to the debunking of the conventional images and concepts of God, traditionally perceived as a patriarchal hypostasis. The feminist dispute about sexist and inclusive language finds its culmination in the attempt to dismantle the androcentric captivity of God and theological discourse. How to retool theological thinking so that God might not be construed as a cosmic paterfamilias is probably the biggest challenge. This might be also the main motif—the search for the female dimensions of God—behind the Latina/Hispanic female theologians marked interest in the narratives and worship of the Virgin of Guadalupe and the biblical Sophia.[43]

A Polyphony of Liberation Theologies

During the last decades, in tandem with the growing polycentric character of Christianity, a spate of liberation theologies have emerged from very diverse contexts: Hispanic/Latino, Native American, Asian, Dalit, African, Minjung, Jewish, Palestinian, gay, lesbian, and queer.[44] If social redistribution was the main emphasis of Latin American liberation theology, the demand for the recognition of disdained identities characterizes recent theological trends. Recognition and identity, not only poverty and redistribution, have become crucial issues of theological dialogue and debate.[45] Personal and communal identities, usually left in the dark by traditional ways of doing theology, are now foregrounded.

Naim Ateek and Mitri Raheb, for example, initiate their texts by telling the readers *who* they are: Palestinian Christians.[46] They are both conscious of the tensions in that process of self-identification: *Christian* Palestinians or *Palestinian* Christians?

Palestinian theological hermeneutics is also able to foreground the usually silenced ominous dimension of the Exodus story, both in its biblical context—the atrocious rules of warfare that prescribed servitude or annihilation for the peoples encountered in Israel's route to the "promised land" (Deuteronomy 20:10-17)—and in the present historical circumstances wherein the Palestinian people are harshly mistreated by the state of Israel. From the painful memory of the *al-nakba* (the "great catastrophe"), it highlights the biblical themes of displacement, dispersion, and captivity, the crucial historical matrixes of the biblical scriptures, as meaningful loci of theological enunciation and reflection. It also, maybe more emphatically than other liberation theologies, underscores the intertwining of justice and reconciliation, truth-telling and forgiveness, prophetic denunciation and peacemaking annunciation.[47]

Possibly the most exciting, intriguing, and controversial contribution to the spreading rainbow of different liberation theologies are the writings of the late Marcella Althaus-Reid, an Argentinean Protestant theologian teaching and writing in Edinburgh, Scotland. In the heartland of conservative Scottish Calvinism, she has been transgressing all possible frontiers that have traditionally marked theology as a "decent" and "proper" endeavor. In 2000 she published *Indecent Theology: Theological Perversions in Sex, Gender and Politics* and in 2003 *The Queer God*.[48] *Indecent Theology* claims to free liberation theology from its prudish inhibitions, resituating it in the perspective of oppressed sexualities, of concrete bodies in love at the margins of "decency," of sexual dissidence. *Queer God* attempts something even more daring: to rescue God from the monotonous, mono-loving closet where the deity has been relegated. God is subjugated by its forced enclosure in the restrictive role of patriarchal purveyor of a repressive code of thinking and acting. God, not only destitute human beings, needs to be freed and redeemed. Althaus-Reid conceives queer theology as going even further than gay liberation theologies, for it is grounded on libertine subversions of both oppressive sexual and political heteronomy. Her queer hermeneutics is a methodology of permutations: a fascinating intertextual reading of the sacred scriptures with transgressive and marginal literature to free biblical exegesis from centuries of patriarchal and homophobic exegeses.

A Latino/Hispanic Contribution

Even in the midst of the new American Empire, within the "entrails of the monster," as José Martí phrased it,[49] recent Latino/Hispanic theological productions bring to the fore a vibrant concept of God as Liberator. Mayra Rivera's *The Touch of Transcendence: A Postcolonial Theology of God* (2007) is a readable and intelligent tome comprising a complex array of topics: a deconstructive analysis of how a number of contemporary theologies construe God's transcendence, being and actions in history, a critical discussion of the possible relevance to theology of the texts of several cultural studies writers (Emmanuel Levinas, Jacques Derrida, Luce Irigaray) and postcolonial authors (Gayatri Spivak, Homi Bhabha, Walter Mignolo), and an examination of the implications of some strands of liberation theology (Latin American, feminist) for the doctrine of God.[50]

It concludes with a very suggestive and seductive proposal to rethink divine transcendence. "Divine transcendence," according to Rivera, "has acquired the reputation of being a tool of patriarchal and imperial self-legitimation."[51] There has been a multisecular collusion between dualistic metaphysical views of transcendence with multiple entwined projects intending to control and dominate subaltern communities. The critique of those dualistic views and colonizing projects is followed by a complex and rigorous attempt to elaborate a model of divine "relational transcendence" that allows a conception of God as constantly embracing and touching human and cosmic reality, while providing for an endless process of human liberation and for an ethic of solidarity with those "others" whose singularities (national, ethnic, cultural, racial, gender, sexual orientation) are socially signified as emblems of disdain, marginalization, or exploitation. "We will seek a model of transcendence that is attentive to the concrete sociopolitical significance of otherness . . . Our aim to open ourselves to transcendence in the face of the Other leads us to give special attention to our relationships with those who are marginalized in our communities or simply excluded from them."[52] The touch of divine transcendence is ethically fulfilled in the embracing touch of the pariahs and untouchables.[53]

This is a coherent and impressive theological venture to overcome the dominant dualistic schemes (transcendence/immanence, spirit/body, sacred/profane) that have served as ideological matrices of human subordination and subjugation. Simultaneously, a manner of God-talk is forged that might be faithful both to the biblical witness about the Creator and Sustainer and to the contemporary challenges for social emancipation.

> This model of relational transcendence refuses the "hard boundary" between the divine and the created. Instead it affirms that the beginning, sustenance, and transformation of the cosmos are intrinsically divine . . . Intracosmic and intercreaturely transcendence are thus inherently linked; both are theologically grounded in an assertion of the beginning of creation in God . . . We aspire to give and receive that which may open for us new paths for continuous liberation.[54]

Rivera is well aware that in these times of ours, when new forms of imperial domination are devised, the cross dialogue between polychromic liberation theologies and postcolonial critical studies acquires theoretical relevance and political urgency.[55] Joerg Rieger has well expressed the challenge that this transdisciplinary exchange poses for the concept of God: "What happens when God-talk is turned loose from the powers that be, when it comes from those who bear the marks of colonialism and neocolonialism in their flesh?"[56] From my Latin American and Caribbean context, however, this requires the overcoming of the narrow historical vista of most postcolonial authors, who tend to focus their critical gaze to post-Enlightenment imperial formations.[57] After all, modern Western imperial domination began with the sixteenth-century Iberian conquest of the Caribbean archipelago and the Latin American territories.[58]

Provisional Predictions

Although several observers have predicted the demise of liberation theology, a better way to describe its actual condition is its proliferation by means of the fragmentation of subversive identities. What is striking is its ability to morph from its antecedents into a plethora of new movements. The original intuition of "preferential option for the poor" has been widened to the "excluded," "marginalized," "victims," "disdained," "downtrodden." There are even signs of a vigorous reawakening of liberation theology, for its main sources are still with us:

1. The worldwide growing social and economic inequities entailed by the global hegemony of a neoliberal capitalist system of free market that validates profit as the hallmark of success. Poverty and injustice still prevail, tragically distorting the fate of millions of human beings all over our planet. Transnational corporations play lucrative chess games with their lives and labors, aborting illusions and shattering dreams.

2. But also everywhere the "wretched of the earth," as Franz Fanon called them, demand a different and alternative social order and forge innovative models of protest and resistance. Their particular struggles might be different but not incompatible or incommensurable. Some resist poverty and economic misery, others demand full recognition for their racial, ethnic, or cultural identity, others assert the integrity and dignity of their gender or sexual orientation. These diverse perspectives complicate but also widen significantly the horizons of today's struggles for liberation.

3. The constant retrieval, by many Christians, of the rebel and subversive memories hidden in the biblical texts and Christian traditions. It is impossible to silence or repress completely the rebellious tones of the Exodus narrative, the denunciatory voice of the prophets, Jesus' disturbing proclamation of good news for the poor and the captives, the attempts by the early Christian movement to shape a participatory and sharing community, or the anti-imperial tone of Revelation. Those memories, which constitute the core of the sacred scriptures, precipitate in the mind and heart of many readers the commitment for liberation. They lead to multiple and diverse meaningful efforts to shape for theology a public emancipatory role.[59]

4. God still matters. Even in these postmodernist and cybernetic times people care about God. In the midst of present disturbances and con-

flicts, the "battle for God," as Karen Armstrong so aptly has named it,[60] rages ferociously. In the fascinating and perplexing kaleidoscope of human social existence, God is reimagined as the ultimate source of hope for the oppressed and downtrodden. When the social miseries that afflict so many communities become unbearable, beyond and besides the tiresome quarrels of religious fundamentalism and dogmatic secularism, the memory of God the Liberator erupts again and again: "When the Egyptians treated us harshly and afflicted us . . . we cried to the Lord, the God of our ancestors; the Lord heard our voice and saw our affliction, our toil, and our oppression. The Lord brought us out of Egypt with a mighty hand and an outstretched arm" (Deuteronomy 26:6-8). As the meaningful and influential 1985 South African *Kairos* document categorically states: "Throughout the Bible God appears as the liberator of the oppressed."

These are the factors that counter and resist the ruling imperial project of controlling and policing the frontiers of human imagination. They preserve the relevance and urgency of liberation theology. Several examples suffice: Jürgen Moltmann's memoir, *Experiences in Theology* (2000), devotes a substantial segment to discuss what he names "mirror images of liberating theology."[61] The last section of the splendid *Oxford Illustrated History of the Bible* (2001) deals exclusively with liberationist polyphonic and heteroglossic hermeneutics.[62] The fine contributions to the 2005 World Forum of Theology and Liberation clearly manifest the renewal of liberation theology, this time in an international arena.[63]

Deeply felt fears and hopes, as the astute David Hume noted more than two centuries ago,[64] are able to agitate hearts and spirits and to move minds to think the otherwise unthinkable. Suddenly, at the end of the epoch so aptly named the "Age of Extremes" by Eric Hobsbawm,[65] two tendencies clash: the first announces with glib satisfaction "the end of history," the obliteration of transformative social utopias;[66] the second, from the entrails of the subordinated subjects,[67] proclaims a new insurrection of human hopes for "another possible world."[68]

The essential imperative might be to remember and radicalize the prophetic words written by the imprisoned Dietrich Bonhöffer, in a note surreptitiously preserved by his friend Eberhard Bethge: "We have for once learnt to see the great events of world history from below, from the perspective of the outcast, the suspects, the maltreated, the powerless, the oppressed, the reviled—in short, from the perspective of those who suffer."[69]

Notes

1. The most famous of them, and a model for many, were the Algerian Front of National Liberation, established in 1954, which led the revolt against French colonial domination (brilliantly depicted in Gillo Pontocorvo's 1966 film *Battle of Algiers*); the

National Liberation Front for South Vietnam, created in December 1960, which successfully fought against the division of Vietnam and the military invasion of the United States; and the Palestine Liberation Organization, founded in 1964 to organize the struggle for Palestinian statehood. See Alistair Horne, *A Savage War of Peace: Algeria 1954-1962* (New York: Penguin Books, 1987); Frances Fitzgerald, *Fire in the Lake: The Vietnamese and the Americans in Vietnam* (Boston: Little, Brown and Company, 1972), chapter 4: "The National Liberation Front"; and Helena Cobban, *The Palestinian Liberation Organization: People, Power and Politics* (Cambridge: Cambridge University Press, 1984).

2. Ernst Bloch, *Atheismus im Christentum* (Frankfurt am Main: Suhrkamp, 1968).

3. Herbert Marcuse, *An Essay on Liberation* (Boston: Beacon Press, 1969); Franz Fanon, *The Wretched of the Earth* (New York: Grove Press, 1965).

4. Paulo Freire, *Educação como prática da liberdade* (Rio de Janeiro: Paz e Terra, 1967); idem, *Pedagogía del oprimido* (Montevideo: Tierra Nueva, 1968).

5. See Austin P. Flannery, ed., *Vatican Council II: The Basic Sixteen Documents: Constitutions, Decrees, Declarations* (Northport, N.Y.: Costello, 1996).

6. Jürgen Moltmann, *Theologie der Hoffnung* (München: Chr. Kaiser Verlag, 1966); Johannes Baptist Metz, *Zur Theologie der Welt* (Mainz: Matthias-Grünewald Verlag, 1968).

7. See Dorothee Sölle, *Politische Theologie: Auseinandersetzung mit Rudolf Bultmann* (Stuttgart: Kreuz-Verlag, 1971).

8. Alfred T. Hennelly, *Liberation Theology: A Documentary History* (Maryknoll, N.Y.: Orbis Books, 1992), 114, 116, English translation somewhat amended.

9. See Gustavo Gutiérrez, "The Meaning and Scope of Medellín," in *The Density of the Present: Selected Writings* (Maryknoll, N.Y.: Orbis Books, 1999), 59-101.

10. It is translated and reproduced in Hennelly, *Liberation Theology*, 62-76.

11. Gustavo Gutiérrez, *Teología de la liberación: Perspectivas* (Salamanca: Sígueme, 1973), 67-69; ET: *A Theology of Liberation* (Maryknoll, N.Y.: Orbis Books, 1973).

12. Hugo Assmann, *Opresión—Liberación: Desafío a los cristianos* (Montevideo: Tierra Nueva, 1971), 50.

13. See the important book on the origins of the Latin American liberation theology by Samuel Silva Gotay, *El pensamiento cristiano revolucionario en América Latina: Implicaciones de la teología de la liberación para la sociología de la religión* (Salamanca: Ediciones Sígueme, 1981), translated into Portuguese as *O pensamento cristão revolucionário na América Latina e no Caribe (1960-1973)* (São Paulo: Edições Paulinas, 1985), and into German as *Christentum und Revolution in Lateinamerika und der Karibik: Die Bedeutung der Theologie der Befreiung für eine Soziologie der religión*, Würzburger Studien zur Fundamentaltheologie 17 (Frankfurt am Main: P. Lang, 1995).

14. José Porfirio Miranda, *Marx y la Biblia* (Salamanca: Ediciones Sígueme, 1972); ET: *Marx and the Bible* (Maryknoll, N.Y.: Orbis Books, 1977). Juan Luis Segundo, *Liberación de la teología* (Buenos Aires: Ediciones Carlos Lohlé, 1975); ET: *The Liberation of Theology* (Maryknoll, N.Y.: Orbis Books, 1976).

15. José Severino Croatto, *Exodus: A Hermeneutics of Freedom* (Maryknoll, N.Y.: Orbis Books, 1981); Jorge V. Pixley, *Exodo: Una lectura evangélica y popular* (México, DF: Casa Unida de Publicaciones, 1983); ET: *On Exodus* (Maryknoll, N.Y.: Orbis Books, 1987).

16. Walter J. Houston, *Contending for Justice: Ideologies and Theologies of Social Justice in the Old Testament* (London: T & T Clark, 2006).

17. Jon Sobrino, *La fe en Jesucristo: ensayo desde las víctimas* (San Salvador: UCA, 1999); ET: *Christ the Liberator* (Maryknoll, N.Y.: Orbis Books, 2001).

18. Leonardo Boff, *Jesus Cristo libertador; ensaio de cristologia crítica para o nosso tempo* (Petrópolis: Vozes, 1972); ET: *Jesus Christ Liberator* (Maryknoll, N.Y.: Orbis Books, 1978); Jon Sobrino, *Jesucristo liberador: lectura histórico teológica de Jesús de Nazaret* (San Salvador: UCA, 1991); ET: *Jesus the Liberator* (Maryknoll, N.Y.: Orbis Books, 1993).

19. Leonardo Boff, *Igreja, carisma e poder: ensaios de eclesiologia militante* (Petrópolis: Vozes, 1981); ET: *Church: Charism and Power* (New York: Crossroad, 1986).

20. Jorge V. Pixley and Jean-Pierre Bastian, eds., *Praxis cristiana y producción teológica* (Salamanca: Ediciones Sígueme, 1979).

21. Jonathan Pimentel Chacón, *Modelos de Dios en las teologías latinoamericanas* (Heredia, Costa Rica: Universidad Nacional de Costa Rica, 2008).

22. See Leonardo Boff, *Eclesiogênese: as comunidades eclesiais de base reinventam a Igreja* (Petrópolis: Vozes, 1977); ET: *Ecclesiogenesis* (Maryknoll, N.Y.: Orbis Books, 1986).

23. Gustavo Gutiérrez, *Las Casas: In Search of the Poor of Jesus Christ* (Maryknoll, N.Y.: Orbis Books, 1993).

24. Oscar Romero, *Voice of the Voiceless: The Four Pastoral Letters and Other Statements,* introductory essays by Ignacio Martín-Baró and Jon Sobrino (Maryknoll, N.Y.: Orbis Books, 1998), 50-51.

25. Reproduced in Hennelly, *Liberation Theology*, 394, 411-12.

26. See the strong response of Juan Luis Segundo, *Teología de la liberación: Respuesta al Cardenal Ratzinger* (Madrid: Ediciones Cristiandad, 1985); ET: *Theology and the Church: Response to Cardinal Ratzinger and a Warning to the Whole Church* (London: Geoffrey Chapman, 1986).

27. Reproduced in Hennelly, *Liberation Theology*, 498-506.

28. See Ignacio Ellacuría and Jon Sobrino, eds., *Mysterium liberationis: Conceptos fundamentales de la Teología de la Liberación* (Madrid: Editorial Trotta, 1990); ET: *Mysterium Liberationis: Fundamental Concepts of the Theology of Liberation* (Maryknoll, N.Y.: Orbis Books, 1993). On November 16, 1989, Ellacuría, then rector of El Salvador's Central American University, five other Jesuits priests, and two domestic servants were assassinated by a group of soldiers.

29. See the defense of Sobrino by almost forty theologians in *Bajar de la Cruz a los Pobres: Cristología de la Liberación*, ed. José María Vigil (México, DF: Ediciones Dabar, 2007).

30. See Alan P. Neely, "Protestant Antecedents of the Latin American Theology of Liberation" (Ph.D. diss., American University, 1977).

31. Rubem Alves, "Towards a Theology of Liberation: An Exploration of the Encounter between the Languages of Humanistic Messianism and Messianic Humanism" (Ph.D. diss., Princeton Theological Seminary, May 1968).

32. Richard Shaull, *Hombre, ideología y revolución en América Latina* (ISAL: Montevideo, 1965). Cf. Neely, "Protestant Antecedents," 253: "it is doubtful if any theologian has more consistently and directly contributed to the shaping of the contemporary Protestant theologians of liberation than Richard Shaull."

33. Rubem Alves, *A Theology of Human Hope* (Washington, D.C.: Corpus Books, 1969), 163. On the theological trajectory of Alves, see Leopoldo Cervantes-Ortiz, *Serie de sueños: la teología ludo-erótico-poética de Rubem Alves* (Quito, Ecuador: Consejo Latinoamericano de Iglesias, 2003).

34. See Albert Raboteau, *Slave Religion: The "Invisible Institution" in the Antebellum South* (Oxford: Oxford University Press, 1978); idem, *A Fire in the Bones: Reflections on African-American Religious History* (Boston: Beacon Press, 1995).

35. *A Call to Conscience: The Landmark Speeches of Dr. Martin Luther King, Jr.*, ed. Clayborne Carson and Kris Shepard (New York: Warner Books, 2001).

36. James Cone, *Black Theology and Black Power* (New York: Seabury Press, 1969; repr., Maryknoll, N.Y.: Orbis Books, 1997), 42.

37. James Cone, *A Black Theology of Liberation* (Philadelphia: Lippincott, 1970; Maryknoll, N.Y.: Orbis Books, 1990), v, 3.

38. Including the Caribbean, with its long and dense tradition of Black slavery. See Noel Leo Erskine, *Decolonizing Theology: A Caribbean Perspective* (Trenton, N.J.: Africa World Press, 1998).

39. See James Cone, *The Spirituals and the Blues* (New York: Seabury, 1972; repr., Maryknoll, N.Y.: Orbis Books, 1992).

40. Tertullian, *On the Apparel of Women*, book I, chapter I, introduction. Reproduced from http://www.newadvent.org/fathers/0402.htm.

41. Letty Russell, *Human Liberation in a Feminist Perspective: A Theology* (Philadelphia: Westminster Press, 1974); Elisabeth Schüssler Fiorenza, "Feminist Theology as a Critical Theology of Liberation," in *Theological Studies* 36 (1975): 605-26; Phyllis Trible, *God and the Rhetoric of Sexuality* (Philadelphia: Fortress Press, 1978).

42. Elisabeth Schüssler Fiorenza, *In Memory of Her: A Feminist Theological Reconstruction of Christian Origins* (New York: Crossroad, 1994), 29f.

43. Jeanette Rodríguez, *Our Lady of Guadalupe: Faith and Empowerment among Mexican-American Women* (Austin: University of Texas Press, 1994); Mayra Rivera, "God at the Crossroads: A Postcolonial Reading of Sophia," in *Postcolonial Theologies: Divinity and Empire*, by Catherine Keller, Michael Nausner, and Mayra Rivera (St. Louis: Chalice Press, 2004), 186-203.

44. *Inter alia*, Fernando Segovia, "From 1968, through 2008: A Call to Action for Latino/a American Religious and Theological Studies," *Apuntes* 28, no. 1 (Spring 2008): 4-28; George E. Tinker, *Spirit and Resistance: Political Theology and American Indian Liberation* (Minneapolis: Fortress Press, 2004); Aloysius Pieris, *An Asian Theology of Liberation* (Maryknoll, N.Y.: Orbis Books, 1988); Sathianathan Clarke, *Dalits and Christianity: Subaltern Religion and Liberation Theology in India* (Delhi: Oxford University Press, 1998); Jonathan Gichaara, "Issues in African Liberation Theology," *Black Theology: An International Journal* 3, no. 1 (2005): 75-85; Kim Yong Bock, ed., *Minjung Theology: People as the Subjects of History* (Singapore: Commission on Theological Concerns, Christian Conference of Asia, 1981); Marc H. Ellis, *Toward a Jewish Theology of Liberation* (Maryknoll, N.Y.: Orbis Books, 1989; 3rd expanded ed., Waco, Tex.: Baylor University Press, 2004); Naim Stifan Ateek, *Justice and Only Justice: A Palestinian Theology of Liberation* (Maryknoll, N.Y.: Orbis Books, 1989); Elizabeth Stuart, *Gay and Lesbian Theologies: Repetitions with Critical Difference* (Burlington, Vt.: Ashgate, 2003).

45. Nancy Fraser and Axel Honneth, *Redistribution or Recognition? A Political-Philosophical Exchange* (London/New York: Verso, 2003).

46. Ateek, *Justice and Only Justice*, 13-17; Mitri Raheb, *I Am a Palestinian Christian* (Minneapolis: Fortress Press, 1995), 3-14.

47. Ateek, *Justice and Only Justice*, chapter 7 ("A Dream of Peace"), 163-75; Raheb, *I Am a Palestinian Christian*, conclusion ("I Have a Dream"), 112-16. See also Naim Stifan Ateek, *A Palestinian Christian Cry for Reconciliation* (Maryknoll, N.Y.: Orbis Books, 2008).

48. Marcella Althaus-Reid, *Indecent Theology: Theological Perversions in Sex,*

Gender and Politics (London: Routledge, 2000); eadem, *The Queer God* (London: Routledge, 2003).

49. José Martí, "Carta a Manuel Mercado," *Obras escogidas* (La Habana: Editora Política, 1982), 3:576: "Viví en el monstruo, y le conozco las entrañas:—y mi honda es la de David" ("I lived inside the monster, I know its entrails—and I have David's sling"). See José Martí, *Inside the Monster: Writings on the United States and American Imperialism* (New York: Monthly Review Press, 1975).

50. Mayra Rivera, *The Touch of Transcendence: A Postcolonial Theology of God* (Louisville: Westminster John Knox Press, 2007).

51. Ibid., 1.

52. Ibid., 82.

53. Here Rivera quotes one of Althaus-Reid's transgressive texts: "God is to be found in the presence of the untouchables . . . [Transcendence] is God touching its own limits in the untouchables." Marcella Althaus-Reid, "El Tocado (Le Toucher): Sexual Irregularities in the Translation of God (the Word) in Jesus," in *Derrida and Religion: Other Testaments*, ed. Yvonne Sherwood and Kevin Hart (New York: Routledge, 2004), 394.

54. Rivera, *Touch of Transcendence*, 133, 140.

55. Keller, Nausner, and Rivera, *Postcolonial Theologies: Divinity and Empire*; Kwok Pui-lan, *Postcolonial Imagination and Feminist Theology* (Louisville: Westminster John Knox Press, 2005); Wonhee Anne Joh, *Heart of the Cross: A Postcolonial Christology* (Louisville: Westminster John Knox Press, 2006); Rivera, *Touch of Transcendence*; Joerg Rieger, *Christ and Empire: From Paul to Postcolonial Times* (Minneapolis: Fortress Press, 2007); Kwok Pui-lan, Don H. Compier, and Joerg Rieger, eds., *Empire: The Christian Tradition. New Readings of Classical Theologians* (Minneapolis: Fortress Press, 2007).

56. Joerg Rieger, "Liberating God-Talk: Postcolonialism and the Challenge of the Margins," in *Postcolonial Theologies*, 220.

57. See Fernando Segovia's sharp and critical exposition of the theoretical convergences between postcolonial studies and anti-imperial biblical hermeneutics: "Mapping the Postcolonial Optic in Biblical Criticism: Meaning and Scope," in *Postcolonial Biblical Criticism: Interdisciplinary Intersections*, by Stephen D. Moore and Fernando Segovia (London/New York: T & T Clark, 2005), 23-78.

58. Enrique Dussel, *1492: El encubrimiento del otro (Hacia el origen del "mito de la modernidad")* (Bogotá: Ediciones Antropos, 1992); Walter Mignolo, *The Darker Side of the Renaissance: Literacy, Territoriality, and Colonization* (Ann Arbor: University of Michigan Press, 1995); Luis N. Rivera-Pagán, "Doing Pastoral Theology in a Post-Colonial Context: Some Observations from the Caribbean," *Journal of Pastoral Theology* 17, no. 2 (Fall 2007): 1-28.

59. See Benjamín Valentín, *Mapping Public Theology: Beyond Culture, Identity, and Difference* (Harrisburg/London: Trinity Press International, 2002).

60. Karen Armstrong, *The Battle for God* (New York: Knopf, 2000).

61. Jürgen Moltmann, "Mirror Images of Liberating Theology," in *Experiences in Theology: Ways and Forms of Christian Theology* (Minneapolis: Fortress Press, 2000), 181-299.

62. John Rogerson, ed., *The Oxford Illustrated History of the Bible* (Oxford: Oxford University Press, 2001), 293-355. See also Christopher Rowland, *The Cambridge Companion to Liberation Theology* (Cambridge: Cambridge University Press, 1999).

63. See Marcella Althaus-Reid, Ivan Petrella, and Luiz Carlos Susin, *Another Possible World* (London: SCM Press, 2007).

64. David Hume, *The Natural History of Religion* (London: A. & C. Black, 1956).

65. Eric Hobsbawm, *Age of Extremes: The Short Twentieth Century, 1914-1991* (London: Michael Joseph, 1994).

66. Francis Fukuyama, *The End of History and the Last Man* (New York: Free Press, 1992).

67. Franz Hinkelammert, *El grito del sujeto: Del teatro-mundo del evangelio de Juan al perro-mundo de la globalización* (San José, Costa Rica: DEI, 1998).

68. Jorge Pixley et al., *Por un mundo otro: Alternativas al mercado global* (Quito, Ecuador: Consejo Latinoamericano de Iglesias, 2003).

69. Dietrich Bonhöffer, *Letters and Papers from Prison*, ed. Eberhard Bethge (London: Folio Society, 2000), 16.

2

La Tierra Theologies' Contribution to Creation Theologies

Jeanette Rodríguez

Before reading and writing developed, our religious and cultural ancestors carried an incredible knowledge. Formed by their experience and relationship with all that lived, they understood the human as one who needed to be grateful for every day of life. They respected the gifts of life provided by nature, and thus nature itself. In this essay, I will draw from my own Catholic tradition, including some of our more contemporary theological voices, sources of a wider Hispano/Latino(a) culture, and my familial religio-cultural sources. In addition I will integrate the legacy of Latin American religio-cultural ancestors through their philosophy of *flor y canto*.[1] This integrated approach generates a theological perspective as it emerges in what I call La Tierra theologies.

Catholic and Contemporary Theological Voices

For an overview of the doctrines of creation, I draw primarily from Justo Gonzalez, Anne N. Clifford, Zachary Hayes, and the U.S. and Latin American bishops. Standard creation theologies aim to reconcile reigning cultural opinions and scientific theories about cosmological and cosmogonic (origins) beliefs with claims in sacred texts and traditions.[2] As the Catholic Catechism states, "creation is the beginning and the foundation of all God's works."[3] Rooted in biblical accounts, these theologies emerge out of the experience of the people in the various contexts in which they find themselves.

The works of Justo Gonzalez provide deep insights on the doctrine of creation that are generally held by Christians everywhere. First and foremost, all that is exists because it was created by God. While the Bible opens up with two parallel stories of creation, most scholars agree that this is not the most ancient part of the Scripture. In fact, Israel's conviction that Yahweh was redeemer and liberator precedes the doctrine of creation.[4] As some maintain,

the creation narratives beginning in Genesis 1:1 and in Genesis 2:4b
are examples of the Priestly (P, sixth-fifth centuries B.C.) and Yahwist
(J, tenth-ninth centuries B.C.) traditions respectively. Each account has
a long prehistory; the writers of these accounts received a tradition and
shaped what they received into a new form. Each narrative is a product of a different period in Israelite history, a period that expressed its
belief in God in a manner that reflects its own concerns and needs.[5]

The interpretation of these two accounts surfaces two main points that
relate to what I will later develop as La Tierra theologies. First, the Gen. 2:4b-
25 account, the oldest of the two, presents a very intimate, tender description
of Creator God molding the human from the humas (Heb, 'adam from the
'adamah).

> In highly symbolic form, the text presents the humble origins of human-
> ity, the very name expresses our rootage in the earth. Adam is one who
> is of the earth. In this understanding, the earth is not separate from us,
> rather we are drawn from the same matter present in the world around
> us. Yet we receive from God the gift of life.[6]

In this view, God creates humans to live in community and intimacy with all
of creation. This theological anthropology in particular challenges the "western
world where the sense of the many levels of relations that make up human life
have often yielded to an extreme form of individualism and disregard for the
world of nature."[7]

In 1973, Phyllis Trible proposed a new reading of Genesis 2 and 3 where she
focused on the Hebrew word ha'adam, which is a play on words with 'adamah,
meaning "earth." Ha'adam is found in Gen. 2:7. Trible contends that this first
use of ha'adam is better translated as "earth creature." She argues that this is
significant, since until woman is created, sexuality does not enter the picture.
And only then does ha'adam refer to the male, Adam. Before that, the reference
is to all of humanity, as it is in the first creation story of Gen. 1:26-27. Trible's
reading is supported by the Inclusive Hebrew translation. In that text, unlike
the NRSV (New Revised Standard Version of the Bible), Gen. 2:7 reads "So our
God fashioned the earth creature out of the clay of the earth, and blew into its
nostrils the breath of life. And the earth creature became a living being."[8]

Further, Wes Howard-Brook contends that this understanding provides a
clue to the meaning of Gen. 1:26-27's mysterious "in the image of God" they
were created. He continues that we are now called to envision humans as a
lovely expression of "inspired earth," topsoil animated by the breath of God
(2:7).[9] Thus the second creation story thoroughly grounds humans in the earth
while animating them with participation in God's life, God's very breath. This
emphasis on God as creator, and la creatura or earth creature coming from the
breath of God and earth, becomes a significant starting point for La Tierra
theologies.

Second, the Gen. 1:1-2:4a story of creation emerges out of oppression and links God as Creator-Liberator. A brief review of salvation history lends some insight to understanding the link between creator God and liberator God. When the Babylonians invaded Judah and destroyed Jerusalem and its temple, they crushed hundreds of years of hopes and dreams that had crystallized around the belief and the power of the Israelite's God.[10] From a specific context, very specific questions emerge. In this case, the questions that emerge from the exile were questions of meaning. Why were we here? How is it that we were brought into captivity? Will we ever go back? Are we Babylonians now? How do we teach our children who we really are?

The Genesis 1 creation account contrasts with the surrounding Babylonian myth that the Israelites were exposed to. The purpose of the creation myth within the Israelite epistemology was to praise God. In the Babylonian myth, the purpose of human creation was as service to the gods. This is in opposition to Genesis 1 where humans, male and female, are made in God's image. Clifford mentions an important point, when she states that "in Genesis 1, creation takes place simply through God's word and not a cosmic battle. It is through God's word that a good, orderly world is created."[11]

The first narrative in the "Elohim" tradition emphasizes "'amar," the Hebrew word for "to say" and "to speak," as the tool that "Elohim" uses to bring order into existence. Scholars argue that this is an exilic reading that needed to legitimate the Torah as the source of knowledge for the only true and real God of Israel. Through the spoken word order is brought into the community, and it's that order, that "spoken word," that controls and domesticates chaos. This *tohu wabohu* (Gen. 1:2), the chaos that the spirit of God hovers over, is the chaos that God brings into order. All through Genesis 1, the spoken word defeats chaos, and so it is this aspect of the creation tradition that we see emphasized extensively in the exile, and even in later traditions among the rabbis who believe that the Torah was present as a blueprint (remember Torah wisdom is female) to help God create. These features of religious thought emerge strongly in the exile.

Twenty-first-century religious leaders often gravitate toward the first book of the Bible, Genesis, to understand the theme of creation from a biblical point of view. Contemporary scholars, however, challenge us to examine the rereading and the reception of the creation story by socially locating it in the crisis of empire, exile, and the destruction of the temple in Jerusalem in 587 B.C.E. Through this lens one can see how the creation tradition of Israel emphasized certain themes. First and foremost, that God is the sole creator of the universe, and second, that disobedience to this God leads to exile.

Using this creation story, Gonzalez unpacks the development of the doctrine of creation. He looks at the development of the doctrine by comparing what Christians were affirming in light of what they were rejecting. And in Gonzalez's reflection, the Christian doctrine rejected polytheism, dualism, and radical monism. This entails a rejection that the world is a hostile or capricious place; that there are two eternal principles, one good one evil; and that all reality is one.[12] Thus, within the Christian doctrine, Gonzalez stresses creation as an act of God's will.

Fundamental to this narrative is the free and sovereign decision of a loving God and that all that God created is good. God is the Creator. God creates with an intention that becomes known and is lived out within the history of the people of the Hebrew Scriptures. Thus, Justo Gonzalez maintains that the key element to keep in mind in reflecting on the doctrine of creation is, first and foremost, that the entire universe and everything in it was created by the loving action of a redeemer God. He further stipulates that "we must remember that even from its very origins in the faith of Israel, the doctrine of creation was an expression and a consequence of God's care and redemption . . . That salvation is not salvation from creation, but rather salvation into the combination or perfection of creation." Gonzalez distinguishes between creation and emanation, affirming that there is a difference between God and the world. The world that is God's creation is not God. God transcends the world. And, all that God created is good. The world is also a faulty world. That is to say, however you discern the origins, the bottom line is that the world is not what God intended it to be. And yet, creation is good. It is not to be despised, abused, or neglected. It deserves respect. All creatures are part of the same creation. "This affirmation has become increasingly urgent as we come to realize the degree to which human mismanagement is affecting and polluting the rest of creation—and humans themselves."[13]

Franciscan Zachary Hayes suggests that critically reading biblical sources is not merely a question of interpreting the Genesis accounts but rather "a question of reading and interpreting the many texts that speak of creation in terms of what seem clear facts in the historical development of the Bible." He continues, "If one examines the non-negotiable subtexts of every source, one discovers that God's creative action is an abiding reality and is always the precondition for salvation." The theology of creation, in both Hebrew and Christian scriptures, is a "theology of history deeply tied to the gradually emerging future consciousness of the Jewish and Christian community."[14]

Finally, Phyllis Trible tells us that the Genesis narrative is really a narrative about life and death. This cycle of life and death is found in all living things, throughout all the seasons.[15] This life-death dynamic does not involve a natural process of dying and living, but a death that really refers to being put to death. Jon Sobrino references this when he talks about the people of Latin America as a crucified people. He says, "To die crucified, does not mean simply to die, but to be put to death. It means that there are victims and that there are executioners . . . The truth is that the Latin American people's cross has been inflicted on them by the various empires that have taken power over the continent." Sobrino reminds us of a phrase used by modern Jesuit Ignacio Ellacuría, in which he states, "Creation has turned out badly for God."[16]

This life-death dynamic as lived in Latin America shapes its theological contribution to La Tierra theologies. It is estimated that by the end of the century, 170 million Latin Americans will be living in dire poverty, with an additional 170 million in life-threatening conditions. In addition, wars and repression, according to the Latin American bishops, have created "'the misery that marginalizes large human groups,' which 'as a collective fact is an injustice crying to heaven.'"[17] This death is experienced by millions of Latin Americans, and by the poor all over the world. And yet, our tradition tells us "that the crucified people themselves are bearers of salvation."[18] A crucified people, Sobrino writes,

> offers values that are not offered elsewhere . . . the poor have evangelizing potential . . . spelled out as the gospel values of solidarity, service, simplicity, and readiness to receive God's gift . . . the poor have a humanizing potential because they offer community against individualism, cooperation against selfishness, simplicity again opulence . . . the crucified peoples also offer us hope."[19]

And with this hope comes the potential for new life. Latin American theologians interpret Genesis, therefore, in the context of increasing conditions of poverty.

The early Christian community reflected this consciousness and its ensuing spirituality in their writings. New Testament accounts reveal that Jesus himself walked, prayed, preached, and ministered within the "Cathedral of Creation"[20] making references to the desert, garden, lake, field, and mountain. His parables include birds and sheep as well as seed, wheat, and harvest. Similarly, the accounts of the first communities recorded that "the multitude of believers had but one heart and a single soul. No one called their belongings their own, but everything was held in common among them" (Acts 4:32-34). Not surprisingly, then, the teaching body of the church has articulated and reflected on such themes as property, the role of earthly goods, and the demands of social justice. While the church has always recognized the right of all people to all property, it has also held that a right to property "constitutes for no one an unconditional and absolute right. There is no reason to reserve for one's exclusive use that which goes beyond our need while others are lacking essentials."[21]

In 1988 Guatemalan bishops used this process of reflection in their pastoral letter concerning land.[22] "It is a cry from 'The People of Corn' who, on the one hand, identify with furrows, sowing, and harvest. And who, on the other hand, find themselves expelled from the land by an unjust and punitive system."[23] In this pastoral letter, the bishops highlight agrarian problems in Guatemala and critique the political system of land ownership that has existed since colonial times to the present, the unequal distribution of land, and the discriminatory practices and marginalization of the campesinos. The bishops' theological insights focus on the earth as a gift of God. They refer to the first oral traditions of Genesis that, first of all, acknowledges and recognizes the dignity of the human person. In the context of systemic and institutional violence, the bishops remind believers of the inherent dignity of the human person as expressed both in the Scriptures and in the subsequent theological constructs. They move on to expressions of joy in the Psalms (Pss. 67:7; 85:13), which pronounce humanity's joy as the fruit of their labors on the earth, the joy with which the people gather their fruits, and culminate with the fiesta in God's honor (Deut. 16:1-15). They note that the earth is a sign of a covenant between God and humanity, and that the earth does not belong to humanity but to the Dios de la Vida/God of Life. Finally, the letter denounces avarice and excessive wealth, urging believers to imitate Jesus' encounter and commitment to the poor.

Creation theologies, then, allocate each of us a place in which we feel a special relationship with the land. Often this relationship with the land bursts forth in special places: the desert, the ocean, a mountain or field. These insights presume an understanding of tradition that needs to be made more explicit. When one is being asked to recover a tradition, one has to ask which tradition? For the reality is that the Christian tradition is really Christian *traditions*. In reflecting on Scripture, we need to keep in mind that we are dealing with texts that evolved over a thousand years of oral tradition and that are riddled with various differing oral traditions. La Tierra theology is close to these ancient Hebrew oral traditions in that La Tierra also carries within itself more than one tradition.

La Tierra Theologies

La Tierra theologies share with the Israelites/Jews a need for counter-narrative in the face of domination. As a response to their captivity, the authors of the first Genesis creation account proclaim, up and against the lived experience of suffering and exile and oppression, that all creation is God's realm, not just the walls of the Babylonian city. In many ways, the account responds to questions that are sewed to the questions of those we share about the La Tierra theologies. Latinos ask those questions too, through their experiences of oppression and violence in immigration, migration, or ruptured treaties. They call out to their God in the hopes of gaining some insight about their situation.

The three strands (or trenza) within Genesis bridging a faith tradition with La Tierra theologies are: (1) the belief that God is the Creator and all that God created is good; (2) the desire to make sense of one's experience in relationship to that God, especially in times of great suffering; and (3) the foundation to all of this is the understanding that the human is intimately tied to both God and to the earth. Like the Genesis narratives, La Tierra theologies are passionate narratives about embodied involvement in the natural world. They draw on the many resources of Latinos/as' memory, including oral traditions, poems, stories, music, literature, and emergent virtual discourses. Deep metaphors speak to experiences of rootedness, interconnectedness, and interdependence of humans. These images are heightened by peoples' shared experience of their environment impacted by (im)migration and sense of homelessness and return.

In *Voices of Time: A Life in Stories*, Eduardo Galeano tells the story of a Catholic priest hearing confessions of the indigenous people in their Tojolobal language in 1992. As the priest listened to the confessions, the translator, Carlos Lenkersdorf, began to think that "no one could make sense of such mysteries." "These mysteries" referred to the sins Carlos translated for the people:

- He says he abandoned his corn . . .
- He says the cornfield is very sad. Many days since he last went.
- He says he abused the fire.
- He says he defiled . . .[24]

"Moreover, the priest had no idea what to do with these things that did not appear anywhere on Moses' list." Perhaps the translator felt that no one could "make sense of such mysteries," because of the different cultural context.[25] Latinos/as' relationships appear to go beyond the individual/interpersonal level to a broader field of relating, which includes family, land/place, and ancestors. This broader field of relating may include animate and inanimate things—or anything that reminds us or connects us to where we come from or to whom we belong. These relationships reflect the deep connection between 'adamah and God's breath.

Luis Valdez, a well-known Chicano filmmaker, insists that he has never "read a single poem by an Azteca, Tolteca, Maya or Yaqui atheist."[26] Valdez captures the Chicano imagination when he speaks about an integral epistemology:

MOVE
con el MOVEMENT
of the Cosmos
with the Nahui ollin
el quinto sol,
SOL DE MOVIMIENTO

It must move with the
EARTH. LA TIERRA,
It must move with the
MORNING STAR, VENUS
Quetzalcoatl, Jesucristo
it must move with God.

RELIGION (re-ligion)
is nothing more than the
tying back
RE-LIGARE
with the cosmic center . . .[27]

Indigenous peoples are sensitive to the human role of harmony and balance in the world. In 1991 the International Organization of Indigenous Women echoed once again at the Women for Our Healthy Planet Conference the wisdom of our ancestors:

Como mujeres de los pueblos indígenas, nuestras vidas están entrelazadas con el mundo natural. Nuestros mitos de la Creación cuentan de

*nuestra emergencia de tierras natales que ahora continúan nutrién-
donos, y que dan razón de ser a nuestras vidas. Somos inseparables de
la tierra de donde fuimos creadas.*

   *Como pueblos indígenas hemos vivido en estas tierras durante
decenas de miles de años, en armonía y equilibrio con toda la natura-
leza. Creemos que todo ser viviente fue dotado de vida por la Creadora
y como tal, somos partícipes de los dones de nuestra Sagrada Madre
Tierra. Dependemos de ella para nuestro sustento; dependemos unas
de otras mutuamente para el desarrollo de nuestras vidas y estamos
interrelacionadas física y espiritualmente. Como seres humanos, es
nuestra responsabilidad cuidarnos entre sí y cuidar a la Natualeza con
el mismo amor que la Creadora nos demostró al darnos la vida.*[28]

As women of the indigenous peoples, our lives are intertwined with the
natural world. Our myths of creation tell the story of our emergence from
the earth, which continues to give us nurturance and the reason for our
lives. We are inseparable from the earth out of which we were created.

   As indigenous peoples, we have lived on this land for tens of
thousands of years in harmony and equilibrium with all of nature.
We believe that all living creatures have been given life by the Creator
[note: the word "Creator" is in feminine form], and as such we are participants in the gift of our sacred mother earth. We depend on her for
our sustenance; we depend on each other mutually for the development
of our lives, and we are interrelated both physically and spiritually. As
human beings we have a responsibility to take care of each other and
to take care of nature with the same love that the Creator has demon-
strated to us in giving us life.

This statement articulated by the women of the indigenous peoples makes clear
that their lives are intertwined with the breathing pulse of all living things. It
demonstrates gratitude and an understanding of the inseparability of the land
with who we are. The statement acknowledges our creaturehood and our dependence, in a positive sense, on the Creator, the giver of life, for whom one lives.

   Earth is our first, our oldest home. Yet many in contemporary society experience a "homeless feeling" often articulated as "not belonging." At times this
"homeless feeling" is concrete. Many people in third world countries and in
developed countries have literally lost their homes. Indigenous people, the poor,
and women have been displaced from their home.

   "*Oikos*, as the experience of belonging somewhere intimate to one's bones,
eludes most moderns."[29] Peter Berger, renowned sociologist, argues that this
homeless mind is a condition of modernity itself. It is a condition that accompanies development and modernization.

   Even apart from homelessness as a matter of mind, it is quite literally
   displacement of one kind or another. The highly mobile rich, living

from hotel to suburbia lot to condo and hotel again hardly have an enduring community they consider their own, even less a binding commitment to a neighborhood. Many advertisements of job descriptions . . . declare the world their "oyster." Every locale is at their disposal, but no particular locale is home in a deep, settled sense.[30]

Would reclaiming the knowledge that the earth is in fact our first and oldest home have an impact on the experience of displacement and aloneness that earthlings feel? I believe this ancestral memory is deep within us. If we are to recall the wisdom of that memory, we must be able to stand firmly on the earth and in reverential silence recall the interdependence and intricate relationship we have, not just with the world, the earth, the land, but with the universe. As Teilhard de Chardin reminds us, "we are the universe reflecting on itself."[31] I find that consciousness and awareness about our common birth home is a starting point for this reflection.

Awareness of our common birth home initiates our understanding that this sacred place on which we stand and on which we make our habitat holds for us the secret of our relationships. In other words, our relationship with the earth is the context of all contexts. Many of us do not begin with this global insight, but with our particular, culturally conditioned experience of home. This is beautifully articulated in a song entitled *Mi Tierra (My Homeland)* written by Estefano and made popular by Cuban artist Gloria Estefan.

Your homeland strikes your soul when you are gone
Your homeland pushes you forth from its roots
Your homeland sighs when you are not there

The land where you were born, you can never forget
Because it holds your roots and everything you've left behind . . .

She flows through my blood . . . My homeland
I carry her inside me, yes indeed
I sing of my homeland, beautiful and holy
I suffer the pain that is in her soul
Although I'm far away, I can feel her.[32]

The classic Chicano literary writer Rudolfo Anaya recognizes the truth expressed in "my homeland flows through my blood" and the longing for home as self-knowledge. He argues that "it was indigenous America that held the tap root of our history; its mythology was the mirror by which to know ourselves."[33]

An example of this classic myth in Chicano literature is that of Aztlán.[34] Aztlán is that place somewhere in the Southwest where migrating groups of Asians came together in the process of becoming indigenous Americans.

There they evolved new levels of spiritual orientation to cosmos, the earth, and community . . . Somewhere in the desert and mountains of what we now call the Southwest, they created a covenant with their gods and from there they moved south to Mexico to complete the prophecy.[35]

In the religious psyche of many Chicanos there is a desire to return to Aztlán, to return to the homeland.[36] I concur with Anaya, who argues that the need for homeland is inherent in the collective memory of any group. It is a covenant with the tribal gods, an encompassing spiritual yearning for homeland.[37]

The Indo-Hispano religious sensibility was deeply influenced by the Pueblo, who held a great respect for the earth. "The recognition of the earth as . . . *la sagrada tierra* permeated the spiritual life of the Hispanic villages, and the process of synthesis fused Spanish Catholicism and Native American thought."[38] The worldview of these indigenous tribes held all things in relationship with one another. In this understanding we are part of the web of life and dependent on one another not just for survival but as a hope for our community. These principles—and the wisdom of the indigenous—continue to emerge from our contemporary writers. Anaya in his discussion about Aztlán reaffirms the values of the indigenous in his description of the Chicanos home of Aztlán:

The true guardians of Aztlán have been the Rio Grande Pueblo people, and the knowledge and love for their homeland has kept their spiritual thought alive in the face of overwhelming odds. They have kept themselves centered with the earth, and that has provided their communities a spiritual and psychological center . . . In a world so in need of ecological and spiritual awareness which would allow us to save the earth and practice democratic principles of love and sharing, these ties to the earth . . . provide hope for our community.[39]

Both the song *Mi Tierra* and the myth surrounding Aztlán manifest a people's affective ties with their environment and, in this case, the land. More permanent and less easy to express are feelings one has toward a place because it is *home* or the locus of memory or the expression of a prophecy, dream, utopia. Reflections about Aztlán and homeland are compelling. They are the carriers of emotionally charged events and situations raised to the level of symbol; they carry the aspirations and hope of a given people or person.

The vision of spirituality around the world, and in particular Indo-Hispano spirituality, focuses on relationships—relationships that include the whole of creation. Many indigenous people call the earth "Our Mother." In this context, all living creatures are related and are made reference to as brothers and sisters. Indigenous words for the earth indicate a sharing and belonging as opposed to possessing or owning.

I remember as a young girl a story my mother told me regarding her migration to the United States from Quito, Ecuador. She told me of her fifteen-hour flight at a time when airplanes consisted of two bleachers on either side. There were no snacks or frills offered. She told us that as she came down the steps of the plane, she felt herself getting weak in the knees and that by the time she had placed her foot on this land, she felt that *all the blood had drained from her body*.[40]

In addition to La Tierra theologies providing deep metaphors of being and aspiration, they also evoke centuries of widespread concern about the fragile character and unjust distribution, consumption, and destruction of these shared natural environments. Their vision of spirituality, lived out in the daily interaction and understanding of the faithful, is more structurally articulated within the Christian tradition. As believing Christians, people ground themselves in the premise that we are part of something much larger, a part of creation formed out of the dust of the earth and the breath of God; we are anchored—if not consciously then in the unconscious knowledge of our embodied life-force—and grounded to the earth. Our *latinidad*—that is, our identity as Catholic Latinos/as, sits upon our *latinidad* and our Catholicism. And within our Catholic tradition we recognize the goodness of all God's creation. We believe that God's wisdom, power, and love is ever present; and it is that love that is creative and unfolding in creation.

It is because we are the creation of a loving and relational God that *la tierra* becomes a gift to all creatures. And when we forget our identity, place, and inherited relationships, God in God's goodness sends the prophets, artists, "ordinary" saints and mystics to remind us of our communal relationship with all creation. Mystics and saints such as Benedict, Hildegard, and Francis have given us a language in which to nurture and sustain our relationship with Brother Sun, Sister Moon. Latin American theologian Leonardo Boff comments: "None of these masters believed that knowledge was a form of appropriation or of domination of things, but rather a form of love and of communion with things."[41] Theologian Thomas Berry beautifully invites us to move from being a collection of objects to a communion of subjects. It is through our embodied selves in the context of being a part of creation and living on this earth that we experience God. "The whole universe is God's dwelling." Earth, a very small blessed corner of the universe, gifted with unique natural elements, is humanity's home; and humans are never so much at home as when God dwells with them.[42]

As a Latina and a Catholic, I see two fundamental questions emerge: How can we move beyond our own ethnocentric boundaries, and at the same time celebrate the distinctiveness we bring as a people? What does our tradition offer in terms of understanding our commitment to justice? The Roman Catholic tradition is one that acknowledges creation as *sacramento*, that is, that nature itself reveals the presence of God. In the pastoral reflection *Renewing the Earth*, the Catholic bishops address the need for Christians to connect their faith with environmental issues. This makes sense in the long Catholic tradition of promoting a consistent ethic of life, one that begins with the acknowledgment and protection of the dignity of the human person, the clear understanding that the human person is a relational, social person.

The church is extending this understanding of the human in relationship to the protection of God's creation. The United States Catholic Conference pastoral statement *Renewing the Earth* (1991) reflects an understanding about the interrelationship and interdependence of life evident in the Judeo-Christian scriptures. This statement also argues for an authentic development that supports moderation and even calls for austerity in the use of material resources. Authentic development, the document states:

> is a balanced view of human progress consistent with respect for nature . . . It invites development of alternative visions of the good society and the use of economic models with richer standards of well being than material productivity alone. Finally, authentic development requires affluent nations to seek ways to reduce and restructure their over consumption of natural resources.[43]

One of the most controversial issues that arises within the environmental movement is the understanding that the impoverishment of people, in particular the most vulnerable of peoples, is closely related to how natural resources, technology, and commerce are distributed, processed, and exploited. It is evident that the level of energy consumption, especially as energy is used in first world countries, is a key issue. Increasingly experts are convinced that the way our generation is using energy will not leave enough for future generations. The web of life is one. Human mistreatment of the created world not only diminishes our dignity and sacrality but destroys the resources made available to us. Perhaps more frightening is that this mistreatment destroys the resources for our future generations.

While I appreciate this development in my own tradition, as expressed in *Renewing the Earth*, I also detect an emphasis on the dignity of the human person *above* all things. The rest of creation is subordinate to the needs of humanity. An alternative Christian view, interestingly enough, was offered by St. Francis of Assisi. Lynn White, Jr., tells us that the key to understanding St. Francis is understanding his belief in the virtue of humility. Humility is not just an individual virtue but a virtue for humanity as a species. "Francis tried to depose man from his monarchy over creation and set up a democracy of all God's creation."[44] Indigenous people emphasize a more mutually interdependent character, while the church's social teachings in conjunction with scripture challenges us to accept our role as caretakers and stewards for the earth and all of creation.

The indigenous traditions teach us that when we separate our existence from the processes of the landscape our hearts become fragmented and all that is "other" is objectified. La Tierra theology reminds us that the land is the source of our nourishment, survival, identity, and, indeed, life. Therefore, the contemporary ecological crisis must impress upon our consciousness a new awareness of our dependence on the earth and on one another. We must help our communities understand that we share a common destiny. This common destiny is linked with the earth because we belong to the earth. It calls for the re-embracing of values laden with the heartfelt meaning of our interconnectedness with creation.

The organic ecological perspective emphasizes interconnectedness and mutual interdependence of the "earth creature" with the earth. This interdependence could provide a resource for a new ethics. Returning to the insights of the indigenous women quoted earlier in this chapter we learn:

Consideramos que es nuestra responsabilidad cuidar a la tierra como si fuera nuestra madre. Como hijas de pueblos indígenas somos testigos de la destrucción de la tierra. Nuestra Sagrada Madre está siendo violada por la devastación de los bosques y las excavaciones para encontrar minerales; está siendo envenenada por desperdicios radioactivos y residuos químicos, y nosotras, sus hijas y sus hijos estamos siendo destruidos en esta despiadada búsqueda por apoderarse de sus recursos naturales, de sus preciosos dones y, así, mantener el consumismo. Sentimos el dolor y el sufrimiento de la MADRE TIERRA como si fuese nuestro sufrimiento.

We believe that it is our responsibility to take care of the earth, as if she was our mother. As daughters of the indigenous people we witness the destruction of the land. Our sacred mother is being violated by the devastation of the forests and the mineral evacuations; she is being poisoned through toxic wastes and radioactive chemicals; and we, her daughters and sons, are being destroyed. We feel the pain and suffering of our Mother Earth as if it were our own.[45]

The most difficult challenge will be to move away from the sole interest in individual lifestyles and ethnocentrism to a more adequate structural and systemic concern—or, as our tradition has called for, a commitment to the common good. First and foremost, it is imperative to understand that the key issue is survival itself, especially as it affects the survival of the more marginalized. K. C. Abraham, director of the South Asian Theological Research Institute, argues that political and social justice are linked to ecological health. He cites connections between economic exploitation and environmental degradation. Global atmospheric changes result from the destruction of forests, and the poor and indigenous peoples are driven out of their habitat for the sake of "development." The uneven distribution, control, and use of natural resources are just a few of the serious justice issues. For example, the natural resources needed to maintain the lifestyle of one person in the United States are equal to what is required for between two and three hundred people in Asia.[46] The rapid depletion of nonrenewable natural resources further raises the question of our responsibility for future generations.

Latino/a Catholics, especially those who can trace their roots to the indigenous or native understanding of "all our relations," have a contribution to make, particularly in relationship with the land.

The argument of survival in our modern world seems to urge us toward the common center of our humanity. When we established our rights to the homeland of Aztlán, we understood that that right belongs to every group or nation, and we understood how we share in all the homelands of world mythology. The children of Aztlán are citizens of the world. We must move beyond the limitations of ethnicity to create a world without borders. Each community rising to its new level of awareness creates respect for self and for others, and we are in need of this awareness before we destroy the Earth and each other.[47]

Alone I cannot surrender myself to the common center of our humanity. This commitment must be communally engaged on global and interdenominational levels.

Ecologists and social ecologists have clashed around the issue of setting the human person apart from the environment. The former want to speak ideally about "communion of subjects" translated as every living thing is equal; however, it is also the human subject who can consciously bear culture and its adaptation. This makes the human ultimately responsible for the balance of the biosphere. This functional separateness of the human person does not alter our need to understand the interrelationship and interdependence of all of creation. This insight leads one to a keen awareness of how the unjust exacerbations that accompany the shift from the productive wealth of land to the productive wealth of persons, which affects the universal destination of material goods, have had an especially great impact on women and ecology.[48]

The issue of the environment became a documented international concern in 1972 at the United Nations conference on human environment held in Stockholm, Sweden. However, it was not until 1983 that planetary survival was linked to the environment. The commission concluded that "to meet the needs of the present generations without compromising the ability of future generations to meet their own needs, environment protection and economic growth would have to be tackled as one issue."[49]

The primary goal of the summit was to find an equitable balance between the economic, social, and environmental needs of present and future generations as well as to lay the foundation for future global partnerships, especially between developed and developing countries. In 1988 the World Commission on Environment and Development published a report entitled "Our Common Future." This linked the environmental crisis to the need for sustainable development. It identified the financial practices that were worsening the North/South gap and the fact that women made up the majority of the world's poor and illiterate.[50]

Along with this data, we are reminded by Pope John Paul II in his document "The Ecological Crisis" that at the core, "the environmental crisis is a moral imperative. It calls us to examine how we use and share the goods of the earth, what we pass on to future generations and how we live in harmony with God's creation."[51] Abuse of our eco-balance (interpersonally and naturally) has a devastating effect on the world, but in particular on the most vulnerable links: women, children, and people in the third world. Deforestation, acid rain, soil erosion, and the indiscriminate use of fertilizers and pesticides lead to the breakdown of the local sustenance economy on which most women and children are dependent.[52] The poor, the marginalized, the powerless bear the brunt of the current environmental crisis. Their lands and their neighborhoods are, more likely than not, polluted. The term *environmental justice* has received much attention in recent years. Environmental justice refers to the inequitable distribution of environmental hazards. Unsurprisingly, the poor and minority communities are exposed to higher levels of toxic chemicals.

In the United States, the civil rights movement made explicit the connections between race, poverty, and pollution. Not only are activists in poor and minority communities focusing on how the environment and our people are affected by such things as toxic wastes and the larger global issues of deforestation, acid rain, and so forth, but more and more activists are articulating and demonstrating the impact that environmental issues have on the very health and overall quality of people's lives.

> While environmental injustice might be regarded as merely a reflection of similar disparities and inequalities that exist in other sectors of society (e.g. education and health care) and over other scales (the poor areas of cities compared with the rich areas, or more broadly, the poor developing countries and the industrialized countries) there are several good reasons why it should be of special importance to health professionals . . . the question of environmental justice reconnects people, and with them, public health and medicine, to their lived environment. It makes housing, heating, clean air, clean food and water and safe play areas for children as central to environmental health as the most complex problems.[53]

A 1993 report from the Center for Policy Alternatives warned that "people of color were 47 percent more likely than whites to live near a commercial hazardous-waste facility."[54] It is in their neighborhoods that toxic wastes are dumped and in their communities that, more likely than not, the poor and marginalized have undrinkable water. Their children are deformed and sick. They are the ones driven out of their lands and homes for the sake of development. As a community of faith what will be our response to the ethical challenge these situations raise?

The ecological movement and the feminist movement joined together to work not only for justice and peace but for the integrity of all of creation.

> [E]cofeminism is born of daily life, of day-to-day sharing among people, garbage in the streets, bad smells, the absence of sewers and safe drinking water, poor nutrition, and inadequate health care. The ecofeminist issue is born of the multiplication of rats, cockroaches and mosquites, and of the sores on children's skin . . . This is no new ideology. Rather, it is a different perception of reality that starts right from the unjust system in which we find ourselves and seeks to overcome it.[55]

Chung Hyun Kyung echoes my belief that a reintegration of the wisdom of the First Peoples and La Tierra theology will add to a more holistic spirituality and theology of creation. Indigenous wisdom will restore that which has been breached by the development of institutionalized patriarchal systems.

Although much contemporary rhetoric espouses "value language," we need to remember the *meaning* that incarnates these values. For example, the modern "value" of "land" is either neutral or reduced to an economic or functional value. On the other hand, Indian spirituality recognizes the intrinsic sacrality of La Tierra. This meaning and sense of the sacred are not confirmed by humanity but are revealed to us in the created and formational interplay with la tierra. This heartfelt *meaning* is foundational to the values that we must nurture and/ or regain if we are to continue to contribute to the web of life.

All great religious traditions recognize and acknowledge that life is a sacred gift. Ecologists, scientists, and theologians are asking how we can live with our Mother Earth, *Pachamama*,[56] in a way that promotes sustainability. And as we come to learn from La Tierra theologies, the concept of *Pachamama* is integral to the identity and culture of the people. For the Quechua and Aymara people of the Peruvian highlands, the land that they inhabit is more than just a commercial commodity. Land is not a product to be bought and sold. Kenyan environmentalist, political activist, and 2004 Nobel Peace Prize Laureate Wangari Maathai once said: "We are called to assist the earth to heal her wounds and in the process heal our own—indeed, to embrace the whole creation in all its diversity, beauty, and wonder."[57]

The earth is in danger, and it is very possible that the next generation of human beings will not have a livable earth to inherit. Thus today, through land reform laws, the Quechuas and the Aymaras are reclaiming the land of their ancestors as their birthright.

Members of communities of faith are not the only ones challenging the tradition and other religious communities to respond to this crisis. In 1990 a group of international scientists headed by Carl Sagan called on religious leaders and churches to react to the crisis as "the only social agents with the ethical power to respond to 'crimes against creation.'"[58] One response to this crisis and call for direction comes from theologian Leonardo Boff of Brazil. He argues for development that is in solidarity with those generations yet to come. Boff challenges those economic policies and structures that function from a vision of relentless growth. "The model of unlimited growth is possessed by a demon."[59] He states:

> it is constructed only on the basis of exploitation of the working classes, on the underdevelopment of dependent nations, and on the rape of nature. The result is that economic development does not give rise to simultaneous social development. The benefits are available only to a restricted group of nations or to the upper classes of a nation, and they do not include the well being of nature.[60]

The ecological crisis challenges us to examine our way of thinking and behaving in general and, more specifically, our attitudes about nature and development. Chung Hyun Kyung states, "Ecologists enable us to see our anthropocentric sinfulness in relation to other living beings. They call us to a new pattern of relations with all beings in the cosmos based on mutuality, interdependence and life-giving values."[61]

La Tierra theologies join the voices of ecologists to reclaim and reinterpret symbols and imagine new and hopeful ways to affirm life. The theologies honor the subject, respect the language and affectivity of the heart, realize the importance of teaching our future generations how to humanize their will, and increase one's ability to understand and draw from an intuitive nature of thinking that is dynamic, fluid, creative, searching, and excludes no one. These theologies call for a radical openness to all, placing as paramount the work of relationships as a consequence of being. We as theologians must play an active role in this conversation and bring to the table both the life-affirming aspects of our religious and cultural traditions and our skills and commitment to transformation.

In addition, we would like to turn our attention to the wisdom found in the spirituality of many indigenous people. As Chung Hyun Kyung states, "This spirituality gives full value to creation as a dynamic and highly integrated Web of Life. It exudes life-giving values: sacredness of the land, reverence for all creatures, judicious use and conservation of the earth's resources, compassion for the weak, oppressed and marginalized."[62]

Finally, these values make possible the aspirations articulated by Valdez:

> we must re-identify
> with the center and proceed
> outward with love and strength
> AMOR Y FUERZA and
> undying dedication to justice.[63]

This dedication to justice begins with the recognition of the myriad voices that must remain in conversation with one another, including those bold enough to defend La Tierra.

Creation theologies began with indigenous peoples in the Middle East responding to their experience of God in their context. Christians built on their experience as recorded in Jewish Scriptures—and western European experience informed the evolving Christian theologies, with some insights from mystics such as Francis, Eckhart, and Hildegard. The increasing separation from land and from creation itself led to privileged people subjugating others and using creation to fuel greater privilege, creating a crisis for the earth. As theologians consider again creation, they are informed by contemporary indigenous people's theologies, which both return us to Jewish/Christian roots and invite a newer and deeper understanding of the interdependent web of creation.

Notes

1. The sixteenth-century Spaniards believe that, through a process of abstraction, the intellect was capable of obtaining truth and communicating it through words. In contrast, the Nahuatl believed that only the heart was capable of obtaining truth. Words were not enough: only through *flor y canto* (flower and song) can truth be obtained and communicated (Virgilio Elizondo, *Mestizaje: The Dialectic of Cultural Birth and the Gospel* [San Antonio: Mexican American Cultural Center, 1978], 114-15). The Nahuatl wise men and wise women did not believe that they could form rational images of what is beyond, but they were convinced that through metaphors, by means of poetry, truth was attainable (Miguel León-Portilla, *Aztec Thought and Culture*, trans. Jack Emory Davis [Norman, Okla.: University of Oklahoma Press, 1963], 79).

2. I am grateful for the insights of my colleague Dr. William J. Buckley. See also Frank Moore Cross, *Canaanite Myth and Hebrew Epic: Essays in the History of Israel* (Cambridge, Mass.: Harvard University Press, 1997).

3. Catechism of the Catholic Church (United States Catholic Conference), #198.

4. Justo Gonzalez, *A Concise History of Christian Doctrine* (Nashville, Tenn.: Abingdon Press, 2005), 35.

5. Anne M. Clifford, "Creation," in *Systematic Theology: Roman Catholic Perspectives*, vol. 1, ed. Francis Schüssler Fiorenza and John P. Galvin (Minneapolis: Augsburg Fortress Press, 1991), 198.

6. Zachary Hayes, O.F.M, *What Are They Saying about Creation?* (New York: Paulist Press, 1980), 66-67.

7. Ibid.

8. Phyllis Trible, *God and the Rhetoric of Sexuality* (Philadelphia: Fortress Press, 1978), 94-105.

9. Wes Howard-Brook, *Come Out, My People: God's Call out of Empire from the Beginning to the End* (Maryknoll, N.Y.: Orbis Books, 2010).

10. Ibid., chapter 3.

11. Clifford, "Creation," 199.

12. Gonzalez, *Concise History*, 43.

13. Ibid., 49, 51.

14. Hayes, *What Are They Saying?* 30.

15. Trible, *God and the Rhetoric of Sexuality*, 74.

16. Jon Sobrino, *The Principle of Mercy: Taking the Crucified People from the Cross* (Maryknoll, N.Y.: Orbis Books, 1994), 50, 49.

17. Ibid., 49-50.

18. Ibid., 53.

19. Ibid., 55.

20. "The Cry for Land," joint pastoral letter by the Guatemalan Bishops' Conference, in *"And God Saw That It Was Good": Catholic Theology and the Environment*, ed. Drew Christiansen, S.J., and Walter Grazer (Washington, D.C.: United States Catholic Conference, 1996), 283. Available online at http://faculty.theo.mu.edu/schaefer/ChurchonEcologicalDegradation/documents/CryforLand_000.pdf.

21. Ibid., 286.

22. Ibid.

23. Ibid., 275.

24. Eduardo Galeano, *Voices of Time: A Life in Stories*, trans. Mark Fried (New York: Metropolitan Books, 2006), 84.

25. Ibid.

26. Luis Valdez, *Early Works: Actos, Bernabe and Pensamiento Serpentino* (Houston: University of Houston, Arte Publico Press, 1990), 176.

27. Ibid.

28. "Madre Tierra, Madre Creadora," in *Con-Spirando*, no. 2, Octubre 1992, *Revista Latinoamericana de ecofeminismo, espiritualidad y teologia*, 16-17.

29. Larry L. Rasmussen, *Earth Community, Earth Ethics* (Maryknoll, N.Y.: Orbis Books, 1996), 96.

30. Ibid. (Rasmussen is paraphrasing Berger.)

31. Lorna Green, *Earth Age: A New Vision of God, this Human and the Earth* (Mahwah, N.J.: Paulist Press, 1994), 125-26.

32. Estefano, *Mi Tierra*, Foreign Imported Productions and Publishing, Inc. (BMI, 1993).

33. Rudolfo Anaya and Francisco A. Lomeli, *Aztlán: Essays on the Chicano Homeland* (Albuquerque: Academia/El Norte Publications, 1989), 238.

34. For Chicanos Aztlán referred back to an ancient Aztec myth, a myth that articulates the longing for a homeland, a homeland that was somewhere north of present-day Mexico City. "Aztlán meant that Chicanos and Mexicans shared a common historical origin and identity, identity grounded in a mestizo people proud of their Indian roots." Richard Griswold del Castillo and Arnoldo De Leon, *North to Aztlán: A History of Mexican-Americans in the U.S.* (New York: Twayne Publishers, 1996), 131.

35. Ibid., 238.

36. This affect-laden image and desire for a return to Aztlán may have eschatological implications. Traditionally eschatology referred to "last things" and dealt with the themes of death and judgment, heaven and hell. In addition to being a systematic reflection on the content of our Christian hope, Monika Hellwig has eschatology focused on the "realization of the promised reign of God in all human experience and in all creation." I resonate with Hellwig's interpretation of eschatology in light of La Tierra theology for two reasons. One, she incorporates in this understanding God's reign and the promise of that reign for all human experience and all of creation. Two, the key, and many times dismissed or undervalued, contribution is the notion of hope. For Christians the content of hope is based on the person of Jesus. For Chicano theology there is an additional nuance to this hope, a return to the homeland, Aztlán. Monika K. Hellwig, "Eschatology," in *Systematic Theology: Roman Catholic Perspectives*, vol. 2, ed. Francis Schüssler Fiorenza and John P. Galvin (Minneapolis: Fortress Press, 1991), 349-50.

37. Anaya and Lomeli, *Aztlán*, 238.

38. Ibid., 239.

39. Ibid., 240.

40. Jeanette Rodríguez, "La Tierra: Home, Identity and Destiny," in *From the Heart of Our People: Latino/a Explorations in Catholic Systematic Theology*, ed. Orlando Espín and Miguel Díaz (New York: Maryknoll, 1999).

41. Leonardo Boff, *Ecology and Liberation: A New Paradigm* (Maryknoll, N.Y.: Orbis Books, 1995), 38.

42. *Renewing the Earth: An Invitation to Reflection and Action on the Environment in Light of Catholic Social Teaching* (pastoral statement of the United States Catholic Conference, November 14, 1991), 6.

43. Ibid., 9.

44. Lynn White, Jr., "The Historical Roots of Our Ecologic Crisis," in *Readings*

in Ecology and Feminist Theology, ed. Mary Heather MacKinnon and Moni McIntyre (Kansas City: Sheed & Ward, 1995).

45. "Madre Tierra, Madre Creadora," 16.

46. K. C. Abraham, "A Theological Response to the Ecological Crisis," in *Ecotheology: Voices from South and North,* ed. David Hallman (Maryknoll, N.Y.: Orbis Books, 1994), 69-70.

47. Anaya and Lomeli, *Aztlán,* 241.

48. *Centesimus Annus,* encyclical of Pope John Paul II (1991), 30-37.

49. "Sustaining the Future," Earth Summit +5, Special Session of the General Assembly to Review and Appraise the Implementation of Agenda 21 (New York, June 23-27, 1997).

50. "Women and Sustainable Development," Earth Summit +5, Special Session of the General Assembly to Review and Appraise the Implementation of Agenda 21 (New York, June 23-27, 1997).

51. *Renewing the Earth.*

52. Kwok Pui-Lan, "Ecology and the Recycling of Christianity," in *Ecotheology,* 108.

53. Editorial, "Less Equal Than Others," *Lancet* 343, no. 8901 (April 2, 1994): 805.

54. Rasmussen, *Earth Community,* 76-77. See Benjamin A. Goldman and Laura Fitton, *Toxic Waste and Race Revisited: An Update of the 1987 Racial and Socio-economic Characteristics of Communities with Hazardous Waste Sites* (Washington, D.C.: Center for Policy Alternatives, 1994), 77.

55. Mary Judith Ress, *Ecofeminism in Latin America* (Maryknoll, N.Y.: Orbis Books, 2006), 126.

56. *Pachamama* is the generous earth mother of Andean culture.

57. Conversation with LeeAnne Beres, executive director of Earth Ministry.

58. James Burbank, "Can Eco-Justice Go Mainstream?" *National Catholic Reporter,* June 6, 1997, p. 4.

59. Ibid., 20.

60. Ibid.

61. Chung Hyun Kyung, "Ecology, Feminism and African and Asian Spirituality" in *Ecotheology,* 175.

62. Ibid., 177.

63. Valdez, *Early Works,* 177.

3

Creation

A Cosmo-politan Perspective

CARMEN NANKO-FERNÁNDEZ

Introduction: Where Buffalo Roam?

"Oh give me a home where the buffalo roam . . ." begins a patriotic classic sung by generations of schoolchildren across the United States. Like millions of diasporic and migrating Latin@s and Hispan@s who have made their home on the U.S. Atlantic coast, I too was born and raised in la tierra of the iconic roaming buffalo—the Bronx, New York.[1] Grazing contentedly in the bucolic human-made setting of the Bronx Zoo are the descendants of the appropriately named "Mother Herd." The Bronx ancestors of these urban American bison were sent west from New York City in the early twentieth century to repopulate the species in order to forestall extinction.

This preservationist initiative to breed bison in urban captivity and then relocate them into their native habitat was at the heart of the founding of the New York Zoological Society. Begun in the 1890s, the initiative was not without its perils. The first herd did not survive because the alien diet of indigenous Bronx grasses proved deadly. Members of the subsequent city herd, raised on hand-fed prairie grasses, eventually made their way to the Wichita Mountain Preserve in Oklahoma from Fordham Station in the Bronx, via Grand Central Depot on October 11, 1907. Instrumental throughout the process was Theodore Roosevelt and, appropriately, during his term as president of the United States, the bison return "home." In Oklahoma, thousands of Plains Indians gathered to "witness the return of the 'Great Spirit's cattle.'"[2]

Considered sacred to a number of indigenous peoples in what is now the United States, the buffalo, a misnomer for bison, become an iconic symbol of an imaginary western frontier consumed by Manifest Destiny. With the decimation of the bison population came a longing for conservation perhaps best captured in the movement that results in the establishment of the federally protected

41

national parks system. The apparent inconsistencies of these preservationist inclinations are best illustrated in the person of Theodore Roosevelt, born and raised in New York City. An avid hunter and amateur naturalist, "Roosevelt made conservation a vital, almost violent pursuit. It went with being manly, brave, patriotic. It was as populated with animals as any children's book. It was scientific and yet saturated with religious meaning, patrician but populist, global and yet fueled by jingoistic fervor."[3]

Deeper critical investigation of this particular slice of the restoration of the American bison first reveals the multiple layers, ambiguities, and even contradictions that accompany the construction, communication, and interpretation of creation stories and re-creation praxis, ancient as well as contemporary, sacred and secular. Second, this little-known episode in the history of complicated interconnections among the created/creatures reflects the power of empires and the religious impulses that ground imperial actions and their relational networks. Third, the Bronx bison and their ancestors situate the construction of creation and re-creation narratives and actions in the heart of the metropolis.

A View through an Hurbano Postcolonial Lens

The notion that we are in a postcolonial age seems a bit presumptuous to me, a resident of the District of Columbia with an affinity for Puerto Rico. Nuyorican scholar Juan Flores cautions, "for the purpose of identifying the conditions faced by Puerto Rican, Mexican American, Dominican and other Latino peoples in the United States, and the economic and political domination of their home countries, the term postcolonial seems to be jumping the gun at best."[4] However, postcolonial criticism, as a spectrum of perspectives that attend to imperial and colonizing influences and consequences in texts and contexts, provides an optic for exploring select biblical, ancient, national, and contemporary creation narratives latinamente. In the "shadow of empire," such an analysis "presupposes and demands a specific optic with clear implications for both the representation of the past and the representation of the present."[5] In this case, with respect to biblical texts, "it is necessary to speak not just of one empire but of a succession of empires involving, depending on the locality of the center in question, the Near East as well as the Mediterranean Basin: Assyria, Babylon, Persia, Greece, Rome."[6] The additional texts that shape the varying lenses of Latin@ theologies also make it necessary to consider imperial contexts of sixteenth- through eighteenth-century Spain, nineteenth- through twenty-first-century United States, and the often-ignored empires of the indigenous Americas prior to Iberian conquest.

Postcolonial analysis attends not only to the interrelated and complex worlds of texts but also to the equally complicated contexts of particularly situated readers and interpreters. For example, Jean-Pierre Ruiz observes, the Bible played a crucial role among the colonizers themselves as they sought to frame their enterprise in the terms of a worldview shaped in large measure by their understanding of the Bible. While several important studies address the religious dimension of the conquest of the Americas, scholars of religion have devoted relatively little attention to this period in the history of biblical interpretation, or to the place of the Bible in shaping the Spanish colonial enterprise in the Americas.[7]

A focus on readers/interpreters de carne y hueso, across time and geography, shifts attention to the multivalent and polyvocal dimensions revealed by privileging "contextualization and perspective, social location and agenda, and thus on the political character of all compositions and texts, all readings and interpretations, all readers and interpreters."[8] The political character highlights the network of relations constitutive of those on the peripheries and in the centers, as well as those who mark their relationships to power in the vast range of distances in between.

The significance of space and place concerning texts and their subsequent interpreters is key to understanding the ways in which texts map and remap worlds of meaning. This *locating* of meaning is particularly imperative for theological reflections on creation, as expressed through narrative and praxis. Too often overlooked in the theological interpretation of cosmological texts is the complex role of the metropolis in the construction of narratives, in the shaping of authors' and interpreters' cosmovisions, and as ritual or ceremonial cosmic topography. The implicit message sent is that creation themes are antithetical to the city, that nature and culture inhabit separate spheres, that the rural is preferred over the urban as a site of creaturely communion. On the contrary, drawing on the scholarship of Mircea Eliade, Jaime Lara, in his study of the Spanish colonial city at the intersection of religion and urban planning, suggests:

> If the world is going to be lived in, it must be consciously and ritually founded . . . Such ritual orientation and construction of sacred space have cosmogonic value, for space is efficacious in the measure to which it reproduces the work of the gods, especially that human intervention in space: the city.[9]

The United Nations estimates that by 2030 over 60 percent of the global population will reside in urban areas, a rapid growth predicted on the basis of the historic reality that as of 2008, for the first time ever, over half of the world's population resides in cities.[10] In their 2007 report on the state of the global population, the UN notes that this urban explosion will not be without environmental consequences. "The conventional wisdom has been that the expansion of urban space is detrimental in itself. Since many cities are situated at the heart of rich agricultural areas or other lands rich in biodiversity, the extension of the urban perimeter evidently cuts further into available productive land and encroaches upon important ecosystems."[11] However, the report concludes, "there is increasing realization that urban settlements are actually necessary for sustainability. The size of the land area appropriated for urban use is less important than the way cities expand: Global urban expansion takes up much less land than activities that produce resources for consumption."[12]

As shifting Latin@ populations continue to reshape and fuel the growth of any number of U.S. cities and their suburbs, it is appropriate and timely to employ critically an urban optic, especially in viewing matters of creation. This distinctive perspective from the city is grounded in a hybridity characteristic of Latin@ experiences of la vida cotidiana in the United States. These are experiences marked by fluidity in languages, traditions, migrations, cultures, identities, and even in the ethnic and racial constitution of families. To underscore these dynamic and fluid interactions, characteristic of a Latin@ theological hermeneutic emerging from urban contexts, I borrow the term Hurbano, Spanglish for a new programming format for contemporary music that is both Hispanic and urban. "The format has been taking over stations, bringing in crossover-friendly bilingual disc jockeys and playlists that feature reggaeton, along with Latin pop and hip-hop."[13] These featured musical genres are intentional and creative in their hybridity. They draw on traditional Latin music styles as well as more contemporary and varied expressions, fuse languages and cultures with ease, often reflect the local contexts out of which they arise, and for the most part are producible at the grassroots level with minimum resources. While the mainstreaming of these genres into a marketable commodity is a matter for another discussion, it is precisely the locating of urban Hispanic perspectives that drives this proposal for an Hurbano theological lens.[14]

What has la ciudad to do with creation? What do Babylon, Jerusalem, Patmos, Madrid, Salamanca, Tenochtitlán, Cuzco, San Juan, Mexico City, San Antonio, Los Angeles, New York, Washington, D.C., among others, have to do with one another when it comes to theologizing latinamente on the texts and contexts of creation? Using postcolonial lenses with a cosmo-politan optic, that is, a perspective that intentionally attends to intersections of cosmos and city, this exploration of creation begins by considering a biblical text from Genesis 1 that has particularly influenced reflections by Latin@ theologians. A critical examination of select scholarship by divergent yet representative Latin@ theologians follows, centering on the work of Jeanette Rodríguez, Alejandro García-Rivera, and Virgilio Elizondo. Finally, from insights that link cosmos and metropolis, perhaps contemporary theological cartographies will emerge proposing alternate directions through barrios that may be absent on previous maps. Such an engagement may result in "voice and visibility to a whole series of social, ethnic, cultural and sexual persons and sectors that are usually deprived of any voice or image, and that are never represented on maps or in tourist guides."[15]

What Does Babylon Have to Do with Jerusalem?

A survey of Latin@ theologies reveals a tendency to emphasize theological anthropology with a starting point grounded in Genesis 1:26-28. It should come as no surprise that theologians who belong to communities traditionally marginalized and even deprecated because of race, ethnicity, and language would gravitate toward a scriptural affirmation of all humanity, male and female, as bearing the divine image. This integral connection between theological anthropology and creation, in the words of Miguel Díaz,

> has been reflected in U.S. Hispanic efforts that analogously relate the intentional divine plan to create a diversity of creatures with the intentional U.S. Hispanic goal to affirm and promote sociocultural diversity (*mestizaje/mulatez*). This anthropological focus on creaturely differences sees the horizontal fellowship and asymmetric order of creation as something good and essential.[16]

For a significant number of Latin@ theologians the *imago Dei* is at the heart of creation doctrine. It is the basis for human solidarity and praxis for justice. It is an affirmation of humanity's creatureliness in diversity, though the focus is primarily on human diversity and not on the web of creation.[17] Mindful of an indigenous inheritance of respect for the natural world, participation in the creative agency of God is qualified by a cautious understanding of dominion. As articulated by Justo González, this domination "is not that of an autocrat but rather that of self-giving governance. What is surprising is that this was known as early as the time when these words were written, long before modern technology. But given the fact of that power, the biblical author sets a limit to it: It is power given to be used after the likeness of God's power. It is creative power."[18]

A quarter of a century ago biblical scholar Richard Clifford cautioned theologians of the day about their use of Hebrew Scriptures in their formulations of theologies of creation. He warned of the temptation to read back into these ancient texts through lenses crafted in a "modern spirit." He identified "four significant differences between the ancient West Semitic and modern concept of creation: the process, the product or emergent, the description, and the criteria for truth." Clifford noted that ancient Near Eastern texts lack a dichotomous distinction between nature and humans found in contemporary constructions of creation and that their concern is not so much the physical world but "human society organized in a particular place." For Clifford, "Ancient cosmogonies were primarily interested in the emergence of a particular society, organized with patron gods and worship systems, divinely appointed king (or some other kind of leader), and kinship systems." Within this framework, Clifford observes, narrative served as the favored means of communication, allowing for a flexibility where variations on a theme or multiple versions not only allowed for alternate perspectives but were tolerated. In this sense, drama not theory is the criterion for truth for cosmogonies. "Drama selects, omits, concentrates; it need not render a complete account."[19]

With Clifford's caution in mind, what happens if Genesis 1 is reread through a postcolonial optic that restores the Priestly (P) authors to a context, whether exilic or postexilic, that is in the shadow of empire? What does Babylon have to do with Jerusalem? Does this text, often read by Latin@s with a particular focus through the lens of the *imago Dei,* offer other insights into understandings of creation if consideration is given to P as part of a people on the margins "who find themselves in imperial, colonial, and neocolonial contexts"?[20] Will there emerge, as biblical scholar David Sánchez contends, a challenge to "centers of power in patterned ways . . . the subversion of the imperial myths used to justify and maintain such claims to power"? Sánchez uses the expression *imperial myth* intentionally in a "cosmological sense, referring specifically to the way in which these myths function in justifying claims of imperial and colonial power and in the ongoing maintenance of such power."[21]

Both Sánchez and biblical scholar Kenton Sparks cite mimetic behavior as a response to colonizing activity that threatens peripheral communities. The complexity of relationships in imperial contexts defies simplistic categorization. There is a spectrum of postures possible between complicity and resistance, "a complex mix of attraction and repulsion" that complicates constructions of margins and centers.[22] For Sánchez this draws attention to "the actual multi-texturedness of cultural contacts."[23] For Sparks, this suggests the possibility of a particular intertextual relationship of elite emulation whereby the "Priestly Pentateuch . . . imitates specific Mesopotamian textual traditions for polemical reasons."[24] This act of imitation establishes difference or otherness as well. From Sparks's perspective, P's emulation of Mesopotamian texts was a means to "bestow upon Israel, and upon Israel's religion, that air of antiquity and authority that was attached to all things Mesopotamian."[25] In this way, the colonized validate their legitimacy by strategically reshaping their own traditions in a manner that situates Israel in the stream of the neighboring cultures past and present. This cross-pollination of cultural literatures is possible prior to the Babylonian exile; however, the experiences of diaspora and return, displacement and colonization under the imperial aegis of Babylon and Persia, increase the probability of interaction and intertextuality. Sparks contends,

> It is one thing to imagine that P was miming Mesopotamian literature from afar . . . But it is quite another thing for P to do so in the exilic or postexilic period, when many Jews—especially of the Diaspora intelligentsia—lived in close quarters with non-Jews. In this context, it seems to me more likely that P's mimetic strategy reflects a context of cultural competition, in which he labored to protect the identity and integrity of his Israelite community against the threat of cultural assimilation.[26]

For Sparks, the response of P to this perceived threat to identity is the construction of "Israelite tradition—its history and institutions—as authentic and attractive alternatives to the dominant culture of Mesopotamia." He concludes that the fruits of this labor are borne out by the "vibrant communities of Judaism that emerged in Mesopotamia, Palestine, and the far-flung Diaspora."[27]

Scholars have long maintained a connection between the Priestly account of creation in Genesis 1 and the Babylonian *Enūma Elish*, enumerating similarities and correspondences as well as vast theological differences. "Yet even these differences sometimes reveal the underlying influence of Mesopotamian ideas. In terms of anthropology, P goes beyond *Enūma Elish* by tracing humanity's divine animation to the creator rather than to the blood of a rebel demon. Humanity bears the 'image of God.'"[28] Scholars note that typically the representation of deities is the realm of monarchs, thus legitimating their earthly authority. Helen Schüngel-Straumann observes, "P relies on the ancient oriental ideology of the monarchy found quite frequently in Egypt where the king or queen represented the deity."[29] What distinguishes P's usage, according to Schüngel-Straumann, is that it is not restricted to earthly rulers but the image of God applies to all humanity. Therefore, male and female are God's representatives, and as such, "humankind is responsible for the creatures, just as God is for the whole of creation."[30]

If, as Clifford maintains, ancient Near Eastern cosmogonies are about the organization of given societies in particular places, then culture and community are the primary concern, not the modern presumption of creation and the relationship to the physical universe. In the *Enūma Elish*, for example, "The victory of Marduk establishes the institutions of divine and human governance (Babylonian kingship and related institutions), which a great people required in order to exist."[31] In response, the P cosmogony in Genesis 1 subverts the very literature it mimics by positing instead that it is God alone, no representative monarch, who provides structure, security, and identity for the people Israel. Therefore whether living in diaspora as a foreigner or in a colony as a returning settler, or at "home" as a colonized other, the community needs to understand that their allegiance is owed to the God who brings them together as a people. At the same time, implicit is a responsibility as well as an identity as bearers of the image of God. What are the implications for God's representatives in light of what Schüngel-Straumann describes as an impressive example of the "democratization of an ancient oriental concept"?[32]

From a Latin@ perspective, a postcolonial exploration of Gen 1:26 adds a critical level of depth to an appropriation of P's passage that emphasizes the relationship among divinity, diversity, and identity. However, naïve inattention to the layers of meaning in the cosmovision that produces the P account and to the concrete imperial circumstances that drive its construction and initial transmission mitigates the power of the narrative to speak anew in Latin@ contexts. The possibility that P's creation composition seeks to preserve the identity of a colonized community from imperial assimilation certainly resonates with the experiences of any number of contemporary Latin@ scholars. The role of creation narratives as being more about the preservation of a people and the establishment of the relationships that govern their existence has been lost in layers

of interpretation that derive their perspectives from a premise of the separation
of the "natural" or physical universe and humanity. The role of cosmogonies,
whether they are deployed by those in power seeking to affirm the order they
need to maintain their control or by those who in their powerlessness find a
means of articulating a counternarrative that sustains their existence, remains
to be explored. The role of these theological dramas in the creation of culture
and community in particular places and for the organization of particular peoples deserves critical reflection.

Latin@ Theologies of Creation

Theologizing about creation has been limited in Latin@ scholarship. Three
distinctive approaches are evident in the works of Jeanette Rodríguez, Alejandro García-Rivera, and Virgilio Elizondo. For the purpose of this survey,
each selection chosen provides a window into a particular aspect of creation,
yet all posit an appreciation for the interconnectedness of the cosmos. They
draw on sources from the Christian tradition, including expressions of popular
religion, as well as on indigenous cosmogonies. Rodríguez in her La Tierra
theology seeks to attend to the earth. García-Rivera in his anthropology of
creatureliness proposes a cosmic fellowship among *criaturas de Dios*. Elizondo
finds a new humanity in the *mestizaje* that arises from the suffering imposed by
the legacy of the conquest.

Jeanette Rodríguez: La Tierra Theology

In 1999, Jeanette Rodríguez's nascent reflections in ecotheology focus on "*la
tierra* as it is expressed within the notions of home, identity, and destiny."[33]
Her La Tierra theology is drawn from a variety of disparate sources including
interpretations of Nahua concepts, some contemporary Chicano authors, and
various strands within the Roman Catholic tradition. These initial explorations
attempt to establish la tierra as "an authentic category" based on its potential
to "bridge the variety of issues that emerge in ecological reflection: the term in
Spanish (*la tierra*) can indicate either the earth, the land, or one's country." She
further suggests that mestizaje is integral to interpreting "the Latino/a relationship to the earth" as both ecological reflections and mestizos/as are "neither
totally this or that but rather a bit of this *and* of that, which is its identity and
its strength."[34] The work remains underdeveloped, though what is striking is the
attempt to link relationally matters of identity to ecological matters of sustainability via an eclectic retrieval of sources that in the end appeals to an undefined
mestizaje.

The choice of sources employed by Rodríguez presumes Latin@ intimacy
with the land that is inseparable from other relationships with "family, com-

munity, and even the cosmos." She contends *our relationship with the earth is the context of all contexts* and as such is the primal homeland. With Chicano authors like Rodolfo Anaya she regards the spiritual yearning for homeland as inherent in communal collective memory. Rodríguez also attempts to connect la tierra to both identity and destiny, an understanding that keeps humans grounded in the web of life.[35]

Rather ambitiously, La Tierra theology "joins the voices of ecologists to reclaim and reinterpret symbols and imagine new and hopeful ways to affirm life."[36] This occurs through appeals to a limited number of works—poetry, songs, novels—contemporary and ancient that apparently support Rodríguez's contention that La Tierra theology is essentially aesthetics. However, the arguments lack substance and the selective and uncritical use of Chicano literature, campesino songs and Chicano appropriations of Nahua concepts such as Aztlán, tend toward a romanticized imaginary that raises the question of whether it resonates with a Latin@ population that, as census data continues to document, is more likely to live within metropolitan areas.

Alejandro García-Rivera: An Anthropology of Creatureliness

Alejandro García-Rivera is among the more prolific Latin@ theologians writing in the area of theological cosmologies.[37] Among the themes he develops across his scholarship is an understanding of the human as a creature among creatures. He explores what he calls an anthropology of creatureliness in one of his earliest works, his theological reflections on the "little stories" surrounding St. Martín de Porres.[38] For García-Rivera, the image of God functions as the "dynamic force that continually shapes the human creature" and as the catalyst for fellowship.[39] Through fellowship, human creatures participate in their own creatureliness, "entering into the very process of creation which the Creator graciously has offered to share with this very special creature."[40] He goes on to assert that this participation in one's own creatureliness is also the basis for the human creatures' participation in the "creatureliness of the cosmos." In accepting and participating in one's status as created, as criaturas, humans in effect become co-creators with God, and among their creative acts is establishing relationships. In relationship, each informs and expands the other's understanding of *imago Dei*, so much so that one becomes a new creature.

Central to García-Rivera's proposition is an appreciation for and an affirmation of difference. He locates sinfulness in the Iberian conquest and subsequent colonization, in part, in the simultaneous denial of another's difference while defining an artificial identity for the self. He points to the Encomienda system as example. "The encomenderos did this by defining an artificial identity for themselves (the civilized adult) that led to the exploitation and slavery of millions (the natural children)."[41] For García-Rivera, this imposition of identities that subsume differences "under the conditions of symmetry is ultimately a violent act, an act against the cosmic order which was created not so much as a hierarchy but as a fecundity of different creatures."⁴² Symmetric relationships, conceptualized by García-Rivera from the perspective of "hegemony masked as harmony," preserve the power to "mask the strains of domination, making some forms of hierarchy appear 'natural,' even graceful."⁴³

With cosmic diversity and the potential for fellowship in mind, García-Rivera turns to the popular "little stories" of Lima's St. Martín de Porres. He sees the stories as a challenge to the artificial and often unjust relationships contrived in a colonized New World. These stories of the boundary-crossing Martín call into question the behavior of his contemporaries by offering an alternate way of being in relationship that is faithful to the intentions of the Creator, a way of living and being as a *criatura de Dios*. "St. Martín's anthropology of creatureliness was not so much a dismantling of the hierarchy of being but a protest that the metaphor of a ladder with a special rung of rationality where the human stood was not only inappropriate but dangerous." In retrieving the image of Martín depicted with a dog, cat, and mouse sharing a bowl of human food, García-Rivera posits a cosmic fellowship enabled by Martín, a restructuring of creation by the human creature capable of healing relationships. For García-Rivera "the dog, cat and mouse story reveals the creatureliness of the human, an identity found through the capacity for cosmic fellowship given the human creature by the Creator." At the same time, Martín, through his charity for these criaturas of Lima, "transformed natural enemies into natural fellows . . . Creatureliness and identity had been transformed and interrelated into the cosmic fellowship enabled by St. Martín."⁴⁴

Respect for human creatureliness that does not collapse differences but embraces them as part of the Creator's cosmic intention opens possibilities for graced fellowship across the spectrum of criaturas de Dios. At the same time, it is the capacity for healing, a process of restoration, that ties human creatures to the cosmic order. For García-Rivera, it is the little stories of Martín's actions of feeding, sustaining, and healing all criaturas de Dios, not only across the socioeconomic and racial strata of his time but across the rational/irrational divide as well, that challenge, reinterpret, and remap Old World anthropology into a New World anthropology.⁴⁵ "The healing of dogs as if they were people, for example, pointed out what is at stake in loving God and having fellowship with one's Creator. One must cross the gap of asymmetry inherent in the created order. God created the world in marvelous diversity, a garden of fecund asymmetries."⁴⁶

Virgilio Elizondo: Mestizaje and the New Creation

Virgilio Elizondo engages the Guadalupan event and the text of the *Nican Mopohua* through a hermeneutical lens of mestizaje in his book *Guadalupe: Mother of the New Creation*. In his interpretation, "the image is poetry that is seen while the poem is imagery that is heard." A reading of Elizondo suggests that this poetic text functions for him as a creation narrative, "a highly complex mestizo (Nahuatl-European) form of communication" containing elements of both Nahuatl and Iberian worldviews that together "say new things that neither alone could have expressed." However, at the same time he insists that story must be understood through the cosmovision of the Nahuatl peoples because it is the "indigenous account of the real new beginnings of the Americas . . . sacred narrative as remembered by the victim-survivors of the conquest who were equally the first-born of the new creation."[47]

Elizondo establishes the text within the tradition of Aztec creation narratives through its use of particular recognizable indigenous symbols as well as its employment of literary formulae such as "when it was still night (*Nican Mopohua*, v. 7)." He points to the usage of this phrase and others in Nahuatl mythology as indicative of a period immediately prior to and/or at the dawn of creation. Within an Aztec cosmovision built on cyclic creations, the timing coincides with a possible expectation of a new creation out of a destructive end. For Elizondo, it is the creation of mestizos/as born of a violent conquest that bears theological significance. As expressed by Néstor Medina, "in Elizondo's *mestizaje* scheme, the significance of Guadalupe corresponds to the first biological-cultural *mestizaje* that took place and the spiritual *mestizaje* that followed expressed concretely in the devotion of Guadalupe."[48]

Elizondo interprets the *Nican Mopohua* from within the context of the largest city with a Hispanic majority in the United States. He recalls in the opening pages of the book the impact of his childhood pilgrimage to Mexico City from San Antonio, Texas. This family trip to the basilica that houses the image of La Virgen Morena becomes, by his own admission, a core moment in his life. His later reflections as a theologian take him from considering Guadalupe as evangelizer of the church and the Americas, to protector and liberator of the marginalized, to "the beginning of a new creation." This identification establishes La Morenita at the center of a cosmovision whereby she becomes "the mother of a new humanity, and the manifestation of the femininity of God—a figure offering unlimited possibilities for creative and liberating reflection. Juan Diego is the prototype of the new human being of the Americas."[49]

For Elizondo, mestizaje is not only the consequence of two conquests, the first by fifteenth-century Spanish conquistadores and the second by nineteenth-century U.S. Anglo-Europeans; it signifies divine creative and necessarily redemptive activity with universal implications. "It meant creation of a new humanity, the humanity of inclusion, where all people would find a place to celebrate the divine. The divine process continued in the ongoing act of creating a *mestizo/a* people, so as to establish a cosmic order characterized by *mestizaje*."[50] In Elizondo's interpretation of the Guadalupan event and the *Nican Mopohua* the role of creation narratives in the preservation of a people and in the delineation of relationships is especially evident. Writing in resistance to the negative experiences of Mexican Americans in the southwestern United States, Elizondo takes that which is a cause for self-deprecation, and re-envisions hybridity as revelatory of the divine. In Elizondo's reconceptualizing of mestizaje as foundation of a new creation, a new cosmic order breaks in marked by "a universality of harmony, a universality of respect for others in their differences, a universality of love, compassion, and mutual aid."[51] In other words, the mixture that is the source of discrimination and pain for the majority population of San Antonio and the doubly colonized southwestern United States is affirmed with divine intentionality in the Guadalupan event as an "anthropological reversal" that is the basis of a new, improved, and inclusive humanity.[52] This has cosmic repercussions in Elizondo's interpretation of the *Nican Mopohua*. Guadalupe merges and enriches "the Nahuatl concept of cosmic determinism and the Western concept of historical absolutism" in a manner that generates "a new metaphysics that recognizes the interconnectedness and interdependence of all creation while equally recognizing the uniqueness and value of the individual within the cosmic."[53]

Rubén Rosario Rodríguez finds a corrective to Christian creation doctrine in Elizondo's explication of Guadalupe as the Mother of the new creation. He sees in Elizondo's appropriation of Nahuatl perspectives a retrieval of aspects ignored in Western tradition, namely, creation "as an interconnected and interdependent organic system" as well as a shift in focus away from humanity as the pinnacle. Rosario Rodríguez also appreciates the theological anthropology that arises when the *imago Dei* embraces not only mestizaje but "as a feminine manifestation of the divine, Guadalupe challenges the church to embrace the full humanity of women." This theology of creation that places mixture, and consequently those who are marginalized, poor, and oppressed, at the center of the *imago Dei*, is then both liberative and inclusive.[54]

A Postcolonial Hurbano Analysis

This survey of three Latin@ approaches is by no means exhaustive, yet it serves to highlight three separate entries into theological reflection on creation. While all affirm a commitment to the interconnection of the created universe, inevitably the prime focus is the human creature, in relation to tierra (Rodríguez), in relation to other creatures (García-Rivera), and in relation to other humans (Elizondo). A critical analysis of these three perspectives through a specifically Latin@, postcolonial, and urban lens reveals both the contributions of these theologies to the greater discourse on creation as well as lacunae.

A Clash of Empires

Curiously, the postcolonial hermeneutic stance adopted by a number of Latin@ biblical scholars is often missing in the scholarship of Latin@ theologians, even in their interpretations of scripture. Sustained and critical attention to multiple empires and imperial contexts is pervasive in Latin@ biblical scholarship, yet, as is evident in the three approaches presented, it is limited by theologians to Iberian colonization and secondarily to U.S. expansionism of the nineteenth and twentieth centuries. Totally ignored or glossed over are the implications of imperial contexts in scriptural texts and contexts as well as in indigenous texts and contexts. While Latin@ theologians, Rodríguez and Elizondo in particular, prefer to focus on the flor y canto aspect of the Nahua inheritance, scholar of religious and Mesoamerican studies Davíd Carrasco points to the complexity and contradictions of Aztec life. He writes:

> The fractured image that results from a total view of Aztec life raises questions of the most profound and emotional sort . . . how could a people who conceived of and carved the uniquely marvelous calendar stone and developed one of the most accurate calendrical systems of the ancient world spend so much time, energy, and wealth in efforts to obtain and sacrifice human victims for every conceivable feast day in the calendar? Why did a people so fascinated by and accomplished in sculpture, featherwork, craft industries, poetry, and painting become so committed to cosmic regeneration texts is an image of startling juxtapositions of Flowers, Song/Blood, Cut.[55]

In dealing with cosmogonies, the role of empire cannot be dismissed. As observed by biblical scholar Richard Clifford and noted earlier, these narratives establish social order, organize a people, clarify relationships, and communicate identity through text, space, and ritual. Ethno-historian Johanna Broda's exploration of Templo Mayor, the sacred precinct in Tenochtitlán, the capital city of the Aztec empire, concludes that certain aspects point to an embedded presence of a more ancient Mesoamerican cult associated with the "sacralization of the earth and water." However, she continues,

> the cult of water, mountains, and the earth was imbued with ideological elements through which the Aztecs pursued to legitimate their political dominion. The monumental art of the second half of the fifteenth century clearly expressed this imperial vision and claim to legitimacy. A cosmovision of ancient cultural roots was integrated into Mexican state cult.[56]

The retrieval of sources cannot ignore the intersections with or influences of empire. This is also significant for understanding the relationship with land, which as Rodríguez points out includes considerations of home, earth, and country. This is further complicated in imperial and colonial relationships, whether that empire is Aztec, Spanish, U.S., Babylonian, Persian, or Roman. For peoples on the margins of empires, in colonies, or in diaspora, relationships to imperial centers are measured by tributes and taxation, exploitation of labor and resources, political accommodation and subjugation.

Imperial contexts also give rise to counternarratives that may mimic yet challenge the prevalent cosmovision or propose alternate visions that might be necessary for survival, resistance, or even cohesion in diaspora. For example, is the Guadalupe event (and the *Nican Mopohua*) a tool for evangelizing indigenous populations or is it a counternarrative in support of group identity, crillollo/a or mestizo/a? Reading Elizondo's interpretation of both the Guadalupe event and the *Nican Mopohua* through the lens of mestizaje recognizes a contemporary appropriation that is a counternarrative to the accounts of U.S. national origins that have marginalized peoples on the basis of race, ethnicity, and language. Elizondo's interpretation posits an alternate vision whereby the despised are the new humanity. He reverses the myth that has been responsible for adverse conditions of his people, primarily Mexican Americans across the southwestern United States, and promotes a vision that finds inclusion not in the so-called American Dream but in a future that is mestizo/a.

This interpretation is, at best, somewhat naïve, ignoring the violent, racialized, and imperial history of mestizaje. Néstor Medina demonstrates that this emphasis further marginalizes indigenous peoples and observes that for some first peoples Guadalupe "functions as a symbol imposed upon their communities in order to have them abandon their ancient religious symbols and practices."[57] He further shows that through the lens of mestizaje, the diversity of Latin@s in the United States is homogenized, and the inclusion of all peoples is not possible in an image that is both narrow and historically destructive. The past and potential damage of a metaphor that reinscribes racialized categories that propped up imperial domination should not be minimized or even sanitized. Ignorance of the insidious dimensions of empire and colonization inevitably result in complicity with or replication of power dynamics that are antithetical to respect for creation. Medina's caution cannot be easily synthesized or romanticized; the symbol of our "new humanity" is also "the perennial reminder of the conquest and eradication of the indigenous religious traditions."[58] Attention to imperial and colonial implication of sources for theologizing is imperative in order to develop credible theologies of creation that do not legitimate the tools of empire.

Diversity Yes, Mestizaje No

Among the contributions of Latin@s to theologies on creation is the situating of difference in the *imago Dei*. Respect for difference opens an appreciation for the diversity constitutive of the web of creation and implies that diversity is also constitutive of the divine. García-Rivera establishes cosmic fellowship across criaturas de Dios, through the image of the mulato Martín whose healing activity restores relationships across the creaturely web. The mixture of peoples, identified as mestizaje in the work of Elizondo, finds expression in Juan Diego and Our Lady of Guadalupe. This new creation not only represents the origins of a people but bears eschatological significance for humanity and, by extension, the created universe.

A number of Latin@ theologians and others influenced by Elizondo adopt the term mestizaje to refer to the permutations resulting from colonial-era human mixtures that transgressed racial, cultural, and therefore inevitably socio-economic distinctions. Imbued with theological significance, the term expands beyond its original referent, mestizos/as—children born of Spanish and indigenous peoples of the Americas—to include mixtures of all types, not just human. For example, in developing La Tierra theology, Rodríguez uses the concept to describe ecological reflections that are "a bit of this *and* of that," and one book reviewer uses it to describe Elizondo's writing as a "unique *mestizaje* of pastoral practice with intellectual reflection, an option for the poor with an openness to the rich and influential."[59] Unnuanced and decontextualized appropriations of the term mitigate the violence out of which the expression was literally born and this results, as Medina notes, in a "confusing web of contradictory and competing meanings that make the use of mestizaje increasingly problematic."[60] From Medina's perspective, with the evolution of mestizaje into a synonym for generic intermixture, "Elizondo comes dangerously close to making absolutizing claims that run contrary to his theological proposal . . . all but divorcing the term from the original distinctively historical-social-political specificity of Latinas/os in the United States"—not to mention its divisive usage in Latin America.[61]

In the construction of creation theologies, as a term intended to embrace the diversity of humanity, mestizaje conveys the opposite of inclusion and for some suggests loss and assimilation. Using mestizaje, even with the best of intentions, erases the African presence, subjugates the indigenous, and ignores the complexity of the racial and ethnic categorizations that arise from Iberian colonization. The concept as used theologically posits a new creation in the Americas only when the Iberian is introduced—What of the hybridities, ethnic and cultural, that characterized pre-fifteenth-century, Africa, América, and Iberia?

As catalyst of a new creation, mestizaje and mulatez, do not result in any improvement in the old creation. While the mulato Martín de Porres may be the protagonist for cosmic fellowship, his healing activity across the socioeconomic, racial, and cultural continuum of Lima did not result in a profound altering of relationships in colonial Peru, or an improvement in conditions for enslaved peoples of the African diaspora, or even respect for the lowly Dominican brother within his own house. While the mestiza Virgen de Guadalupe may locate difference in the divine, for Medina, "Elizondo's *mestizo/a* interpretation of Guadalupe amounts to affirming the dual cultural-spiritual ancestry of *mestizos/as* but says nothing of the conditions of oppressions of and struggles of resistance by indigenous people at the time of the apparition or in the present."[62]

The instinct to situate diversity in the *imago Dei* is a promising development for reimagining theologies of creation because from Latin@ perspectives this says as much about God as it does about humanity. Diversity that is understood as dynamic, unfolding, and ongoing is not only a reflection of the divine in the creature but also a reflection of the created in the divine. Creation in the divine diversity and its correlative, creative praxis with divine responsibility, deserves sustained reflection for the possibilities it opens to understanding the network of relationality across the creaturely spectrum. However, a more sophisticated and critical handling of baggage-laden images is necessary lest Latin@ theologies participate in the very universalizing trends our scholarship often critiques.

The Cosmo-polis

Absent from Latin@ theological reflections on creation is consideration of the intersection of city and cosmos. Rodríguez's La Tierra theology raises the connection of tierra with earth and homeland. Her use of sources, however, does not pursue the urban dimension prevalent in both biblical and indigenous texts. Carrasco's mining of sources reveals that for the Aztecs the capital city of Tenochtitlán was "the material expression of the Mexica conviction that they had come to occupy the axis of the cosmos."[63] Rodríguez appeals nostalgically to Aztlán, the primordial home of the Nahua, but neglects to entertain the ramifications that the end of their journey is the founding of their new home, the city. As Carrasco illustrates, dominance and subjugation are part of this narrative, the capital "was remembered as the *axis mundi* of the wider society, subduing others, gathering wealth, and exercising its magnetic political authority."[64] One version of the founding narrative explains:

> Our god orders us to call this place Tenochtitlan. There will be built the city that is to be queen, that is to rule over all others in the country. There we shall receive other kings and nobles, who will recognize Tenochtitlan as the supreme capital . . . let us go among these marshes of reeds, rushes, and cattails, as our god has indicated. Everything he has promised us has come true; thus we shall now find this place for our city.[65]

Scripture and the Christian tradition, too, are replete with urban-based images—so much so that their influence in Christian practice and arts deserves more serious attention. Jaime Lara, scholar of liturgy and Christian art, maintains that similarities between Mexica cosmology and medieval Catholicism were such that Nahuas had no problem "appreciating Christian urban symbolism" especially in light of their own visions of "urban utopia."[66] Lara sees intersections between the New Jerusalem of Revelation 21 and Aztec constructions of what Carrasco calls an urban-centered world. "What is certain is that for Mesoamericans, as for Jews and Christians, earthly cities were modeled after heavenly patterns; they were navels of the earth, pilgrimage centers, and models of ideal living."[67]

Lara holds that Jerusalem, real and imagined, has been the central metaphor for Judeo-Christian constructions of space, time and destiny. "Like the cities of Mexica, it was a hagiopolis and cosmic model."[68] He proposes that for Christians and Jews, the loci of salvation history remain Eden and Jerusalem. "Both the terrestrial paradise of Adam and Eve and the rebuilt city of Jerusalem were embedded in the prophetic literature of the Middle Ages and

the Renaissance."[69] Participation in this biblically informed creative and eschatological thrust is evident in the writings of Cristóbal Colón: "God made me
the messenger of the new heaven and the new earth of which he spoke through
Saint John in the Apocalypse, after having spoken of it through Isaiah, and he
showed me to that location."[70] It is further manifest in what Lara describes as
"the urban-planning treatise employed most frequently in Hispanic America,"
namely, the prophetic book of Ezekiel. Lara suggests that colonial Latin American city design was highly influenced by both the books of Ezekiel and Revelation, and "the invention of the printing press had thus made the construction of
surrogate Jerusalems possible even across the Atlantic Ocean."[71]

García-Rivera, in his most recent explication of a theological cosmology
dismisses the metaphor of the city and instead proposes a move toward a garden
as "the context of our redemption." Contrary to the aforementioned UN population study, which sees planetary sustainability as tied to the city, García-Rivera
insists, "We are now being placed face to face with the fragile facts of our natural existence. The city can no longer be the human habitat that isolates us from
our origins in the dust of the earth. Indeed, the city must either be transformed
or it will be dissolved."[72]

In some ways, his conceptualization of redemption in terms of place is consistent with the centrality of place in the cosmologies of the Mexica and the
Spanish colonizers and evangelizers. For García-Rivera, the relevant question
is not When we will get there? but Where are we going? He believes this shift in
paradigm from time to place may "help us see with renewed and restored eyes
the crucial role that cosmology plays in theology. Where are we going? . . . We
are going to the *garden of God*, our home in the cosmos." In his cosmovision the
garden represents a "successful fusing of nature and art" and "the premier locus
of a theological cosmology."[73] It can be argued that the cosmovisions of both the
Nahua and the Spanish Christians did not make sharp distinctions between time
and space and their respective cosmo-politan perspectives did not see opposition
between nature and art.

García-Rivera's turn to the garden but rejection of the city is curious
because gardens are most frequently associated with urban, and certainly sub-
urban, life. In addition, his first explorations of cosmology through the lens of
the santo Martín are clearly situated in the metropolis. The locus of Martín's
activity is the city of Lima; the cosmic fellowship is established with creatures
who are part of the urban landscape and even domestic life. While mice are
classified as vermin, and cats and dogs scrounge the scraps of the city, in the
spectrum of creatures, they pose the lowest level of threat to humans and their
natural enmity toward one another is often beneficial to humans.

Of the three theologians studied in this survey, Elizondo situates his perspective in the heart of a city. San Antonio, Texas, is the U.S. metropolis with
the largest majority Latin@ presence. Elizondo says explicitly that the experience of being Mexican American in this context is influential in his theological
reflections. This home city and Paris, the metropolis where he completed his
academic work, become for him sites "where the new humanity is emerging and

taking shape." He experiences Paris as a place where the whole world is paraded before him, a "universal city . . . where boundaries did not exist, where differences did not mean barriers." On the other hand, for Elizondo, San Antonio is not only the frontier zone, the border, between two countries constitutive of his identity, but "the meeting point and often the site of violent clash between two radically different civilizations." It is here on the frontera, locus for the second mestizaje, the encounter between mestizos/as and what he calls the Nordic Anglo cultures of the United States, where the new intermingling of peoples is occurring. It is a place where he sees "differences are not being destroyed, but they are being transcended and celebrated as together we usher in the beginning of the new race of humanity."[74]

Elizondo's romanticized and overly optimistic interpretations of his urban contexts provide an entrée into his construction of a mestizaje with universal implications. He quickly shifts his attention from the city to the person of the mestizo/a, in whom he finds that "racial and cultural mixture does not have to be destructive of cultural identity, but that it can even strengthen it."[75] The complexities of urban realities do not receive his critical assessment. For example, Elizondo's experience of Paris is one of privilege, as an international graduate student, or even as tourist. He admits that his creativity emerged from observations of the variety of humanity passing his vantage point in outdoor cafés. The Paris he assumes is embracing of difference and apparently without boundaries is not the reality of the African and Arab immigrants relegated to the banlieue. These residents, *extra muros,* are part of a tradition of those who have lived outside the city's walls, whether eleventh-century poor, fifteenth-century military deserters and thieves, or nineteenth-century social undesirables.[76] In some ways, today's banlieue residents are the collateral damage of French colonization, and the violence, "an expression of post-colonial trauma."[77] Elizondo's hopeful positing of a new humanity in a "universal city" misses the fact that for "many Parisians, the banlieue represents 'otherness'—the otherness of exclusion, of the repressed, of the fearful and despised."[78]

The reality of San Antonio is equally complicated. As Elizondo observes, multiple colonizations and mixtures of peoples and cultures mark this region's history. In a majority Latin@ city within striking distance of the border, matters of migrations and status within the United States are not without conflict, as intralatin@ divisions also dictate variance in response. While he is certainly more fluent in the complex socioeconomic reality of this urban context, Elizondo's tendency is to move quickly beyond the tensions. He conflates matters of difference into mestizaje, thus flattening what would have been a richer reflection on the urban as a site where the intersections of people and cultures indeed do create new ways of a negotiated living together. Such a theologizing, thoroughly cognizant of the complexity of urban human experience in a particular place, might have provided new insights with the city as metaphor for hybridity, for engagement across difference, and possibly for conceptualizing how humanity might coexist in a new way.

A Return to the City

Theological talk of a new creation cannot avoid attending to those "dissident cartographies" that map complicated cityscapes and "different geographies of estrangement or exile" hidden in plain sight.[79] Theological reflection on the intersection of cosmos and polis is certainly not new. For Latin@s, it is part of our multiple inheritances from a number of sources, including but not limited to indigenous conceptions and constructions in the American hemisphere; biblical texts and centuries of situated readers interpreting those texts in their respective contexts; lived experiences of centuries of peoples from across the globe. From the experiences of an exilic people dreaming about their Jerusalem, to the urban dwellers of John's Apocalypse, to Augustine's *City of God* and the urban planners of old and new Spain, cities are poised in constructive visions of origins and ends. Latin@ theological contributions about la tierra, las criaturas de Dios, and on new ways of being human would further advance contemporary reflections on creation by attending to cosmo-politan trajectories. Like the urban communities addressed in John's Apocalypse, Latin@ cosmo-politan theologies, too, invite contemporaries to entertain critically "the ambiguities of their own urban existence, together with the uneasiness with which their own Christian convictions promised to infuse them."[80]

Taking seriously the intersections of cosmos and polis underscores the inextricable relationship among creation, eschatology, and the expectations of a responsible and just convivencia. With tongue-in-cheek, Carlos Monsiváis, Mexican cultural journalist and poet, best reminds us that the ancient concerns remain:

> In the beginning, since the Christian god was running late, Huitzilopochtli and Tlaloc created the heaven and the earth (so called because its most abundant component was water) . . . and the first thing the gods did to improve the appearance of the first city was creating a Centre, since they were aware of its magnetic pull . . . Soon Tenochtitlan was inhabited and organized in its very avant-garde fashion, and then came the creation of the Province to promote migrations to the big city.[81]

Notes

1. This text intentionally uses el arroba (@) with an acute accent @́. The convention of combining the "o" and "a" into one character that is gender inclusive is utilized by other scholars, particularly in culture studies. For me, the symbol for "at" (@) intensifies the significance of social location for doing theology from Latin@ perspectives, i.e., latinamente. The use of @ in electronic communication situates individuals and highlights networks of connection, two aspects constitutive of Latin@ theological methods. I add the acute accent (@́) as a reminder of the hybridity of language, culture, and identity.

Toward this end, this text also does not italicize Spanish, underscoring the fluidity of English and Spanish in daily usage. See Nanko-Fernández, *Theologizing en Espanglish: Context, Community and Ministry* (Maryknoll, N.Y.: Orbis Books, 2010). Thanks to my colleagues from the faculty seminar at the Catholic Theological Union for their helpful input on an earlier draft of this chapter.

2. Douglas Brinkley, *Wilderness Warrior: Theodore Roosevelt and the Crusade for America* (New York: Harper/HarperCollins, 2009), 625. See also the children's book by Neil Waldman, *They Came from the Bronx: How the Buffalo Were Saved from Extinction* (Honesdale, Pa.: Boyds Mills Press, 2001).

3. Jonathan Rosen, "Natural Man," *New York Times* (Sunday Book Review), August 6, 2009, available online at http://www.nytimes.com/2009/08/09/books/review/Rosen-t.html.

4. Juan Flores, *From Bomba to Hip-Hop: Puerto Rican Culture and Latino Identity* (New York: Columbia University Press, 2000), 214.

5. Fernando F. Segovia, "Biblical Criticism and Postcolonial Studies: Toward a Postcolonial Optic," in *The Postcolonial Biblical Reader*, ed. R.S. Sugirtharajah (Oxford: Blackwell Publishing, 2006), 42.

6. Ibid., 38.

7. Jean-Pierre Ruiz, "The Exegesis of Empire: Toward a Postcolonial Reading of Christopher Columbus's *El libro de las profecías*," paper presented at the annual meeting of the Catholic Biblical Association of America, San Francisco, California, 2003, cited with permission; available online at http://www.cwru.edu/affil/GAIR/cba/ruiz.pdf.

8. Segovia, "Biblical Criticism," 34.

9. Jaime Lara, *City, Temple, Stage: Eschatological Architecture and Liturgical Theatrics in New Spain* (Notre Dame, Ind.: University of Notre Dame Press, 2004), 91.

10. United Nations Population Fund (UNFPA), *State of World Population 2007: Unleashing the Potential of Urban Growth*, available online at http://www.unfpa.org/swp/2007/english/introduction.html.

11. UNFPA, chapter 4, "Urban Growth and Sustainable Use of Space"; available online at http://www.unfpa.org/swp/2007/english/chapter_4/index.html.

12. Ibid.

13. Joe Dean, "Genre Watch: Reggaeton," January 5, 2007; available online at http://emusician.com/remixmag/artists_interviews/musicians/reggaeton/index.html.

14. For example, some of the scholarship of biblical scholars Jean-Pierre Ruiz and David Sánchez reflect what I call an Hurbano perspective. See Ruiz, "Biblical Interpretation from a U.S. Hispanic American Perspective: A Reading of the Apocalypse," in *El Cuerpo de Cristo: The Hispanic Presence in the U.S. Catholic Church*, ed. Peter Casarella and Raúl Gómez, S.D.S. (New York: Crossroad, 1998), 78-105; idem, "'They Could Not Speak the Language of Judah': Rereading Nehemiah 13 between Brooklyn and Jerusalem," in *They Were All Together in one Place? Toward Minority Biblical Criticism*, ed. Randall C. Bailey, Tat-siong Benny Liew, and Fernando Segovia (Atlanta: Society of Biblical Literature, 2009), 79-96; Sánchez, *From Patmos to the Barrio: Subverting Imperial Myths* (Minneapolis: Fortress Press, 2008).

15. José Miguel G. Cortés, "Dissident Cartographies," in *Dissident Cartographies*, ed. José Miguel G. Cortés (Barcelona: Sociedad Estatal para la Acción Cultural Exterior [SEACEX], 2008).

16. Miguel H. Díaz, "Theological Anthropology," in *Handbook of Latina/o Theologies*, ed. Edwin David Aponte and Miguel A. De La Torre (St. Louis: Chalice Press, 2006), 70.

17. See for example Javier R. Alanís, "The *Imago Dei* as Embodied in *Nepantla*—A Latino Perspective," *Currents in Theology and Mission* 32, no. 6 (December 2005): 448-53; Ismael García, *Dignidad: Ethics through Hispanic Eyes* (Nashville: Abingdon Press, 1997), 130-37.

18. Justo L. González, *Mañana: Christian Theology from a Hispanic Perspective* (Nashville: Abingdon Press, 1990), 131.

19. Richard J. Clifford, S.J., "The Hebrew Scriptures and the Theology of Creation," *Theological Studies* 46 (1985): 509, 510, 512.

20. David A. Sánchez, *From Patmos to the Barrio: Subverting Imperial Myths* (Minneapolis: Fortress Press, 2008), 45.

21. Ibid., 45-46, 161 n. 24.

22. See ibid., 9, and Bill Ashcroft, Gareth Griffiths, and Helen Tiffin, *Post-Colonial Studies: The Key Concepts* (New York: Routledge, 2000), 12-13.

23. Sánchez, *From Patmos to the Barrio*, 9.

24. Kenton L. Sparks, "*Enūma Elish* and Priestly Mimesis: Elite Emulation in Nascent Judaism," *Journal of Biblical Literature* 126, no. 4 (2007): 631.

25. Ibid., 642.

26. Ibid., 646.

27. Ibid., 647, 648.

28. Ibid., 631.

29. Sparks attributes this insight to Nahum M. Sarna, *Genesis = Be-reshit: The Traditional Hebrew Text with the New JPS Translation* (JPS Torah Commentary; Philadelphia: Jewish Publication Society, 1989), 1 . Helen Schüngel-Straumann, "On the Creation of Man and Woman in Genesis 1-3: The History and Reception of the Texts Reconsidered," in *Biblical Studies Alternatively: An Introductory Reader*, ed. Susanne Scholz (New York: Prentice Hall, 2002), 92.

30. Schüngel-Straumann, "On the Creation of Man and Woman," 93.

31. Clifford, "Hebrew Scriptures," 510.

32. Schüngel-Straumann, "On the Creation of Man and Woman," 93.

33. Jeanette Rodríguez-Holguín, "*La Tierra*: Home, Identity, and Destiny," in *From the Heart of Our People: Latino/a Explorations in Catholic Systematic Theology*, ed. Orlando Espín and Miguel Díaz (Maryknoll, N.Y.: Orbis Books, 1999), 189.

34. Ibid., 205, 206.

35. Ibid., 192, 194-96.

36. Ibid., 203.

37. Alejandro García-Rivera, *The Garden of God: A Theological Cosmology* (Minneapolis: Fortress Press, 2009); idem, "The Whole and the Love of Difference: Latino Metaphysics and Cosmology," in *From the Heart of Our People*, 54-83; idem, "Wisdom, Beauty and the Cosmos in Hispanic Spirituality and Theology," in *El Cuerpo de Cristo*, 106-33.

38. Alejandro García-Rivera, *St. Martín de Porres: The "Little Stories" and the Semiotics of Culture* (Maryknoll, N.Y.: Orbis Books, 1995).

39. Ibid., 101.

40. Ibid.

41. Ibid., 100.

42. Ibid., 101.

43. Robert J. Schreiter, introduction to *St. Martín de Porres*, xvi.

44. García-Rivera, *St. Martín de Porres*, 105, 102.

45. Ibid., 67

46. Ibid., 100.

47. Virgilio Elizondo, *Guadalupe: Mother of the New Creation* (Maryknoll, N.Y.: Orbis Books, 1997), xix, xviii-xix, xviii.

48. Néstor Medina, *Mestizaje: (Re)Mapping Race, Culture and Faith in Latina/o Catholicism* (Maryknoll, N.Y.: Orbis Books, 2009), 122.

49. Elizondo, *Guadalupe*, xi.

50. Medina, *Mestizaje*, 14. See also Alejandro García-Rivera, "Virgilio Elizondo's Place among Theologians of Culture," in *Beyond Borders: Writings of Virgilio Elizondo and Friends*, ed. Timothy Matovina (Maryknoll, N.Y.: Orbis Books, 2000), 254.

51. Elizondo, *Guadalupe*, 134.

52. Ibid., 107.

53. Ibid., 117.

54. Rubén Rosario Rodríguez, *Racism and God-Talk: A Latino/a Perspective* (New York: New York University Press, 2008), 173, 172.

55. Davíd Carrasco, "Myth, Cosmic Terror, and the Templo Mayor," in *The Great Temple of Tenochtitlan: Center and Periphery in the Aztec World*, by Johanna Broda, Davíd Carrasco, Eduardo Matos Moctezuma (Berkeley/Los Angeles: University of California Press, 1987), 125.

56. Johanna Broda, "Templo Mayor as Ritual Space," in *Great Temple of Tenochtitlan*, 106-7.

57. Medina, *Mestizaje*, 123.

58. Ibid.

59. Rodríguez-Holguín, "*La Tierra*," 206; Daniel G. Groody, "*Beyond Borders*, by Timothy Matovina," book review, *Journal of Hispanic/Latino Theology* 9, no. 1 (December 2000): 58-60.

60. Medina, *Mestizaje*, 59.

61. Ibid., 35.

62. Ibid., 123.

63. Davíd Carrasco, *City of Sacrifice: The Aztec Empire and the Role of Violence in Civilization* (Boston: Beacon, 1999), 32.

64. Ibid., 35.

65. Diego Durán, *The History of the Indies of New Spain,* trans. Doris Heyden (Norman, Okla.: University of Oklahoma Press, 1995), 43-44, cited in Carrasco, *City of Sacrifice*, 35.

66. Jaime Lara, *City, Temple, Stage*, 92-93. It is worth reading Lara in conversation with Carrasco.

67. Ibid., 94.

68. Ibid., 109.

69. Ibid., 94.

70. Cristóbal Colón, in a letter to Doña Juana de la Torre, the nurse of Prince Juan, cited in Ruiz, "The Exegesis of Empire." "Del nuevo cielo y tierra que dezía Nuestro Señor por San Juan en el Apocalipsi, después de dicho por boca de Isaías, me hizo mensajero y amostro aquella parte" (from Consuelo Varela, ed., *Cristóbal Colón: Textos y documentos completos* [Madrid: Alianza Editorial, 1982], 243; translation from Djelal Kadir, *Columbus and the Ends of the Earth: Europe's Prophetic Rhetoric as Conquering Ideology* [Berkeley: University of California Press, 1992], 153).

71. Lara, *City, Temple, Stage*, 103, 109.

72. García-Rivera, *Garden of God*, 5.

73. Ibid., 6, 120, 121.

74. Virgilio Elizondo, *The Future Is Mestizo: Life Where Cultures Meet* (New York: Crossroad, 1992), xi, x, 111.

75. Ibid., 95.

76. Andrew Hussey, "The Paris Intifada: The Long War in the Banlieue," *Granta* 101 (2008): 45.

77. Ibid., 58.

78. Hussey, "The Paris Intifada," 59.

79. Cortés, "Dissident Cartographies."

80. Jean-Pierre Ruiz, "No Temple in the City: The Place of Worship in the Apocalypse of John," in *Humanizing the City: Politics, Religion and the Arts in Critical Conversation,* ed. Patrick D. Primeaux (San Francisco: Catholic Scholars Press, 1997), 3.

81. Carlos Monsiváis, "Assembly of Cities," in *Dissident Cartographies.*

4

Who We Are

A Latino/a Constructive Anthropology

MICHELLE A. GONZÁLEZ

Systematic theology is characterized by several classic loci that are shared areas of emphasis for theologians. They include: Christology (the identity and meaning of Jesus Christ), methodology, concept of God, pneumatology, ecclesiology, Mariology, soteriology, and eschatology. This article centers on one such locus, theological anthropology. Within systematic theology, the study of what it means to be human, created in the image and likeness of God, falls under the heading of *theological anthropology*. This has implications for both our relationship with our Creator and our relationship with one another. Theological anthropology speaks to humanity's relationship with the divine and the interrelationship of the human community. Since the writings of the earliest Christians, theologians have attempted to understand and explain what it means to be a creature of God. For every generation of Christians, the significance of our humanity is constantly being reinterpreted based on one's sociocultural, historical, and political context. There is no one unified anthropology, but various anthropologies that are shaped by the diverse communities that struggle to interpret God's revelation.

This essay offers a constructive, contemporary interpretation of theological anthropology rooted in the scholarship and insights of Latino/a theology. A diverse collective of voices that are unified by their self-identification as offering a manner of approaching theology *latinamente*, Latino/a theologians ground their contemporary scholarship in the lives, struggles, identity, and, most importantly, faith of Latino/a people. However, this contemporary interpretation of theological anthropology always remains connected to the historical Christian tradition. After a brief overview of theological anthropology as it functions within systematic theology, this essay introduces two key voices and themes within historical theological anthropology. My second section examines the theological anthropology of Karl Rahner, arguably one of the most influential in twentieth-century theology. I then turn to the constructive theological piece, drawing from the scholarship of Latinos/as in order to present Latino/a theology's contemporary contribution to systematic theology as a whole.

An Introduction to Theological Anthropology

As defined by Kristen E. Kvam, the term *theological anthropology* emerges from, "The Greek work *anthrōpos*, which signifies 'human,' provides part of the name . . . The adjective *theological* underscores that this study differs from the study of humanity in anthropology as a social-scientific discipline . . . the term *theological* stresses that this field of study explores religious considerations of what it means to be God's human creatures."[1] Kvam observes that for centuries anthropology did not stand alone as a theological focus, but was often nestled into writings on Christology or the doctrine of creation. Kvam also notes that historically anthropology was labeled as the "doctrine of man," though there is now a move to more gender-inclusive language. Kvam warns, however, that this move to inclusivity can often eclipse the function of gender in theological anthropologies. Men are often held as paradigmatic for human experience and women's experiences are ignored. In a sense then, given the privileging of men's experience, the doctrine of man can be seen at times as a more appropriate name for this field of study.

Classic theological anthropologies have often emphasized our spiritual relationship with the divine and downplayed its implications for our concrete existence. Otherwise put, "The main focus of theological anthropology has tended to be the supernatural orientation of humankind as beings created (in the words of Gen 1:27) 'in the image of God' (*imago Dei*). As a result of this focus, the other, more material side of existence has been overshadowed, even obscured."[2] This passage emerges from a recent collaborative rewriting of systematic theology that emphasizes the constructive nature of the theological task. As the authors of the chapter on the human being indicate, there are three issues that challenge contemporary theological anthropologies: freedom and responsibility (in light of relativist approaches to ethics and an awareness of the contextual nature of our understandings of sin and evil), identity and alterity (in reference to difference at the level of the individual and community), and time and memory (in light of contemporary emphases on expediency).[3] This article is sympathetic to these concerns. Theological anthropology must remain firmly grounded in the contemporary situation and not fall into abstract speculation that ignores the very materiality of human life.

A pressing concern for theological anthropology is the relationship between humanity as described in the opening chapters of Genesis (which falls from God's original creation, and consequently becomes deficient) and the new creation that Christians claim is found in Christ. The classic formulation of this new creation is found in Paul's letter to the Galatians when he writes, "There is no longer Jew or Greek, there is no longer slave or free, there is no longer male and female; for all of you are one in Jesus Christ" (Gal 3:28). How one constructs the relationship between the old and the new remains a central question for theological anthropology, one that has plagued Christians since New Testament times:

> If the emphasis is placed on the contrast between the new humanity in Christ and the old, it becomes easy to wonder whether the differences of (for example) gender and race that are overcome in Christ are part of God's good creation or signs of some defect in the created order. On the other hand, if abiding significance of these differences is affirmed, then it might seem to follow that social practices designed to reinforce them should be preserved.[4]

At the root of this question is the meaning of our historical particularity in light of salvation history. Another concern that emerges from this discussion is the role of sin and evil within theological anthropology. These are classic topics that are discussed under this heading. Turning to the historical voices that are foundational for contemporary theological anthropologies, I draw from two theologians who have transformed the manner in which we understand our relationship with the divine and consequently with ourselves: Augustine of Hippo and Thomas Aquinas. Because to introduce the scope of these scholars' contributions to theological anthropology is too broad for such a brief essay, I will focus on the manner in which the *imago Dei* functions in their work as a centerpiece to their understandings of humanity.

A Theological Overview

Augustine of Hippo was born in 354 in Thagaste (modern-day Algeria). He is, arguably, the most influential theologian in the history of Christianity. Considered the "father" of the doctrine of original sin, Augustine's monumental corpus covers a variety of themes, including the Trinity, grace, sexual ethics, the nature of the church, and spirituality. Augustine's *Confessions* is considered the first Western spiritual autobiography. He personally encountered and struggled against two of the most significant debates in the early church: Donatism and Pelagianism. His theology offers a North African contribution, one that is shaped by the struggles and concerns of his culture and era. It is difficult to approach Augustine's writings on the *imago Dei*, for as John Edward Sullivan points out, "His teaching about the image does not appear in systematic fashion in any one treatise, but is scattered throughout his letters, his sermons, the exegetical and polemical works, the *Confessions*, the *City of God*, and in the *De Trinitate*, the principal source of his teaching, it is almost inextricably bound up with the trinitarian doctrine."[5] Within this section I will limit my reflections to Augustine's writings within the confines of his reflection on the Trinity and his interpretations of the book of Genesis.

De Trinitate is a fundamental text for understanding Augustine's notion of the divine image. In book 7, chapter 12, Augustine gives his trinitarian exegesis of Gen 1:26: "But *let us make* and *our* are said in the plural, and ought not to be received except in terms of relative names. For it was not that gods might make, or make after the image and likeness of gods, but that the Father, and Son, and Holy Spirit might make after the image of the Father, and Son, and Holy Spirit."[6] For Augustine, the fact that the Genesis account says "Let us" with regard to the creation of the human and "Let there be" with regard to everything else indicates the involvement of the three Persons of the Trinity's involvement in creation. The same sentiment is repeated in *The Literal Meaning of Genesis*. "Because of the three Persons, it is said *to Our image*; because of the one God, it is said *to the image of God*."[7] This leads to an understanding of the *imago Dei* as trinitarian. "Our image" and "to the image of God" indicates that man is made in the trinitarian God's image (not just the Son or the Father).

Book 14 of *De Trinitate* argues that the image of God in the mind is permanent, just defaced. "The mind is God's image *par excellence* in virtue of its capacity for knowing God . . . The perfection of the divine image in the mind is the divine gift of wisdom, by which the mind becomes aware of God, and is not only 'in' God, but 'with' God, through the revival in it of that 'memory of God' which was never entirely obliterated." Sin damaged, but did not destroy, the image. Christ's grace restored the image within us, healing our nature. Following a similar vein as Gregory of Nyssa, Augustine also holds that only when contemplating God is human nature in the image of God. "As we said of the nature of the human mind that if as a whole it contemplates the truth, it is in the image of God; and when its functions are divided and something of it is diverted to the handling of temporal things, nevertheless that part which consults the truth is in the image of God, but the other part, which is directed to the handling of inferior things, is not the image of God" (book XII, chap. 7, 10). We are only truly human when we are fully oriented toward God. Augustine's understanding of the image, therefore, comes to be associated with the intellectual capacities of the human being. "Augustine interpreted *image of God* to mean the rational and moral capacities in human nature."[8] For Augustine the image functions on three levels: that likeness to God in which we were created; the return to that likeness, which was obscured by sin, through the life of grace; and the perfection of that likeness in the kingdom of God.[9] Here we find a notion of the *imago Dei* that is dynamic.

The theology of Thomas Aquinas (1225/1227-1274) offers one of the most extensive and influential contributions to Christian theology. This Angelic Doctor has left a stamp on several central ideas within the history of Christian thought, most notably on Christian understandings of the human. He is best known for his *Summa Theologiae*, a systematic exploration of Christian theology and philosophy written over the course of eight years. My overview of the *imago Dei* in Aquinas's anthropology focuses on two key texts, *The Disputed Questions on Truth* and the *Summa Theologiae*. Beginning with *The Disputed Questions*, one finds various themes that resonate with the theology of Augustine. Like Augustine, Aquinas locates the image of God in the rational capabilities of the human. "In us the mind designates the highest power of our soul. And since the image of God is in us according to that which is highest in us, that image will belong to the essence of the soul only in so far as mind is its highest power. Thus, mind, as containing the image of God, designates a power of the soul and not its essence" (question 10, art. 1, p.6).[10] As representative of the highest capabilities of the human, the mind, for Aquinas, is the locus for the image. Yet it is only when the mind is turned toward higher things that it truly reflects the image.

Also echoing Augustine, Aquinas has a trinitarian understanding of the *imago*. "Likeness brings the character of image to completion . . . There is a likeness of the uncreated Trinity in our soul according to any knowledge which it has of itself, not only of the mind, but also of the sense, as Augustine clearly shows. But we find the image of God only in that knowledge according to which there arises in the mind the fuller likeness of God" (question 10, art.7, p. 33). We grow in likeness to the image of the Trinity within us as we turn our knowledge toward divine things. As noted by D. Juvenal Merriell, "St. Thomas held that man is the image of the Trinity by virtue of his intellectual nature, inasmuch as by his nature man is inclined to know and love God and is capable of accepting the invitation of grace that the triune God makes when He calls man through Christ to participate in the innermost life of the Trinity."[11] In Aquinas's theology, the human possesses three types of knowledge: knowledge of God, knowledge of oneself, and knowledge of temporal things. We can't express likeness to the Trinity in knowing temporal things. The image of the Trinity is in the mind, as far as it knows God, and in self-knowledge, insofar as we reflect the image of God.

Several of these themes also appear in Aquinas's masterpiece, the *Summa*. In question 93 Aquinas adds the dimension of biological sex into his analysis of the image. For Aquinas, the *imago Dei* exists in humanity in three ways: "First, inasmuch as man possesses a natural aptitude for understanding and loving God; and this aptitude consists in the very nature of the mind, which is common to all men. Secondly, inasmuch as man actually or habitually knows and loves God, though imperfectly; and this image consists in the conformity of grace. Thirdly, inasmuch as man knows God actually and loves Him perfectly; and this image consists in the likeness of glory" (art. 4, p. 890).[12] This threefold understanding of the image reveals its dynamic nature. On one level, the image functions on the basic level in which we are created to understand and love God. This is, in a sense, the foundation of the image. Second, through the gift of grace we come to know God imperfectly, thus growing in the image. We can achieve the final level of knowing and loving God perfectly, reflecting the image in all its glory. Well, some of us can. As the following statement indicates, for Aquinas men and women do not reflect the image equally. "The image of God, in its principal signification, namely the intellectual nature, is found both in man and woman . . . But in a secondary sense the image of God is found in man, and not in woman, for man is the beginning and end of woman, just as God is the beginning and end of every creature" (art. 4, p. 890). Women are not able to achieve

and reflect the image in such an elevated manner as men. The foundation of
this belief, one that represents a radical break from the theology of Augustine,
is that for Aquinas the body reflects the image. "Although the image of God in
man is not to be found in his bodily shape, . . . the very shape of the human body
represents the image of God in the soul by way of trace" (art. 6, p. 894). This is
based on the Aristotelian belief that the body reflects the soul. Woman has the
first degree of the image, but doesn't have the second in the same way that men
do. This is based on their bodily weakness, which represents a weakness of the
soul and mind. Ultimately, however, the image dwells in the highest rationality
of the human, where there is no distinction between the sexes. Aquinas contends that woman's imperfect creation, as expressed in her bodiliness, reveals
her inferior status. This connection between bodiliness and the image of God is
especially significant in light of Latino/a theology's emphasis on sacramentality
and Latina feminist theological concerns.

One Contemporary Anthropology: Karl Rahner

For many Roman Catholic theologians, the work of the Jesuit priest Karl Rahner remains the greatest and most significant theological achievement of the
twentieth century. "Even before his death at Innsbruck on March 30, 1984, Karl
Rahner had been hailed as *the* religious thinker who had contributed more than
any other to the renewal of Catholic theology in the twentieth century."[13] Rahner is a student of scholastic and modern German philosophy and is extremely
influenced by the spirituality of Ignatius of Loyola. Rahner considers the church
a significant audience for theology. He believes that theology must serve the
church and be its voice in the contemporary context. While he was not a dogmatic theologian, Rahner argues that academic theology must always remain
connected to pastoral theology. Rahner ran into several problems with the Vatican throughout his career. His text on Mariology, for example, was prohibited
from publication and remains unpublished even today. In Vatican II, however,
he is vindicated. His theology marks the spirit of the Council and his openness
to world religions and the world in general is a clear stamp of his theology. Due
to his broad significance to all Christian theologies, his clear link between the
pastoral and academic realms, and his theological imprint on Vatican II, Rahner
is a fundamental source for Latino/a theologies.[14]

  For Rahner, the starting point of theology is anthropology. The foundation of Rahner's theology is the human being, who is the hearer of God's message. Geffrey B. Kelly links the fundamental insight of Rahner's theology to his
anthropological insights: "Rahner's genius was to link the human search for
fulfillment with the restlessness implanted in the individual's heart by God and
to correlate God's trinitarian presence in historical, somatic reality with what
he affirmed to be signs of God's grace investing human life with dignity and
beatific destiny."[15] The human is by nature open to receive revelation—we are
recipients of God's gracious self-communication. In other words, we are created to be saved. Rahner argues that we are oriented toward the horizon that

we know as God, and that the ground for the reception of grace is in the structure of the human. Within us is the experience of grace, and only in grounding our self-reflection of that experience of transcendence will we truly understand ourselves. We have a restlessness in our hearts that is only satisfied by God. It is in human nature to be open to the unlimited quest for meaning, where "The horizon of the human spirit as the infinite question is fulfilled by this ineffable self-communication of God with the believing trust that this infinite question is answered by God with the infinite answer which God is, it follows that through this grace the event of free grace and of God's self-communication is already given at all times."[16] We become conscious of ourselves as selves through radical questioning; this is the transcendent present in ordinary experience. The foundation of our everyday thinking is this unthematic deeper consciousness of which we are not consciously aware.

Due to the transcendent nature of the human, theology is essential to anthropology. As "hearers of the Word," humanity is the starting point of theology. For Rahner, humanity is able to understand that which is incomprehensible and to be seized by that which is beyond the intellect's capabilities.

> Hence the original knowledge of God is not the kind of knowledge in which one grasps an object which happens to present itself directly or indirectly from outside. It has rather the character of a transcendental experience. Insofar as this subjective, non-objective luminosity of the subject in its transcendence is always oriented towards the holy mystery, the knowledge of God is always present unthematically and without name, and not just when we begin to speak of it.[17]

These unthematized, unsystematic experiences (and knowledge), that which we experience yet can never fully articulate, are the subject matter of theology. "The effort to grasp and to thematize this reality is what Rahner calls the function of theological anthropology."[18] What Rahner names the *potentia oboedientialis* is the obedential potency for a possible revelation, our openness to God. In all our transcendental acts of knowledge we know God implicitly. Another key term in Rahner's anthropology is *supernatural existential*. This refers to our orientation to God's intended transformation via grace. If God intended us for a life of grace, Rahner argues, then the possibility of grace must be in our nature. "Creation is intrinsically ordered to the supernatural life of grace as its deepest dynamism and final goal. The offer of this grace, then, is an existential, an intrinsic component of human existence and part of the very definition of the human in its historical existence."[19] The supernatural existential is ultimately humanity's orientation to God's intended supernatural transformation through grace.

Rahner understands that our ordering toward God leads to an endless search for meaning. As we become aware of ourselves we are open to everything, though nothing is completely satisfying. Our spirits are open to the unlimited quest for meaning. Rahner's anthropology has been described as an anthropology open to the transcendent. On the basis of the Thomistic understanding that we can know beyond the senses, yet answering to the Kantian claim that all knowledge is rooted in the sensory, Rahner posits God as the principle of human knowledge. Rahner will always say, however, that we have the freedom to say yes or no to God. God is the ground of the very freedom to reject God. "God's self-communication as offer is also the necessary condition which makes its acceptance possible."[20] The supernatural existential does not require us to accept God in our lives; it makes us capable of accepting God's invitation. In his analysis of Rahner's anthropology, Miguel Díaz highlights that, for Rahner, all human experience is an experience of grace. Religious activity merely makes "explicit for ourselves what we already know implicitly about ourselves in the depths of our personal self-realization."[21] In his depiction of Rahner's anthropology, Díaz emphasizes the importance of the everyday in his theology, for Rahner situated the experience of grace in everyday experiences. Díaz interprets this, and Rahner's positive interpretation of popular religious practices, as a precursor to contextual theologies.[22]

Constructive Latino/a Proposal

Constructive Latino/a theology draws from and expands on historical and contemporary theological voices in order to elaborate a theology that is grounded in and reflects the faith and lives of Latino/a communities. The methodology of Latino/a theology is one where the Latino/a context is the starting point of theological reflection. However, this contextual approach is not in contradiction with a more faith-based starting point. Instead, Latino/a theologians argue, one must embrace a holistic sense of Latino/a culture where matters of faith are not compartmentalized but instead saturate every aspect of Latino/a lives and cultures. In terms of theological anthropology in particular, Miguel Díaz outlines several themes that are central: "(a) the relationship between Creator and creation, (b) the relationship between anthropology and Christology, (c) the relationship between human freedom (agency, liberation, and the building of just societies) and God's grace (gift, salvation, and the coming reign), and (d) the relationship between the communal human and the triune life of God."[23] While Díaz's themes are extremely helpful for our envisioning of theological anthropology broadly, in this section I highlight the particular Latino/a contribution to this broader discourse. I emphasize four themes that Latino/a theologians offer as their distinctive contributions to systematic theology as a whole: *mestizaje/mulatez* (plurality and difference), community/family, relationships, and grace and culture.

Mestizaje/Mulatez: a.k.a. Plurality and Difference

The category of *mestizaje* has come to saturate Latino/a theology. The privileging of *mestizaje* is intimately linked to Latino/a theology's emphasis on culture.

For Benjamín Valentín, both *mestizaje* (which he defines as "Latino(a) cultural hybridity") and popular religion are concepts that function as categories to explain and promote Latino/a culture.[24] This is the primary site of struggle for Latinos/as. Anthropologically, *mestizaje* functions to name the ambiguity and in-betweenness of Latino/a identity. Contesting a monolithic understanding of Latinos/as as a single race, Miguel de la Torre and Edwin Aponte note, "Hispanics are a *mestizaje* (racial mixture or combination of ethnicities), a *mestizaje* of races, a *mestizaje* of cultures, a *mestizaje* of kitchens, a dense stew of distinct flavors."[25] In the concluding section of their text, Aponte and de la Torre describe the diversity of the current Latino/a community as an "evolving *mestizaje*." The category, for them, no longer represents the mixture of Indigenous and Spanish; it now refers to cultural mixture in any sense of the word, as long as it applies to Latino/a communities.

Mestizaje/mulatez function to designate the mixed reality of Latino/a peoples. It is also transformed to describe Latino/a hybridity in general. In Isasi-Díaz's words, "*Mestizaje/mulatez* is the Hispanic/Latino incarnation of hybridity and diversity."[26] This new conceptualization of *mestizaje/mulatez*, Isasi-Díaz argues, opens avenues for discussions with other marginalized groups and grounds an understanding of difference that is not exclusive or oppositional. They represent the in-betweenness of Latino/a culture within dominant U.S. society and its accompanying worldview. This racial and cultural mixture, the sense of people living between two worlds, reflects the context from which Hispanic theology emerges. "Because we choose *mestizaje* and *mulatez* as our theological locus, we are saying that this is the structure in which we operate, from which we reach out to explain who we are and to contribute to how theology and religion are understood in this society in which we live."[27] *Mestizaje/mulatez* not only portrays the Latino/a context; these terms also reflect the epistemological standpoint from which Latinos/as exist in the world as hybrid people. This mixture and ambiguity is also the hermeneutical lens through which Latinos/as see the world and has ontological implications for the methodology of Latino/a theology. "This 'from there to here' is also part of our multiple, shifting identities, a fluid social ontology that is one of the constitutive elements of *mestizaje-mulatez*, the racial-ethnic-cultural-historical-religious reality that is the *locus* of the Hispanic/Latino community in the USA."[28] In embracing *mestizaje-mulatez*, Latinos/as are expressing solidarity with other marginalized people of color and attempting to dismantle dualistic constructions of race that plague identity politics. For Isasi-Díaz, the intentional choice to embrace the *mestizo-mulato* condition is a manner of contesting hegemonic constructions of identity within the academy and society.

Since the earliest writings of Virgilio Elizondo, *mestizaje* and then later *mulatez* have become central markers of Latino/a theological elaborations. They represent a manner of approaching Latino/a identity and hybridity. However, these terms do not function without a certain level of scrutiny. In my own research, I have critiqued the overemphasis on *mestizaje* as a manner of eclipsing *mulatez* and consequently Mexicanizing Latino/a identity.[29] And while I agree with both Manuel A. Vásquez and Miguel de la Torre that we must be suspicious of the manner in which *mestizaje* and *mulatez* are problematic in terms of diluting, overgeneralizing, and whitening Latino/a identity, I am a bit wary of their critique that the term is divorced from the contemporary Latino/a community.[30] *Mestizaje* and *mulatez* are living terms in our communities, not merely academic constructions, and their fundamental role in Latino/a theologies reflects their centrality among Latinos/as.

Community and Family

Miguel Díaz highlights the communal life of Latino/a communities as the starting point of Latino/a anthropologies.[31] This emphasis on the communal Latino/a experience does not negate the diversity of the Latino/a community or undermine the theocentric nature of theological anthropology. Similarly, Roberto S. Goizueta presents community as central to Latino/a anthropology. "This is not to say that the individual subject, or ego, is subsumed within community, but that the subject is constituted by community (more precisely, by communities), which, in turn, functions as a collective or communal subject."[32] The relationship between the individual and the community is dialectical. Linked to this communal understanding of the self is an emphasis on *familia* as a defining dimension of who we are.

The Spanish word *nosotros* (we) is fundamental within Latino/a theological anthropologies. "In an authentic community, the identity of the 'we' does not distinguish the 'I'; the Spanish word for 'we' is '*nosotros*,' which literally means 'we others,' a community of *otros*, or others."[33] As Goizueta highlights, the we-otherness of we is reflective of how Latinos/as understand themselves and those whom they embrace into the we of their families and communities. Latinos/as recognize that the individual cannot exist outside of the communities and families that both define her and with whom she has relationships. I would add to this that the communities that define us are not always those we choose. Latinos/as must be aware of the ways in which we are grouped and categorized by others and how our communities function in the dominant culture, which can at times be distinct from and even in tension with the understanding of community and family that we claim.

Perhaps no other scholar has examined the theological value of Latino/a community more than Goizueta. For him, the communal Latino/a theological anthropology is revealed in Latino/a popular religion:

If a central aspect of Good Friday and Guadalupe—and, by extension, other forms of popular Catholicism—is the affirmation of the intrinsic value of the concrete and particular as a prerequisite for an encounter with the spiritual and universal, this affirmation reflects an underlying understanding of the human person and human relationships. To suggest that the particular mediates the universal is to suggest that there is no such thing as an isolated, individual entity that is not intrinsically related to others: every human person is a concrete, particular, and unique mediation of the universal. In other words, every "individual" is a particular, unique mediation of universal humanity, universal creation, and, in the last analysis, a unique mediation of the Absolute. Each person (precisely *as a* person) is defined and constituted by his or her relationships, both personal and impersonal, natural and supernatural, material and spiritual.[34]

We are intrinsically relational, and our relationships are constitutive of who we are. Also, Goizueta contends, relationships come prior to the individual. These relationships include our ancestors and the institutions that are a part of or perpetuate our identity. Language also highlights the communal nature of who we are. "Presupposed in this modern liberal anthropology is a dichotomy between the individual and community. That is, the community is always extrinsic to individuality. Community is, at best, an addition or supplement to the individual and, at worst, a threat to and limitation of the individual." Community is also placed in opposition to institutions, and instead of a constitutive idea of community, there is a "sentimental" one. In the anthropology of Latino/a popular Catholicism, community is seen as preexistent and constitutive. Goizueta notes that the Trinity offers us a symbol of God's communal nature. Jesus reveals theology (God) and anthropology (who we are). Popular Catholicism does not separate the Jesus of history from the Christ of faith. "It is in our common accompaniment of Jesus on the cross that *he* constitutes *us* as individuals and a community." Through popular Catholicism our relationships with the sacred constitute who we are in the here and now.[35]

In Ada María Isasi-Díaz's *mujerista* theology, three phrases are critical to anthropology: *la lucha, permítame hablar,* and *la comunidad/la familia.*[36] These are not the only sources, nor are they necessarily exclusive to Latinas. However, "these phrases offer a valid starting point for an anthropological exploration of Latinas." To speak of these three phrases is to offer an arena for Latinas' theological contributions: Latinas' daily lives (*lo cotidiano*), their contributive voices, and their relational conception of selfhood. Family and community are fundamental dimensions of human nature. "*Familia/comunidad* for Latinas/os does not subsume the person but rather emphasizes that the person is constituted by this entity and that the individual person and the community have a dialogic relationship through which the person reflects the *familia/comunidad.*" In other words, the communities to which we belong, from the most personal to the broader societal, constitute humanity. In her emphasis on community, Isasi-Díaz not only highlights the relational nature of humanity but also adds the dimension of humanity's established relationships.[37]

Community and family, however, cannot be accepted uncritically as good. Instead, Latino/a theologians must now turn to articulating a clearer sense of what types of communities are reflective of the sacred and our intended human nature. After all, communities can be destructive, oppressive, and violent. Similar to the manner in which Orlando O. Espín has challenged Latino/a theologians to critically examine the category of "the people," we must also engage the category of "community." As he writes, "Has Latino/a theology been romanticizing Latino/a family life and Latino/a culture and history, thereby contributing to the perpetuation of sins and idols; and if so, how do we defend our *Latinidad* while we also seriously critique our own dehumanizing behaviors and attitudes?"[38] I agree with Espín's concern and would argue that in the same way Latino/a theology has idealized the people, we have also romanticized community and family. This does not take away from the central theological insight on the communal nature of the individual; it just calls for more development.

Relationships and the Trinity

Emerging from the Latino/a emphasis on the communal nature of humanity is a focus on relationships. This is an obvious offshoot from a communally centered anthropology. Communities do not exist outside of relationships. Goizueta highlights that in the theology of Latino/a popular Catholicism, "The human person is defined, above all, by his or her character as a relational being. Yet this relationality is not merely some static 'essence' of the person, but an *active* relating in and through which the person defines him or herself, in interaction with others."[39] Relationship is an action. We only recognize ourselves as individuals when we encounter another. This does not deconstruct and erase the individual but instead understands her in a more fluid and dynamic fashion.

The relational nature of humanity is grounded in God's trinitarian nature as relational and our reflection of this nature through the *imago Dei*. Catherine Mowry LaCugna grounds her theological anthropology in her trinitarian theology, emphasizing a relational God in communion with humanity. While not a Latina, her theology, as well as Mary Catherine Hilkert's, are helpful conversation partners on this point. LaCugna's relational ontology "understands being as being-in-relation, not being-in-itself." "Relationship, personhood, and communion" become the heart of *theologia* and *oikonomia*. "The mysteries of human personhood and communion have their origin and destiny in God's personal existence." This relational ontology understands God's nature as in relationship, and God's relationship with us reveals God's nature. LaCugna defines personhood as interpersonal, intersubjective, and unique. Personhood must balance autonomy and heteronomy, individuality and relationality. Right relationship in communion becomes LaCugna's foundation for Christian faith.[40]

Sixto J. García offers a trinitarian anthropology grounded in his assertion that, "The Trinity thus stamps its profile on every human being's personal reality and by extension on every human society and political structure. There is a perichoretic activity in society in whose structures the trinitarian God images godself."[41] This trinitarian image of God is not only expressed in individual human beings but also in human collectivities. García's insight bridges a trinitarian, relational understanding of the human with the Latino/a emphasis on community. Linking this to a justice-infused understanding of the Trinity, as done by Anglo and Latina feminist theologians, gives us insight into the very nature of the communities that Latinos/as want to celebrate in their theologies.

The trinitarian nature of God fuels an anthropology that envisions the human as social. These relationships must be characterized by mutuality and equality. As Mary Catherine Hilkert indicates, "If the trinitarian model offers the ideal paradigm for social and political relations, then unity-in-diversity and radical equality become ethical and political mandates." The nature of humanity is relational. The mystery of what it means to be human is grounded in the relational mystery that is the Triune God. Human beings do not image God as individuals but in their right relations. Hilkert adds the dimension of justice into her relational vision of the human. "The image of God is reflected most clearly in communities characterized by equality, respect for difference and uniqueness, and mutual love." Jesus' life, ministry, and death reveal the true nature of the Trinity. This image of Christ is grounded in Jesus' teachings, where the last are first. Through baptism and embracing a Christian life we image Christ. The image of Christ reveals the image of the Trinity that is reflected in our practical actions. In a world marked by the systematic degradation of other human beings, the image of God is found in the crucified people who image the crucified Christ. Only through our protest and action against that which violates the image of God in all of humanity is the image as "compassionate love in solidarity" revealed. The image of Christ is a vocation we are called to fulfill. Hilkert's dynamic notion of the *imago Dei* presents the image as something we embody through our ethical actions, a challenge we must meet in order to truly reflect our intended nature. We are called to image God through our actions and relationships with one another.[42]

Echoing Hilkert's insights, Ada María Isasi-Díaz's Christology is inextricably linked to social justice, placing an emphasis on a praxiological and ethical understanding of *Jesucristo*, where discipleship requires our active participation in the kin-dom of God as it is realized here and now. "All who commit themselves to proclaim with their lives and deeds the kingdom of God are mediators of the kingdom."[43] This mediation is grounded in humanity's *imago Dei* and calls followers of *Jesucristo* to realize God's kingdom concretely here on earth, though never in its fullness. The commitment is informed by the concrete struggles of the poor and the oppressed. Underlying Isasi-Díaz's Christology is the sense that we grow in the image of Christ as we engage in these concrete struggles. Isasi-Díaz presents a justice-infused notion of the self that is grounded in her christological starting point.

For Isasi-Díaz, another dimension of Latino/a anthropology that highlights the significance of justice is the focus on *mestizaje* and *mulatez*. She understands them both as descriptors of Latinos/as' cultural condition and an explicit decision by Latinos/as to embrace an identity within the dominant U.S. paradigm.[44] In other words, especially for those Latinos/as who can "pass" and are not readily defined as people of color, to define as *mestizos* or *mulatos* is an ethical choice. We choose to be in solidarity with marginalized communities, even beyond our own. This is especially significant for the Latino/a with privilege. Whether it be based on economic class, education, race, or gender, to answer to the Christocentric ethical call to justice is to situate oneself in the midst of marginalized peoples. For obvious reasons as an educated elite this is a vital concern for the professional theologian.

In his own work on theological anthropology, Goizueta defines *fiesta* as a form of cultural resistance by demonstrating a new type of anthropology where "agency (doing, making) is grounded in an attitude of receptivity and response; more specifically, the former mediates the latter. In turn, it is precisely in his or her character as receiver and respondent that the person is *capable* of celebrating."[45] Fiesta creates a notion of the human as one who receives rather than produces. This is a political act in a culture that devalues Latino/a culture and scorns the unproductivity of fiesta. Fiesta is characterized as celebration or commemoration. It cannot be romanticized or seen as escapist; it can be civil and religious. Fiesta rejects the subject as agent and the dichotomy of subject-object; it affirms (1) an expression of community; (2) human action in the subjunctive; (3) confluence of play and action; (4) liturgical action. "As a liturgical act, the fiesta reveals an understanding of the human person and human action which, though not necessarily expressly religious or spiritual, represents a *theological* anthropology in the truest sense—that is, an understanding of human life as *gift* and, consequently of the human person as one who (in gratitude) *receives* and *responds* to that gift."[46] Fiesta is reception and response to the gift of life—a gift that is not abstract but tied to the Giver. The response is not only through celebration, but also through love and neighbor and ethical-political action; fiesta is grounded in a commitment to social justice.

Grace and Culture

In his monograph *On Being Human*, Miguel Díaz pinpoints grace as a central dimension of Latino/a theological anthropologies. He understands the Latino/a emphasis on context as a manner of expressing Latino/a culture and religion as a site of God's grace. Grace is a cultural and engendered experience. "Grace is encountered in the ordinary (*lo cotidiano*) private and public spaces of U.S. Hispanic experiences."[47] This Latino/a emphasis on contextualization leads to a stronger emphasis on the social dimension of sin. Perhaps no other Latino theologian has lifted the centrality of grace to Latino/a theological anthropology than Orlando O. Espín. For Espín the central question for theological anthropology is not, "*What* is the human person?" but instead "*Who* are human persons?"[48] Espín's emphasis on *humanitas* is a manner of prioritizing living, breathing human beings and not an abstract sense of humanity divorced from real-life human beings. Contextualization becomes fundamental for understanding the human who cannot be abstracted from his or her concrete historical context.

In "Grace and Humanness: A Hispanic Perspective," Espín bases the thesis of his paper on the idea that, "The experience of grace possible to U.S. Hispanics, in order to be authentically an experience of God-for-us, must be culturally Hispanic."[49] God being for Hispanics must express Godself in the realm of Hispanics. Underlying his assertion is the contention that humanity cannot be understood outside of human culture. One cannot, as Espín notes, escape one's culture. "We are in culture as in a womb from which there is no birth, because we are already born into it."[50] Similarly, because the human experience of God's grace cannot be outside of human culture, God's grace is always expressed contextually and culturally. Not every cultural expression is an expression of God's grace; however, God's grace cannot be experienced outside of human culture.

Espín is not alone in his assertion that Latino/a cultural expressions are one avenue for expressing God's living presence in this world. He is, however, the theologian that has placed this insight in the explicit language of grace. For all of Latino/a theology, whether implicit or explicit, the emphasis on culture as the medium to express God's grace is a pervasive theme. This is linked to Latino/a theology's heavy contextual emphasis and its insight that all experiences of God's grace and expressions of God's revelation are culturally contextualized. This goes against an abstract, theological method that divorces theological insights and theological expressions from concrete, historical, living, flesh and blood communities.

A Constructive Summary

Latino/a theological anthropology draws from and expands on the Christian theological tradition in light of the contemporary Latino/a condition in order to articulate an anthropology that speaks *of* and *to* yet *not only* about Latinos/as' particular way of being human. From Augustine we gather the foundational insight of the communal nature of humanity with his trinitarian starting point. Yet unlike Augustine, the person in Latino/a theology is historically contextualized and this relational self is explored in light of her or his historical condition. Aquinas's emphasis on embodiment resonates with Latino/a theology's aesthetic sensibility, mirrored in our privileging of popular religion as a theological source. Rahner's grace-infused worldview and his anthropological starting point are also key points of reference. However, Latino/a theologians push all of these thinkers further, presenting a historically conditioned vision of the human that is not an abstract, universal theoretical category.

A Latino/a anthropology is informed by the various dimensions that shape and color this community, all with an eye to revealing something about the human condition, one that is inextricably linked to humanity's relationship with the divine. One cannot, however, hold a romantic understanding of community. "If U.S. Hispanic subject is born out of the confluence of communities and cultures, that confluence is initially conflictual and, indeed, violent: it is experienced as non-being, as a rupture, a disjunction, an extinction, and a crucifixion. This historical fact precludes idealistic or sentimental interpretations of either subjectivity or community."[51] Our understandings of community cannot be naïve, silencing the realities that divide and marginalize. Not all communities must be celebrated. One cannot accept community uncritically as a value in and of itself. A community that is constructed at the expense of certain members is not one that can be celebrated within a Christian vision of the human. At the foundation of a communal anthropology is an understanding of the human as relational. We are intrinsically relational and our relationships are constitutive of who we are. Relationships come prior to the individual. These relationships include our ancestors and the institutions that are a part of or perpetuate our identity; language also highlights the communal nature of human be-ing.

In the anthropology of Latino/a popular religion, community is seen as pre-existent and constitutive. Popular religious rituals unite us not only to our communities of worship but also to the community of the sacred. Popular devotion to Mary is another example of this communal, relational anthropology. Mary is also defined by her relationships; she too accompanies and is accompanied. Mary reveals not only something about the divine, but also about the nature of humanity. As the ideal disciple, Mary's preferential option for the marginalized and her accompaniment of marginalized communities, as seen in devotion to both La Caridad del Cobre and Our Lady of Guadalupe, reveals a vital dimension of the human condition and the manner in which our relationships with one another mirror our relationship with the divine. As the Magnificat teaches us, "Mary's song is a war chant, God's battle song enmeshed in human history, the struggle to establish a world of egalitarian relationships, of deep respects for each individual, in whom the god-head dwells."[52] Mariology reveals vital dimensions about both humanity and God. Mary in her openness to God's saving plan reveals the kingdom of God to humanity: a God "who does not cease to perform wonders on behalf of the poor, overthrowing the powerful and filling the hungry."[53] This in turn sheds light on the nature of humanity and the significance for intrahuman relationships for theological anthropology.

Relationality, however, is not some stagnant essence of the human but is instead dynamic. Relationships define who we are. It is through our relationships with others, and our relationships with the divine, that our identity is formed. Fundamental are those relationships and actions that constitute our daily lives. The dynamic character of these relationships brings forth the interactive and interdependent nature of humanity. Not only is this relational community characteristic of interhuman communities, it also marks humanity's relationship with the divine. The human person is not solely constituted by human relationships; one's relationship with the divine as giver of life is foundational. Our relationship with God is the foundation of all our other relationships.

Using the complexity of Latino/a identity as the starting point of their theologies, Latino/a theologians bring forth the importance of relationships in their anthropologies. Because there are various elements that shape and color identity, one must center on the relationships that unite them as the key factor that is constitutive of humanity's *imago Dei*. The Christian God is a God that exists in relationship. The foundation of the communal understanding of human nature is the community that is the Trinity. This understanding of the image of God in humanity mirrors the trinitarian life of relationships, and just as God relates within God's-self and relates to God's creation, so do we humans have relationships with ourselves and our Creator. In a similar manner, the God of Christian faith is a God of community, where the three persons of the Trinity exist as one in relational community. We as humans mirror that communal nature as people who are individuals yet whose individuality can only be understood through the very communities and relationships that form our humanity. A Latino/a anthropology must take into serious consideration, however, the ambiguous nature of humanity and the manners in which power and dominance function in communal settings. In these moments the image of the Trinity in humanity is distorted, resulting in communities that do not reflect divine relationship.

Underlying much of this discussion of theological anthropology is a worldview that holds the material and the spiritual worlds as organically interconnected. The sacred is present in the everyday. As noted by Goizueta, this is seen perhaps most clearly in Latino/a and Latin American literature. "One of the most widely recognized cultural manifestations of this particular characteristic of Latino/a culture is the so-called spiritual realism of so much Latino and Latin American literatures, where the historical and the spiritual worlds often intermingle almost willy-nilly."[54] This magical realism, as it is often described, is in fact the everyday worldview and life of many Latinos/as. The presence of the spiritual within the material world that is everyday for Latinos/as, yet is often depicted as quaint or superstitious by outsiders, is a fundamental insight in Latino/a anthropology. Our human community expands beyond those who are merely alive, and the spiritual realm plays a central role in our everyday existence. Whether it is the pouring of rum on the ground before serving the bottle in order to offer some to the *orishas*, or leaving a glass of fresh water at one's bedside and drinking it upon awakening, or bringing flowers to a statue of La Caridad, these everyday acts reveal the presence of the sacred in the material world. Thus our actions in this world have direct implications for our relationship with those in the beyond, and these relationships are vital. They inform of our understanding of human identity.

One dimension I would like to add to this discussion is the function of race within our notions of the human. For many, the centrality of race within theological anthropology seems questionable. However, as Eleazer S. Fernandez rightfully reminds us, "Racism undergirds a certain way of construing and constructing the human. In this regard, racism is a question of anthropology, of who we are in relation to others. Racism involves our deepest beliefs about the human, beliefs that have often acquired the status of essentiality and eternality."[55] An anthropology that takes seriously how race and consequently racism have functioned within theology reveals that in our constructions of humanity as created in the image of God certain aspects of human existence have been privileged at the expense of others.

Liberation theologies remind us that Jesus did not become incarnate in an abstract, dehistoricized human being, but in a marginalized Galilean Jew. In the straightforward language of James H. Cone, "God did not become a universal human being but an oppressed Jew, thereby disclosing to us that both human nature and divine nature are inseparable from oppression and liberation."[56] To understand our humanity we must focus on Jesus' status as an oppressed man and his preferential option for the marginalized. Only when we follow this path will our true humanity be revealed. For Cone this is the *imago Dei*, struggling against anything that denies any one person's full humanity. Sin, consequently, is defined as that which dismantles the human community. In Virgilio Elizondo's *mestizo* Jesus we again find Jesus' marginalization as a central christological principle with heavy anthropological implications. Our full humanity is realized only when we are in the active struggle against those forces that oppress our sisters and brothers.

Central to Latino/a anthropology is the assertion that one cannot understand the human condition without reference to the divine. As creatures created in the image of God, our humanity is inextricably linked to divine being. As Alejandro García-Rivera notes, "What is human cannot be known without reference to God, and that reference lies not with the distinctiveness of the human but with the connectedness of creation."[57] Our humanity is revealed through our relationships with the divine and with God's creation. Our humanity, however, always exists within our contextual particularity, where the diversity and unity that is the human condition manifests itself within our limited cultural context. Culture is the inescapable reality in which we are born, one that shapes every interpretive horizon of humanity, including our understandings of the divine. As noted by Espín, "What is commonly catalogued in our society as 'human,' as 'experience,' and as 'God,' is all culturally allowed."[58]

Latino/a anthropology takes its cue from the poetry, stories, and essays that emerge from this community and highlights the significance of race within human identity and the human community. Far from negating the existence of race, Latino/a anthropology must delve deeply into questions of race and how they shape the image of God within us. Such an anthropology must learn its lessons from a racist past and attempt to image a human community not dominated by hierarchy and power. In the spirit of a trinitarian anthropology, such a vision of the human strives to image who we are in all of our distinctiveness and unity.

Notes

1. Kristen E. Kvam, "Anthropology, Theological," in *Dictionary of Feminist Theologies*, ed. Letty M. Russell and J. Shannon Clarkson (Louisville: Westminster John Knox Press, 1996), 10.
2. M. Shawn Copeland, Dwight N. Hopkins, Charles T. Mathewes, Joy Ann McDougall, Ian A. McFarland, and Michele Saracino, "Human Being," in *Constructive*

Theology: A Contemporary Approach to Classical Themes, ed. Serene Jones and Paul Lakeland (Minneapolis: Fortress Press, 2005), 79.

3. Ibid.

4. Ibid., 84.

5. John Edward Sullivan, O.P, *The Image of God: The Doctrine of St. Augustine and Its Influence* (Dubuque: Priory Press, 1963), ix.

6. See Augustine, *The Trinity*, in *Augustine: Later Works*, ed. John Burnaby (Philadelphia: Westminster Press, 1955).

7. All citations taken from Augustine, *The Literal Meaning of Genesis*, vol. 1, *Books 1-6*, trans. John Hammond Taylor, S.J. (New York: Paulist Press, 1982), book III, chap. 19. "For man was not made to the image of the Father alone, or of the Son alone, or of the Holy Spirit alone, but to the image of the Trinity." Augustine, *On the Literal Interpretation of Genesis: An Unfinished Book*, trans. Roland J. Teske, S.J. (Washington, D.C.: Catholic University of America Press, 1991), 187.

8. Tatha Wiley, *Original Sin: Origins, Developments, and Contemporary Meanings* (Mahwah, N.J.: Paulist Press, 2002), 65.

9. John Burnaby, introduction to *The Trinity*, 30-31.

10. All citations from Aquinas, *The Disputed Questions on Truth*, in *Truth*, vol. 2, *Questions X-XX*, trans. James V. McGlynn, S.J. (Chicago: Henry Regnery Company, 1953). "Thomas understood that Augustine found the image of the Trinity at its best in man's acts of knowing and loving God because in these acts man reflects the eternal processions of the Son as the eternal Word from the Father and of the Holy Spirit as Love from the Father and the Son. Thus Aquinas conceived of the image of God as an ineradicable capacity for God in man, the foundation for man's participation in the life of the divine Trinity to which man is called by God's grace. In this he faithfully followed Augustine." D. Juvenal Merriell, *To the Image of the Trinity: A Study in the Development of Aquinas' Teaching* (Toronto: Pontifical Institute of Mediaeval Studies, 1990), 4.

11. Merriell, *Image of the Trinity*, 245.

12. All citations from Aquinas, *Summa Theologiae*, in *Basic Writings of Saint Thomas Aquinas*, ed. Anton C. Pegis (New York: Random House), question 93.

13. Geffrey B. Kelly, introduction to *Karl Rahner: Theologian of the Graced Search for Meaning*, by Karl Rahner, ed. Geffrey B. Kelly (Minneapolis: Fortress Press, 1992), 1.

14. There are a number of theologians I could have chosen for this section: Hans Urs von Balthasar, Paul Tillich, or Karl Barth, to name a few. For the reasons stated above I find Rahner to be the most appropriate choice. In addition, Rahner's anthropological starting point to theology is very in tune with Latino/a theology's contextual starting point. His contribution to Vatican II also gives an excellent example of a pastoral, academic, and public theologian.

15. Kelly, "Introduction," 1.

16. Karl Rahner, *Foundations of Christian Faith: An Introduction to the Idea of Christianity*, trans. William V. Dych (New York: Crossroad, 1997), 172.

17. Ibid., 21.

18. Kelly, "Introduction," 42.

19. William V. Dych, S.J., *Karl Rahner* (Collegeville, Minn.: Liturgical Press, 1992), 36.

20. Rahner, *Foundations of Christian Faith*, 128.

21. Ibid., 53.

22. Miguel H. Díaz, *On Being Human: U.S. Hispanic and Rahnerian Perspectives* (Maryknoll, N.Y.: Orbis Books, 2001), chap. 4.

23. Díaz, "Theological Anthropology," in *Handbook of Latino/a Theologies*, ed. Edwin David Aponte and Miguel de la Torre (St. Louis: Chalice Press, 2006), 67.

24. Benjamín Valentín, "*Oye, ¿Ahora Qué/*Say, Now What? Prospective Lines of Development in U.S. Hispanic/Latino(a) Theology," in *New Horizons in Hispanic Latino(a) Theology*, ed. Benjamín Valentín (Cleveland: Pilgrim Press, 2003), 105.

25. Miguel de la Torre and Edwin Aponte, *Introducing Latino/a Theologies* (Maryknoll, N.Y.: Orbis Books, 2001), 13.

26. Ada María Isasi-Díaz, "*Burlando al Opresor*: Mocking/Tricking the Oppressor: Hispanas/Latinas' Dreams and Hopes," in *La Lucha Continues: Mujerista Theology* (Maryknoll, N.Y.: Orbis Books, 2004), 137.

27. Isasi-Díaz, "*Mujerista* Theology: A Challenge to Traditional Theology," in *Mujerista Theology: A Theology for the Twenty-First Century* (Maryknoll, N.Y.: Orbis Books, 1996), 66.

28. Isasi-Díaz, "La Habana: The City That Inhabits Me: A Multi-Site Understanding of Location," in *La Lucha Continues*, 113.

29. See Michelle A. González, *Afro-Cuban Theology: Race, Religion, Culture, and Identity* (Gainesville: University of Florida Press, 2006).

30. Manuel A. Vásquez, "Rethinking *Mestizaje*," and Miguel de la Torre, "Rethinking *Mulatez*," in *Rethinking Latino(a) Religion and Identity*, ed. Miguel de la Torre and Gastón Espinosa (Cleveland: Pilgrim Press, 2006), 129-74.

31. Díaz, "Theological Anthropology," 68.

32. Roberto S. Goizueta, "*Nosotros*: Toward a U.S. Hispanic Anthropology," *Listening* 27, no. 1 (Winter 1992): 57.

33. Ibid.

34. Roberto S. Goizueta, *Caminemos con Jesús: A Latino/a Theology of Accompaniment* (Maryknoll, N.Y.: Orbis Books, 1995), 49-50.

35. Ibid., 60, 68.

36. Ada María Isasi-Díaz, "Elements of a Mujerista Anthropology," in *Mujerista Theology*, 129. These phrases are translated: the struggle, allow me to speak, and the community/family.

37. Ibid., 129, 143.

38. Orlando O. Espín, "The State of U.S. Latino/a Theology," in *Hispanic Christian Thought: At the Dawn of the Twenty-First Century: Apuntes in Honor of Justo L. González*, ed. Alvin Padilla, Roberto Goizueta, and Eldin Villafañe (Nashville: Abingdon Press, 2005), 111.

39. Goizueta, *Caminemos con Jesús*, 72.

40. Catherine Mowry LaCugna, *God for Us: The Trinity and Christian Life* (San Francisco: HarperSanFrancisco, 1993), 246, 288-92.

41. Sixto J. García, "United States Hispanic and Mainstream Trinitarian Theologies" in *Frontiers of Hispanic Theology in the United States*, ed. Allan Figueroa Deck (Maryknoll, N.Y.: Orbis Books, 1992), 99.

42. Mary Catherine Hilkert, "Cry Beloved Image: Rethinking the Image of God," in *In the Embrace of God: Feminist Approaches to Theological Anthropology*, ed. Ann O'Hara Graf (Maryknoll, N.Y.: Orbis Books, 1995), 199, 200.

43. Isasi-Díaz, "Christ in *Mujerista* Theology," in *Thinking of Christ: Proclamation, Explanation, Meaning*, ed. Tatha Wiley (New York: Continuum, 2003), 162.

44. "*Mestizaje* and *mulatez* for Hispanas/Latinas are not a given but a conscious choice made obvious by how we move in and out of Latino and Anglo-American culture according to need and desire." Eadem, "Creating a Liberating Culture: Hispanas/Latinas' Subversive Narratives," in *La Lucha Continues*, 59.

45. Roberto S. Goizueta, "Fiesta: Life in the Subjunctive," in *From the Heart of Our People: Latino/a Explorations in Systematic Theology*, ed. Orlando O. Espín and Miguel H. Díaz (Maryknoll, N.Y.: Orbis Books, 1999), 90.

46. Ibid., 91.

47. Díaz, *On Being Human*, 56.

48. Orlando O. Espín, "*Humanitas*, Identity, and Another Theological Anthropology of (Catholic) Tradition," in *Grace and Humanness: Theological Reflections Because of Culture* (Maryknoll, N.Y.: Orbis Books, 2007), 51.

49. Orlando O. Espín, "Grace and Humanness: A Hispanic Perspective," in *We Are a People: Initiatives in Hispanic American Theology*, ed. Roberto S. Goizueta (Minneapolis: Fortress Press, 1992), 147

50. Orlando O. Espín, "An Exploration into the Theology of Grace and Sin," in *From the Heart of Our People*, 123.

51. Goizueta, "*Nosotros*," 58.

52. Ivone Gebara and María Clasa Bingemer, *Mary, Mother of God, Mother of the Poor* (Maryknoll, N.Y.: Orbis Books, 1989), 72.

53. Ibid., 175.

54. Goizueta, "Reflecting on America as a Single Entity: Catholicism and U.S. Latinos," in *Many Faces, One Church: Cultural Diversity and the American Catholic Experience*, ed. Peter C. Phan and Diana Hayes (Lanham, Md.: Sheed & Ward, 2005), 77.

55. Eleazer S. Fernandez, *Reimagining the Human: Theological Anthropology in Response to Systemic Evil* (St. Louis: Chalice Press, 2004), 141.

56. James H. Cone, *A Black Theology of Liberation*, 20th anniversary ed. (Maryknoll, N.Y.: Orbis Books, 1994), 85.

57. Alejandro García-Rivera, *St. Martín de Porres: The "Little Stories" and the Semiotics of Culture* (Maryknoll, N.Y.: Orbis Books, 1995), 94.

58. Orlando O. Espín, "The God of the Vanquished: Foundations for a Latino Spirituality," in *The Faith of the People: Theological Reflections on Popular Catholicism* (Maryknoll, N.Y.: Orbis Books, 1997), 17.

5

Who Do We Say He Was and Is?

Jesus and Christology among Latino/a Theologians

BENJAMÍN VALENTÍN

The subject of Jesus of Nazareth has held a special place in the archives of U.S. Hispanic/Latino(a) theology. If one studies the published contributions of Latino/a theologians one will notice that from very early on they dealt with the question of the meaning of Jesus for Christian thought and practice and for the human quest for the sacred more generally. This interest is not only understandable but also commendable. After all, Christianity does profess that Jesus reveals the nature and will of God, that Jesus makes known the ultimate potential of humankind, and that Jesus exemplifies the standard of conduct that humans should emulate and promote. Given the crucial character of these religious assertions, it makes sense that Latino/a theologians would feel the need to reflect on the person of Jesus of Nazareth and the question of his continuing significance: they have properly recognized that no Christian theology would be complete without serious reflection on the person and relevance of Jesus of Nazareth. Thus they have dutifully inquired into the meaning of Jesus and have produced a body of writings that belongs to the realm of Christology—that is, to the realm of the historical and theological study of Jesus. But what is the sum and substance of this body of literature? What are some of the hallmarks of these Latino/a christological writings? What are the strong points and weak points of these compositions? And what patterns of christological thought can we detect in the writings of Latino/a theologians? These are appropriate and worthy questions. These are also questions that merit more extended consideration than they have received thus far.

In the pages that follow I will seek to give at least a partial response to these fundamental questions. I say partial because my focus here will be on the work of three Latino/a theologians who have contributed to the christological discussion: Virgilio Elizondo, Marina Herrera, and Luis Pedraja. To limit the length of this essay, and to ensure analytical depth, I've chosen to restrict my survey of

Latino/a Christology to the work of these three writers.[1] It is my hope, however, that this limited study will still serve to give us a hint of the contents, characteristics, and patterns of Latino/a Christology.

I will proceed in the following way. First, I will review the works on the life and meaning of Jesus put forth by Virgilio Elizondo, Marina Herrera, and Luis Pedraja. This review will include not only an examination of the themes that appear in these works but also an evaluation of the importance and vulnerabilities of these works. Second, I will elucidate three patterns of christological thought in the writings of Elizondo, Herrera, and Pedraja. In this interpretive segment of the essay I suggest that the writings of these three Latino/a theologians display a gravitation toward a Christology from below, a high Christology, and a liberationist Christology. As a whole, this essay aims to contribute to a better understanding and interpretation of Latino/a Christology.

Three Case Studies in Latino/a Christology

A chronological approach is, I believe, most useful in our case studies in Latino/a Christology. So, following a trajectory of publication dates, we begin our study with the christological intimations of Virgilio Elizondo, as he began writing on the topic of Jesus in the early '80s. We will then move on to Marina Herrera, who writes on our topic of interest in the early '90s, and finally on to Luis Pedraja who writes on Christology in the late '90s.

From Jesus of Galilee to Mestizo Christ:
The Christological Intimations of Virgilio Elizondo

It can be said that any commentary on Hispanic/Latino(a) theology must start off with a statement regarding the literary work of Virgilio Elizondo. This deduction is reasonable because the advent of Latino/a theology as an intentional and self-defined academic discourse begins with his work. But in the case of our particular subject matter it makes even more sense. First, Elizondo was the first Latino theologian to reflect on the identity of the historical Jesus; second, among the various Latino/a theologians he is the one who has written most extensively on the topic of the saving or liberating significance of Jesus; and third, he has come forward with the most creative and provocative christological overture we will find in Latino/a theology to date. Two of his books concentrate on the matter of the significance of Jesus for present-day life and especially for Mexican American and Hispanic/Latino(a) life (i.e., *Galilean Journey: The Mexican-American Promise* and *A God of Incredible Surprises: Jesus of Galilee*), and a third contains central sections that touch on this topic (i.e., *The Future Is Mestizo: Life Where Cultures Meet*).[2] This generous body of work shows that the question of the meaning of Jesus has occupied the mind of Elizondo for quite some time now, so it is sensible that we begin our survey of Latino/a theological interpretations of Jesus with a review of his treatises on the subject.

A perusal of Elizondo's writings on the topic of Jesus reveals something else that is unmistakable and captivating, however—it is that Elizondo makes much of the Galilean identity of Jesus. In fact, his books insist upon the thesis that in order to arrive at a sense of the meaning of the concrete human existence of Jesus we must close in on the particularity and connotations of his Galilean heritage. What's more, they intimate that people of the hyphen and the periphery—people who live in and between cultures and may experience psychic dislocation, rejection, marginalization, and disrespect in society because of it—should especially take stock of the importance of the Galilean identity of Jesus. This suggests that Mexican Americans and Latinos/as should want to study the life story of Jesus because they themselves have often felt doomed to nonidentity and marginalization by reason of their mestizo/a background, by reason, in other words, of their mixed-race or mixed-ethnic origins. But why should Mexican Americans, Latinos/as, and other mestizo/a peoples of the world inquire into the importance of the "earthly" identity of Jesus? According to Elizondo it is because in Jesus the Galilean they will encounter one who is quite like them—one who has suffered derision, rejection, and the threat of nonidentity due to heritage and descent. The implication is that by looking into the cultural identity and life story of Jesus, Mexican Americans, Latinos/as, and other mestizo/a peoples of the world will discover someone they can identify with—that is, one who was a mestizo and who experienced disdain and marginalization because of descent and ethnicity just as they do. Furthermore, he suggests that in Jesus of Galilee they will also come upon someone whom they can learn from and take after—one who showed in the flesh the potential of a new mestizo/a consciousness and who exemplified the transgressive and healing transcendence that inheres within the dual or multiple identity of a mestizo/a existence.

So, one might ask, what is the big deal with Jesus' Galilean provenance? Why is it so noteworthy that Jesus hailed from a bucolic village known as Nazareth in the general region of Galilee? And what exactly is the "saving significance" of his earthly Galilean identity? For Elizondo, what is noteworthy about the Galilee of Jesus' time is that it was a great border region between the Greeks and the Jews of Judea that also served as a natural crossing place for international travel routes. Galilee did not command much attention as a religious or intellectual center during Jesus' time, nor did it wield economic and political influence, but it was a borderland territory that served as a kind of crossroads for many diverse cultures and peoples, he suggests. "It was," therefore, "a land of great mixture and of an ongoing mestizaje,"[3] where different cultures were continuously clashing, interweaving, and fusing to create new syncretic or hybrid cultural traditions. Now, we might think that this would make for marvelous and admirable eccentricity, but Elizondo reports that there is a good chance that this mestizaje, or pattern of cultural intermingling, gave Galilee and the people of Galilee a certain repute or "disrepute." Elizondo notes that, whereas subsequent generations of Christians have glossed over Jesus' earthly identity, the earliest Christian communities highlighted Jesus' Galilean origin and gave it special significance, as evidenced by the fact that "it is mentioned sixty-one times in the New Testament."[4] He surmises that the significance attributed to Galilee and to Jesus' Galilean provenance lies with the notoriety and stigma that came with its border status, with its reputation as a place where various forms of mestizaje were taking place. The point to remember, Elizondo underscores, is that, at the time of Jesus, "Galilee was peopled by Phoenicians, Syrians, Arabs, Greeks, Orientals, and Jews,"[5] and the proximateness of this great diversity of peoples apparently contributed to a tremendous mixing of cultures, a mixing that effectuated the negotiation of identities and mores between the Jews and the gentiles of the land. Elizondo explains and summarizes the outcome of this kaleidoscopic merging in the following way:

> In this mixed, commerce-oriented society, some Jews had allowed their Jewish exclusivism to weaken, but others became more militantly exclusivist. Some of the goyim (non-Jews) converted to Judaism and intermarried with Jews. Religious ideas of other groups were also assimilated, as is evident in the case of the Essenes. A natural, ongoing biological and cultural mestizaje was taking place.[6]

This mestizaje or commingling, however, was not regarded favorably by the dominant social, cultural, and religious hierarchies of Jesus' time, Elizondo asserts. Galilean Jews were often doubly rejected as hybrid, and as border, persons—as people who lived in the crossroads of cultures, in other words. They were, on the one hand, scorned by those gentiles who despised Jews, and, on the other hand, "regarded with patronizing contempt by the 'pure-minded' Jews of Jerusalem":

> The natural mestizaje of Galilee was a sign of impurity and a cause for rejection. The Pharisees looked down upon "the people of the land" because they were ignorant of the law. The Sadducees looked down upon them because they were somewhat lax in matters of religious attendance and familiarity with the rules of temple worship.[7]

Moreover, says Elizondo,

> The Galilean Jews spoke with a very marked accent and most likely mixed their language quite readily with the Greek of the dominant culture and the Latin of the Roman Empire. Peter could deny Jesus, but there was no way he could deny he was a Galilean. The moment he opened his mouth he revealed his Galilean identity.[8]

This all suggests then that, by growing up in Galilee, Jesus assumed the personal identity and circumstances of a cultural mestizo. On the one hand, this implies that Jesus probably embodied and evinced the distinguishing marks of a border-lands person—the spiritual, perceptual, linguistic, and maybe even physical traits of one who is bicultural or of mixed heritage. On the other hand, this implies that in all likelihood he also experienced the pathologies of oppression, the ridicule, the rejection, and at times the shame-filled self-image that often go along with a hybrid identity. In short, Elizondo believes that, as a first-century Jewish mestizo, Jesus probably experienced the vulnerability that comes with a borderlands exis-tence, the uneasy feeling of never being fully accepted and of never being quite at home or comfortable in any of the dominant cultural geographies of his time and, perhaps on occasion, not even quite at home in his own flesh.

This seems interesting enough in a historical or conjectural kind of way. But what is ultimately of substance for Elizondo is the way in which Jesus was able to take in and draw from his mestizo Galilean particularity, turning it into a wellspring of positive identity and a force for social good in face of adversity. In fact, although it was probably regarded with disfavor by most during his time, Elizondo insists that Jesus' mestizo identity was a source of providential consequence. Jesus' beginnings in the mixed environment of Galilee, Elizondo suggests, allowed him the opportunity to learn not just from his Jewish faith but also from the many other traditions that enriched his home territory. This provided fertile ground for the cultivation of an inner capacity in Jesus to move beyond the social and cultural borders of his time, and to break the barriers of separation that those engendered. It was in Galilee, Elizondo intimates, that Jesus first learned to juggle cultures, to develop a plural personality, in order to survive sanely; and it was through the process of this learning that he came to offer something new to his milieu: a mode of being that demonstrated a toler-ance for contradictions and challenged the fixity of the delimiting human bor-ders and categories of his time. Furthermore, Elizondo insinuates that Jesus' identification with the most rejected of society, and the affinity that he demon-strated toward the peoples of the periphery during his ministry, were at least in part the result of his mestizo origins and his own experience of rejection as a borderlands dweller. Having learned of the virulent side of society's absolutes through his own marginalization and suffering as a Jewish mestizo, Jesus, Eli-zondo suggests, was better able to understand the virtue and necessity of an inclusive sensibility and ministry. Thus, rather than being a hindrance and a dis-advantage, Jesus' beginnings and development in multicultural Galilee actually afforded him a privileged point of view on life, on cultures, and even on religion. Elizondo makes the point this way:

> Out of his Galilean mixture, Jesus was able to transgress the segregat-ing limits of purity of his people and begin a new universal fellowship that offered real hope to a humanity torn apart by tribal, ethnic, reli-gious, and racial barriers.[9]

For Elizondo's purposes, then, it is significant that Jesus was able to trans-late his "hyphenated" identity and marginal status into a virtuous life and into a liberating force for good. And the reason this is so suggestive and fraught with meaning is because it allows Jesus to function as the exemplary mestizo, as the representative mestizo, as the mestizo that all other mestizos should emulate. Jesus' attainment of or, dare we say, "work" of self-discovery, self-healing, and self-affirmation amid bias and narrowness surely had an effect in his own time, as it allowed his contemporaries to experience a living and life-giving example of humaneness and transcendent hope. As a matter of fact, Jesus' life and activity opened the way for people to relate to him as a Jewish messiah and as champion or "savior" of humanity in his own day and age. But Jesus' story of confident identity and self-assurance amid narrow-mindedness holds continuing signifi-cance for today, Elizondo suggests, for it illustrates that peoples of the hyphen and the periphery are capable of great things. In fact, Jesus' life story shows that hybridity can bestow a privileged space of liberatory and transcendent possi-bilities. And this is especially indicative for Mexican Americans, for Latinos/as, and for other peoples of mixed race or mixed ethnicity today, because it illus-trates that they too can embrace their mestizo/a identities and carry out a life-changing, life-affirming, life-giving vocation in these days. Indeed, Elizondo sees a certain correspondence between Jesus' mestizo experience and the circum-stances of Mexican American experience today. This is especially the case when it comes to the Mexican American people who live in Texas and in the southwest region of the United States. "Being a Jew in Galilee," Elizondo alleges, "was very much like being a Mexican-American in Texas." Just as the Jews of Galilee were "considered too Jewish to be accepted by the gentile population" and yet "too contaminated with pagan ways to be accepted by the pure-minded Jews of Jerusalem, so have the Mexican-Americans been rejected by two groups": the Anglos in the United States and the Mexicans in Mexico.[10] But, just as Jesus was able to generate new life from the margins of his society, and just as he was able to come to positive terms with his status as an inside-outsider, Elizondo believes that similarly, Mexican Americans now find themselves uniquely positioned to advance a liberating mission not only for their own sake but also for that of others. For example, he declares that because they are heirs to the cultural tra-ditions of the "Anglo people" and the "Mexican people," Mexican Americans are in a better position than most to "appreciate more clearly the best of the traditions of both groups, while also appreciating the worst of the situation of both." Moreover, "as mestizos of the borderland between Anglo America and Latin America," Elizondo writes, "Mexican-Americans can be instrumental in bringing greater appreciation and unity between the peoples of the two Ameri-cas."[11] Hence, similar to the way in which Jesus of Galilee was able to convert his mestizo identity from an enslaving shame into a liberating and conciliatory well-spring, so too can Mexican Americans transform their hyphenated existence into a creative force of coalescence and change in this day and age. But this promise holds not only for Mexican Americans, but also for Latinos/as in general and for other mestizo(a)/mulatto(a) peoples of the world; according to Elizondo all who are of hybrid identity can show in their flesh how dualism, intolerance, dis-crimination, and marginalization can be transcended. All who are of interracial/

intercultural portion can come out of the margins of belonging to embrace their hybridity, to rise above society's dividing walls of separation, and to work for a unity that welcomes and takes in diversity and assortment. To be sure, the very foundation of their multidimensional selves can serve to reveal the possibility of new creation, of new life, of a new humanity. And if anyone doubts any of this all they need to do, Elizondo suggests, is look to Jesus of Galilee, to Jesus the Galilean/mestizo savior, to Jesus the quintessential and exemplary mestizo.

It is noteworthy that Elizondo's interpretation of the significance of the historical Jesus, and that Elizondo's empowering message about the liberating potential that exists in the in-between space created by a mestizo existence, rests on a kind of incarnational theology. My point is that for Elizondo it is significant that God apparently entered humanity in the likeness of a mestizo man from Galilee to reveal the heart and face of God to us for the purposes of our edification or salvation. "The amazing thing about our Christian faith," he writes, "is that we believe that it is through the humanity of Jesus that we come to know of God personally." Moreover, our Christian faith also suggests that it is through the humanity of Jesus that we come to know the true or ideal nature and promise of humankind. This all implies, then, that it is in the actual person and life of Jesus the Galilean that we "discover the truth of God and the truth of the human—who God truly is and what it truly means to be a human being." If this is so, or if we believe this to be so, then we must recognize that, because Jesus was a cultural mestizo who hailed from the multicultural environs of Galilee, it is a mestizo who is both the definitive revelation of God and the divinely chosen illustration of true humanity. And what is so amazing and significant about this inference is that it suggests that the all-powerful, all-knowing, all-loving God chose the physicalness and identity of a marginal mestizo peasant from Galilee to lead humanity to the divine and to its own true calling. What is so amazing and significant about all of this, Elizondo submits, is that God not only became one of us but also "one of those without dignity and considered of inferior human condition by the dominant sector of society." That God would become flesh and make "his" dwelling place among us is surprising enough. But that God would opt to do so in the form of a poor mestizo man from lowly Galilee is simply astonishing and yet also decidedly magnificent, Elizondo suggests, for it means that he who was by nature of divine condition emptied "himself" of all high rank and status and entered humanity in the form of a peripheral, degraded Jewish man of the first century. "In the man from Galilee," Elizondo asserts, "God becomes the exploited, inferior, impure, enslaved human being." And while this business of the incarnation will always remain a theological mystery, Elizondo at least helps one to understand that God may have taken the likeness and condition of such a man in order to "enter into flesh and blood solidarity with the victims of the sin of the world, that is, the 'nobodies' of this world."[12] This ought to be important and "good news" for all who are maligned and rejected in society inasmuch as it implies that God has not only taken on their cause but also their very circumstance and even corporeality to lift it up and to use it to call all of humanity to a greater love for God and humankind.

I think there ought to be no doubt about the ingenuity, the gracefulness, the cogency, and the salience of Elizondo's depiction of Jesus. His work offers us at once a unique rendering of the historical Jesus, an important presentation of the potentiality embedded within hybridity, and an inspiriting theology that urges us all toward greater altruism and emboldens those who are marginalized in society to search for positive identity. These are all worthy credits, and one will doubtlessly find that in the writings of Elizondo there are even more treasures than the ones I have touched on here. Nevertheless, it is important to note that Elizondo's opus is not without its shortcomings. One major drawback is that its claims about the Galilean world of Jesus do not square with recent information and ideas that emerge from the historical exegesis of scriptural texts and the archeological study of Galilee. It is evident that Elizondo's portrait of Jesus rests on the premise that Jesus' Galilee was ethnically and culturally diverse, on the premise that Galilee was a region where a tremendous mixing of peoples and cultures took place and where Jewish identity was being revised in an encounter with Greco-Roman ways and other gentile mores. From Elizondo's vantage point, first-century Galilee appears to be "a crossroads of cultures and peoples with an openness to each other." And it is this image of a multiethnic, multicultural, and melting-pot-like Galilee that impels him to look upon Jesus as a likely cultural mestizo, that is, as one who probably alloyed his Jewishness with the great many non-Jewish traditions that flourished in his home territory and, thus, came to offer something new and liberating to his Jewish milieu. The problem is, however, that recent scholarship does not certify this view. Over the last twenty years or so religious historians and biblical scholars have been finding that there is less evidence than often supposed for the postulation of a gentile informed, a "mesticized," or a multiethnic and culturally variegated Galilee at the time of Jesus. In fact, at present they tend to think that gentiles were not an especially large and influential group in the Galilee of Jesus' day, and that the villages and cities of first-century Galilee were neither centers of Hellenization and Romanization nor zones of ponderous cultural mixture. In other words, historians and biblical scholars now tend to believe that the ethnic, cultural, and religious identity of Jesus' Galilee was prominently and recognizably Jewish.[13]

Historians and biblical scholars are surely aware that Galilee was not far from gentile purlieus, nor far from cosmopolitan areas where Hellenism, Romanization, and other forms of cultural assimilation prevailed (e.g., Tyre, Ptolemais, Caesarea Maritima, Scythopolis, Gerasa, and other municipalities in the loose confederacy of cities known as the Decapolis are some that come to mind). They also realize that there were two cities in Galilee that were growing during the time of Jesus (Sepphoris and Tiberias) and that some level of interaction between the Jews of Galilee and gentiles in the region would have been inevitable in and around these. Furthermore, historians and biblical scholars allow for the probability that Galilee saw changes in its regional identity from time to time, as most other places of human dwelling do. These factors, and the current understanding that all places and cultures experience processes of transculturation through time and space, contribute to a growing recognition among scholars that the conceptualization of a Jewish Galilee need not, indeed should not, rule out the possibility of some level of syncretism or hybridization (whether between Judaism and Hellenism or between Jewish culture and gentile traditions more generally). However, two questions to consider here are: How much hybridization? and, At what point in time? Elizondo would have us believe that gentiles were numerous in the Galilee of Jesus' day, that an unusually high degree of Jewish-gentile interaction took place in first-century Galilee, leading to a good deal of cultural and even biological hybridization there, and that these factors combined to make the region both notable and notorious. Indeed, there have been other biblical scholars and theologians who have made these same, or similar, claims. However, the prevailing view among scholars today is that these claims about Galilee are unsupportable. And this appraisal seems fitting: the evidence for a gentile presence and for the appearance of cultural hybridity in Jesus' Galilee is slight to the point of invisibility.

The literary evidence is most definitely insubstantial, especially when it comes to the all-important testimony of ancient literature. Of the various references that are made to Galilee in the Hebrew Bible, in the Christian Scriptures (the New Testament), in rabbinic texts, and in other pertinent nonreligious texts of antiquity, there are only five that appear to use the phrase "Galilee of the Gentiles." Three of these appear in the Babylonian Talmud. The other two appear in Isa 9:1, and in an apparent reference to Isaiah found in the Gospel of Matthew (Matt 4:15-16).[14] The sparseness of this list of references should already give us a clue that there is little textual data to support the idea of a Gentile or mesticized/culturally hybrid Galilee at the time of Jesus. But the evidence in support of this notion appears to be leaner still and even more inadequate: neither Isaiah nor the writers of the Babylonian Talmud used the phrase "Galilee of the Gentiles" in reference to the Galilee of Jesus' day, and Matthew's use of the phrase strikes one as being wedded to his belief that gentiles should be welcomed into the bosom of the emerging Matthean Jewish-Christian church and to his belief that gentiles will be included in the coming kingdom of God that Jesus spoke about while ministering in Galilee. In other words, it is more likely that these textual references say something about the social fabric of Galilee many centuries *before* the time of Jesus, and about the theology or eschatology of the author of the Gospel of Matthew *after* the time of Jesus, than about the demography of Galilee *in* the time of Jesus. This leaves the notion of a gentile-infused and "mesticized" first-century Galilee with no applicable and reliable textual support.

And it's not like we can find much literary support for the idea of a gentile-informed, culturally hybrid Jesus either, certainly not in the Gospels at least. If anything, the Gospels give one to understand that Jesus was socialized into, fell in with, and operated out of a Jewish socio-religious world. For instance, they divulge that his family was Jewish, as is clear from the traditionally Jewish names of his parents and brothers (cf. Mark 6:3); they inform of his Jewish ancestry (Matt 1:1-17); they reveal that Joseph and Mary observed Jewish ritual obligations (Luke 2:21-24, 41); they indicate that Jesus spoke Aramaic, a sister language of biblical Hebrew and the spoken language of Palestinian Jews in this period (Matt 6:24; Mark 5:41; 7:34; 14:36; John 1:42); they tell that Jesus dressed in Jewish garb, wearing tzitzit or the fringed tassels that Jewish men have been known to wear on their outer garment (Matt 9:20; Mark 6:56); they place him at the Jerusalem Temple and in local village synagogues or in Jewish gathering places where Judaism was known and practiced (Mark 6:1-2; Luke 2:42-46; 4:16-20; 13:10-17; John 7:14); they suggest that Jesus saw his mission to be primarily to Jewish peasants living in the countryside of Galilee and living within the traditions of Judaism (Matt 10:5-6; 15:24); they show him reading from and interpreting the Torah and the writings of the ancient Hebrew prophets (Matt 5:17-48; 7:12, Mark 12:28-34; Luke 4:16-20); and they have him going to the Jerusalem Temple shortly before his death to celebrate the Jewish holiday of Pesach or Passover (Matt 26:17-19; Mark 14:12-16; Luke 22:7-13). These textual citations do not support the picture of a Jesus who was immersed in a gentile or gentile-laden world, who was infatuated with gentile traditions, and who was influenced by gentile practice. Rather, they seem to place Jesus in a Jewish social milieu, to associate Jesus with Jewish foundations, and to project onto Jesus the ceremonial practices of Judaism.

In like manner, it is notable that archeological evidence appears to discredit the idea of a gentile/"mesticized" Galilee and mestizo Jesus, and to support the picture of a recognizably Jewish Galilee and Jesus. Artifacts found inside of domestic spaces in Galilee and believed to date back to the middle of the first century suggest that the ethnic and religious identity of Jesus' Galilee was firmly Jewish. Stone vessels used for Jewish rites of purification; plastered pools, which most people take to be *miqva'ot*, or ritual baths, used for ritual purity customs; signs of secondary burial of human bones, which lead one to believe that inhabitants of Galilee were acquainted with Jewish burial practices of the time; collections of animal bones that reveal the absence of pigs, indicative of a pork-free diet and compliance with kosher laws: these kinds of archaeological discoveries lend credence to the idea that Galilee was essentially Jewish in the first century.[15] They also show that Jesus and Jesus' message should be understood within the context of a stable Jewish environment, instead of within the context of a multicultural, multiethnic, gentile-infused, mesticized, or highly hybridized environment.

So, where then do these exegetical and archeological considerations leave us in regard to Elizondo's reconstruction of first-century Galilee and Elizondo's depiction of Jesus as a mestizo Galilean and savior? I suppose that they leave us with a sneaking suspicion or feeling that Elizondo's claims about Galilee and Jesus build upon and insist upon questionable speculation. There is little in the contemporary literature or artifacts to suggest that Jesus' Galilee was "a land of great mixture" and of "an on-going biological, ethnic, and cultural mestizaje." That being so, there is little to suggest that Jesus was a first-century Galilean mestizo, whether ethnically, culturally, or religiously. Actually, it seems more likely that most Galileans in Jesus' time were faithful and observant Jews, and, therefore, that Jesus was both an unwavering Jew and a devout practitioner of Judaism. And this raises the question of the appropriateness of the image and concept of mestizaje or hybridity in relation to the makeup of first-century Galilee and in relation to the life and times and the teachings and relevance of Jesus.

But there is another complication that besets Elizondo's rendering of Jesus, and it deserves mentioning as it involves the semblance and possible ennoblement of anti-Jewish reasoning. Various emphases found in the writings of Elizondo give one the impression of an anti-Jewish slant, even if unintentionally or by accident. The depiction of Galilee as a mixed and gentile-infused area rather than as one that was predominantly and recognizably Jewish; the suggestion that Galilean Jews became better Jews by virtue of their daily contact with gentiles in Galilee and by virtue of their openness to gentile culture; the tendency to identify Jesus through the aid of a regional designation (i.e., Galilee or Galilean) rather than by way of an ethnic marker (i.e., Jew or Jewish) or the specific practices and beliefs of Judaism; the description of Judean Judaism as legalistic, purity obsessed, and overbearing; the insinuation that Jews were provincial, clannish, ethnocentric, and prone to sectarian and nationalistic interests; the inference that Jesus was able to transgress the segregating limits of his people and begin a new universal fellowship that offered real hope to humanity in great part because of his Galilean mixture and familiarity with non-Jewish traditions: these are determinations and characterizations that appear in the works of Elizondo and that can provoke allegations of a latent anti-Judaism and maybe even of anti-Semitism.

The truth is that these depictions present a contentious and gloomy rendering of Jewish life in the first century, and especially of Second Temple Judaism. Moreover, they also appear to strip Jesus of his "full" Jewish share and to remove him from Judaism to some extent. On that account, it is perceivable that some might determine that Elizondo's determinations give an instance of and contribute to the anti-Semitic attitudes and supersessionist claims that have obscured understanding of the Jewish Jesus.[16] But we should not charge Elizondo with ill will or prejudice. I know Elizondo well, and consider him not only a colleague and friend but also a mentor and a model human being. Furthermore, it is important to note that we are talking about a loving man who has dedicated his entire life to the empowerment and uplifting of people, and to the promotion of greater amity and social solidarity. In fact, these have been prevalent pursuits in his ministry and scholarship. So, if there is any appearance of anti-Jewish thinking in Elizondo's discourse it is likely due not to intolerance but to inadvertence. Actually, I think the error grows out of a longing to herald the uniqueness or distinctiveness of Jesus. That Elizondo would want to play up the particularity and salience of Jesus is neither surprising nor troubling, since this is what Christian theologians are inclined and even called to do. What is problematic, however, is that Elizondo heightens the difference and relevance of Jesus either by projecting a negative image of first-century Jewish life and practice or by erasing these from the picture altogether. It may be that this proceeding allows Jesus to emerge as a heroic individual who is able to rise above the limits of his unsung Galilean provenience and as a religious revolutionary who is able to transcend the confines of his system of religious belief, but it does so at a heavy and undue cost. It does so at the cost of the belittlement of Jewish life and practice in the first century, and at the cost of the devaluation and effacement of Second Temple Judaism. Lost in this contrasting picture is a sense of the variety, beauty, resilience, and cheerfulness of first-century Jewish life, not to mention the loss of a sense of the diversity, agreeableness, and fairness of first-century Judaism. Lost too is a sense of Jesus' rootedness in and deep-rooted love for Judaism and for Jewish practice. And not only is there the possibility of loss in this contrasting portrayal of Jesus and Jewish life and practice but also there is the risk of encouraging anti-Jewish teaching, even if unintentionally.

It seems to me that Christian theologians should keep the following fine points in mind when trying to decipher the particularity and significance of Jesus:

- That Jesus grew up and came to maturity in a Jewish household in a Jewish village in a Jewish social milieu;

- That Jesus belongs within the history of first-century Judaism;

- That Jesus' Jewish socio-religious context does not have to be belittled in order for Jesus to be considered profound and worthy of notice;

- That Jesus cared about amity, neighborliness, outreach, harmony, compassion, and justice *because* he was Jewish and a follower of Judaism;

- That Jesus did not deviate from Judaism or from the traditions of Israel—his aim was to instruct Jews on the true meaning and keeping of those traditions in preparation for the coming kingdom or reign of God;

- That Jesus' critical, prophetic praxis flowed conclusively from the religious tradition he participated in—that is, from Judaism itself.

Acknowledgment of these particulars could help us to avoid a denigration of Judaism and the mistaken notion of a de-Judaized Jesus.

The two drawbacks that I have detected in the writings of Elizondo are serious and require remedy. They do not invalidate the importance of his work, however. The positive points and contributions I alluded to previously still stand. Moreover, I submit that the basic point of Elizondo's overture can be upheld, even if with some revision. The essential point that Elizondo wants to get across is that Jesus accomplished great things in life and carried out a saving and world-changing mission, even though he was a marginal and marginalized Jew from rural Galilee. He is on target with this acknowledgment and premise. Elizondo strays off the mark only when he attributes Jesus' marginality to his mestizo/mixed cultural identity. This particular ascription seems far-fetched and ill-advised in light of the issues noted previously. However, Jesus can be said to have been a marginal and marginalized Jew in other ways. For example, one can note that we hear almost nothing of Jesus in non-Christian literature of the first century, Jewish or otherwise; that Jesus was a humble fellow and ordinary woodworker who hailed from an uninspiring, out-of-the-way rural village in Galilee (i.e., Nazareth); that Jesus never attended any scribal school nor studied under a noted teacher; that around the age of thirty Jesus embarked on an

itinerant mission to the Jewish peasant class, going from town to town to carry
out his teaching and healing ministry but without the backing of official office,
traditional channels of authority, or scribal learning; that Jesus' prophetic and
apocalyptic message was not well received by everyone; and that he was put to
death in a humiliating and brutal way at a public execution outside the gates
of Jerusalem on charges of sedition against the Roman state. These aspects of
Jesus' life, ministry, and death suggest some ways in which he might be considered marginal, whether for reasons of historical obscurity, or humble provenance, or reduced economic circumstances, or lack of education, or itinerant
and charismatic ministry, or rejection, or humiliating death outside the gates of
the city.[17] Jesus can be said to have been marginal or marginalized in all of these
ways. And yet, despite these apparent historical or material limitations (or perhaps because of them), God chose to work in and through Jesus to offer humans
a saving example of love, righteousness, and godliness. This is truly incredible.
And this is something else that Elizondo is right about: our God is indeed a God
of incredible surprises!

As we can see, Elizondo contributes much to the christological discussion.
But are there other Latinos who contribute in like manner, and might we find an
example of a Latina voice in the midst of these? The next segment offers a clue
and response.

Jesus against Western Cultural Impudence: *The Case of Marina Herrera*

A Latina who contributed early on to the discussion on the meaning of Jesus
among Latino/a theologians is Marina Herrera. Her essay on the subject, entitled
"Who Do You Say Jesus Is? Christological Reflections from a Hispanic Woman's
Perspective," appeared in 1993, at the close of the Columbian quincentenary—
the five hundredth anniversary of the arrival of Christopher Columbus to the
land that would become known as the Americas.[18] If we recall, the Columbus
quincentenary of 1992 proved to be a controversial and fractious commemoration. While many in Europe and the United States used the occasion to pay
homage to Columbus's travels and to the "age of discovery" that they seemingly
initiated, many others utilized the moment quite appropriately to call attention
to the conquest, colonization, enslavement, forced migration, disease, destruction of peoples, effacement of cultures, and environmental exploitation that
resulted from them. The efforts of those in this latter group, including many
teachers, academics, museum professionals, journalists, media types, clergy
people, and social activists, worked to set the significance of the event within a
larger and more balanced context of meaning—a context that encompassed not
only the favorable outcomes but also the adverse consequences that Columbus's
encounter with the Americas gave rise to.

Marina Herrera has adopted this cause. For that reason we find that a
good part of her essay on the meaning of Jesus centers on the matter of the

failings of European culture. In fact, it can be said that what Herrera undertakes in this essay is nothing less than a thorough critique of the assumption of European supremacy in Western ways of thinking, and then a corresponding revaluation of non-European, autochthonic religious motifs that endure within Hispanic culture. For example, she offers an opinion that we ought to declaim the dichotomies that were introduced by early European thought and that have paved the way for the persistence of all sorts of prejudiced ways of thinking, including racism, cultural chauvinism, sexism, class consciousness, and the degradation of nature; the West's unremitting disposition toward the ill treatment and control of "the other" by way of conquest, colonization, expropriation, and subjugation; the inadequate understandings of women, children, sexuality, religious experience, and the nature of human knowledge that were passed on to us by European ways of thinking; the self-serving, individualistic, and self-aggrandizing tendencies of European cultures; and the shortsightedness and self-destructiveness of many Western scientific tenets. Basically, Herrera perceives that Western European thought has gravitated toward and steered us toward dualistic, despotic, and egotistic ways of thinking. These critical observations and comments leave no doubt that there is much about our European inheritance that is less than ideal, at least in the opinion of Herrera. Indeed, she is convinced that much of our European cultural and cognitive legacy, including that in the area of religious belief, is flawed and needs fixing.

One area of religious belief where Herrera would like to see some change or perhaps "conversion" is in our ways of thinking about Jesus. In particular, she finds the blond-haired, blue-eyed images of Jesus, and the images of the triumphant, unvulnerable, glorified, transcendent Christ of Northern European and American traditions to be in need of some correction. Not only are these historically improbable, they may also be culturally and theologically disingenuous, Herrera suggests. In the first place, the image of "a black or brown haired man with olive complexion and a Mediterranean look" is more likely to bear resemblance to the Jewish Jesus of Near Eastern provenance than is a blond-haired, blue-eyed man. What's more, the blond and blue-eyed image of Jesus possibly supports an imperial, colonizing, and racist mind-set that exalts Caucasian people but needlessly subtracts from the beauty of nonwhite, non-European peoples. Second, the image of the unbeaten, inviolable, reigning, superhuman Christ so glorified in Euro-American Christian traditions indicates a longing for ascendancy and an uneasiness with the humanity and modesty of Jesus. Better than these, Herrera suggests, are representations of Jesus that make allowances for his humanness, for his estimable character and relational ways of being, for his engagement and passion in life, and for his suffering and death as a result of the principled, justice-minded, and even countercultural attitudes and actions that he personified and made public.

As a matter of fact, Herrera illustrates her points by discussing the imagery suggested by one of her childhood Spanish prayers and by the word pictures of a Spanish poem she learned as an early adolescent. A prayer that she was taught at a tender age goes something like this: "Jesusito de mi vida, tú eres niño como yo; por eso te quiero tanto y te doy mi corazón," which she translates in English as "Dear little Jesus, you're just a child like me; therefore I love you so and I give you my heart."[19] Herrera notes that this early prayer served to distinguish Jesus from God, making him a member of the human race, a down-to-earth human being one could identify with even as a child. The beauty of this prayer, she suggests, is that it conduces to a consideration of the true humanity of Jesus and to an appreciation of his consubstantiality or correspondence with human beings. In this way, the prayer has the effect of putting us in touch with a flesh-and-blood person rather than merely with a theosophical construction or a hyperphysical entity or an omnipresence. Moreover, it can also have the effect of getting us to focus on the human condition and to set a high value on humaneness rather than on loftiness and control.

A second understanding of Jesus that marked Herrera's early adolescence came from a well-known Spanish poem written by Lope de Vega, which Herrera translates thusly: "The heaven you promised, O God, does not move me to love you. The much feared hell does not move me nor stop me from offending you. You move me, O Lord, seeing you nailed to a cross and reviled; I am moved by the sight of your wounded body; I am moved by your sufferings and your death." Attached to this poem, Herrera recalls, was a painting of Jesus on the Cross that graphically depicted the horror and pain of his crucifixion. The appropriateness and potential of this poem and accompanying picture, she surmises, inheres in its ability to convey the tragic nature of Jesus' violent death and in its ability to provide for a sense of the mystery but also the potentiality and consequence of "a suffering man-God, who assumed his powerlessness to show the extent of God's mercy and love."[20]

This last statement should leave no doubt that Herrera believes in the divinity of Jesus: she refers to him as the "man-God." Herrera does not deny the "godliness" of Jesus. It's just that she leans toward and wants to emphasize the concrete human existence of Jesus. To borrow from the schema of christological reflection found in the Johannine prologue, I venture to say that Herrera's purpose is to assert that in Jesus of Nazareth—and, therefore, in Jesus' earthly actions, attitudes, choices, lifestyle, and social involvement—the Word, Spirit, or "activity" of God became Flesh (John 1:14). In other words, although this point is not made explicit nor developed in her essay, I submit that Herrera's choice of words makes it clear that her Christology rests on the conviction that God's spirit, that God's passion and intent, that God's self-expression and self-communication was embodied in the person of Jesus.

That being so, one could perhaps ask, "What was God revealing to humanity in and through the person and life of Jesus?" And what might the significance of this "living revelation" be for life today, especially perhaps for the purposes of meaningful and transformative human orientation in the context of late modern Western society? Herrera ends her essay with various assertions that go a long way toward answering these two questions, I believe. In the first place, she intimates that if Jesus is to mean anything new or different for us today it has to be in the example he offers us of a trustworthy and relational way of being. In other words, Herrera is convinced that Jesus reveals a congenial way of life that not only embodies God's ideals and purposes for the human community but also opens up possibilities for the fruition of fellowship and justice in contemporary Western society. Specifically, there are four model traits that Jesus exemplified. First, Herrera says, Jesus was not possessive. Among other things, this means that he was not acquisitive, greedy, or possession oriented. This also implies that Jesus was not a clinging, controlling person. In fact, Herrera indicates that "he never claimed an attachment to anything, including his mother, his town, his own ideas of who he was." Second, she offers that Jesus was forgiving, "even of those who tortured and killed him." Third, Herrera announces that Jesus was "non paternalistic" in his dealings with people, and particularly with regard to women and those who were often marginalized and disrespected in his society. Especially notable is the fact that he often dealt with women without condescension, treating them as equals in every possible way. This is apparent, Herrera suggests, by virtue of the stories the Gospels relate in reference to Jesus' interactions with women. They make known, for instance, that "he spoke harshly to his mother, to the Canaanite women, to the woman who felt sorry for him on the way to Calvary, and to Mary when she complained about Martha." Herrera submits that the story of the woman at the well also proves this point inasmuch as it shows that "he did not assume that because she was a poor woman who drew water from the well, she was incapable of understanding the deeper realities of life which he wanted to talk about." In fact, this gospel story intimates that Jesus even came to realize that this woman could make for a "better proclaimer of his message among her people than he or his disciples." Herrera suggests that these representative illustrations, and others like them, indicate that Jesus was a person who was willing to engage with women on an equal footing and without impudence or condescension. And other gospel traditions seem to indicate that Jesus treated others in like manner. Finally, Herrera notes that Jesus gave prominence to the virtue of love. Time and again it appears in New Testament passages that Jesus was primarily interested in the acid test of a person's ability to love. "When looking for a successor," Herrera notes, "Jesus did not ask Peter how good a fisherman he was, or how well he knew the prophets or the law. Rather his question pointed to an overriding concern for the relationships he hoped his followers would have: 'Peter, do you love me?'" This suggests that in the eyes of Jesus, leadership potential was not based on knowledge, rank, or prominence but on the willingness to love. And not only leadership but also one's willingness to follow Jesus and one's eagerness to seek the way of the kingdom of God were to be measured by the readiness to love, to care, to be benevolent.[21]

Herrera summarizes this last emphasis and tendency of Jesus with the suggestion that he was above all "a linker and not a ranker." "Linkers," she says, "persuade others to give up their self-appointed importance, their arrogance, or their holier-than-thou attitudes." They also spurn hierarchical, isolationist, categorical, and dogmatic conceptions of truth and association, preferring to work out of "relational, communitarian, integrative, tentative, artistic, spontaneous structures of reality."[22] This, Herrera suggests, is the saving example that Jesus left for us, and this is the exemplary lifestyle that we Christians will need to emulate if we want to be called "followers of Jesus" and if Christianity is to emerge as a force for virtuousness and justice in favor of all of humanity.

So, what can we make of Marina Herrera's reflections and intimations? To begin with, it should be clear that Herrera does not set before us a systematic treatment of Christology nor a creative or constructive rendering of classical christological doctrine. Neither does she give us a detailed historical reconstruction of the life, times, and teachings of Jesus of Nazareth. What Herrera puts forth is a critique of modern Western social culture. This critique rests on a particular understanding of the historical Jesus and on a particular view of the relevance of Jesus' avowed way of life, however. Jesus, Herrera suggests, exemplified a loving, caring, humble, and compassionate way of life that is of significance in a world where selfishness, bigotry, avarice, and injustice reigns supreme. What we need to do today, she believes, is to return to the praxis of the Jesus of history. We also need to take a long, hard look at our images of Jesus to determine whether they are being held for hurtful and self-serving purposes rather than for righteous and true reasons.

It is true that Herrera does little to support her claims beyond generic assertion, as she avoids both the historical study of Jesus' life and ministry and the riches of christological doctrine. It is also true that her denunciation of all things modern and Western comes across as superfluous, unbalanced, and heavy-handed at times. However, Herrera helps us to see that Western culture, and even Western Christianity itself, is disconnected from the praxis of the Jesus of history.

All in the Family: On Luis Pedraja's Jesus Is My Uncle

The third and final illustration of Latino/a Christology that I will reflect on comes from the work of Cuban American theologian Luis Pedraja. Particularly relevant is his treatise entitled *Jesus Is My Uncle: Christology from a Hispanic Perspective*.[23] This book-length monograph on the subject of Jesus and Christology offers insight into the christological positions of Pedraja and gives us a fitting case study in Latino/a Christology.

In this work Pedraja throws light on customs and religious word choices that are common among Spanish-speaking Hispanic Americans in order to illuminate the contributions these cultural traits can make to Christology. The book's title, *Jesus Is My Uncle*, makes an allusion to one of these distinguishing marks. Pedraja points out that he has an uncle named Jesús, and in fact also had a next-door neighbor, a school classmate, and a church deacon with that same name, Jesús. From a tender age then he was able to associate the name Jesus not only with God's Son (i.e., Jesus of Nazareth) but also with relatives, neighbors, and friends in his Hispanic/Latino(a) community. This fact illustrates an interesting difference between Anglos and Latinos. Anglos seldom name their sons Jesus, perhaps out of fear of impiety or sacrilege. This is not the case in the Latino/a community, however. Many Latinos and Latinas name their sons Jesús, considering the choice of name an honor and a constant reminder of God's nearness. And it makes a difference whether one grows up being familiar with and close to someone named Jesus or not, Pedraja suggests. Pedraja recalls that having an uncle, neighbor, school friend, and church deacon named Jesús led him to think of Jesus Christ in more personal and human ways. As he puts it, "I grew up thinking of God's Son as someone who lived near me and who had a human face like those who bore his name."[24] This is a good thing, Pedraja claims, as it laid the foundation for a Christology that appreciates the humanity of Jesus and is comfortable with the doctrine of the Incarnation.

And speaking of the Incarnation, Pedraja suggests that nuances of the Spanish language can help to make the meaning of this important doctrine more explicit. He notes, for instance, that among English speakers the term "incarnation" remains a seldom-used and abstract theological concept. In English the term is also associated with words like *carnal, carnality, carnage,* and *carnivore,* which are words that can carry negative connotations. The Spanish word *encarnación,* however, has more practical and cheerful connotations in the Hispanic community. For example, Pedraja notes that among Mexicans and Mexican Americans the Spanish word *carnal* "can mean 'brother,' 'close friend,' or 'family,'" indicating that a person is either of the same flesh, related, or cherished. This linguistic association alone holds potential for a deeper understanding of the Incarnation, Pedraja suggests, as it can be used to advert to "the incorporation of humanity into God's family."[25] But Hispanic use of the word *encarnación* can strengthen the meaning of the incarnation of God in more ways than this, Pedraja submits. The Spanish word *encarnación,* he points out, is related to *carne,* a common word for "meat" or "flesh." It is also related to and calls to mind words such as *carnicería* (butcher shop) and *carnicero* (butcher). These word associations, Pedraja suggests, conjure up vivid images of flesh and blood and can therefore encourage a more physical and corporal understanding of the Incarnation. When we read the words of John 1:14 and think about the Incarnation in Spanish, for instance, we get the picture that God actually made "himself" flesh and blood in the person of Jesus Christ. In fact, in its common Spanish translation John 1:14 reads as *el Verbo se hizo carne,* which literally means that the Verb (i.e., God's spirit) became "meat" or "fleshly material" in the person of Jesus. One cannot read John 1:14 in Spanish then and not think of fleshly tissue, of physicality, of corporality.

This linguistic and cultural nuance is significant in a number of ways, Pedraja suggests. In the first place, it is consequential because it impels us to take notice of the full humanity and corporeality of Jesus. This can help to keep us from the snare of a Docetic Christology—one that denies the humanity of Jesus. The added sense of physicalness suggested by the Spanish language is propitious in a second manner, Pedraja intimates, as it can help us to bridge the distance between God and humanity and to think of God as immanent and indwelling in the material world. And these two portents could in turn give rise to a third ennoblement, that being a greater regard for the physical world. The Spanish connotations of the word *encarnación*, Pedraja asserts, remind us "that God comes to us in concrete physical forms" and force us "to look not only at humanity's spiritual needs but its physical needs as well."[26] This, he suggests, implies cherishing one's body, caring about the material well-being of others, and showing concern when people are exploited or are denied an adequate material standard of living in society.

The associations, images, and nuances conveyed by the Spanish language can contribute to Christology in a third way, Pedraja claims. Spanish speakers, he notes, have been referring to Jesus as a "verb" for many centuries now. The custom owes much to the fact that Spanish translations of the Bible commonly render the term or concept of *logos* as "Verbo" (i.e., verb) when referring to Jesus. This hermeneutical rendition goes back to 1793, Pedraja indicates, "when Felipe Scio de San Miguel first translated the Latin Vulgate into Spanish with the consent of the Spanish King," and used the word "Verbo" in reference to "God's incarnate logos."[27] Hence, when we read John 1:1 in Spanish we find that it says *"En el principio era el Verbo, y el Verbo era con Dios, y el Verbo era Dios"* (In the beginning was the Verb, and the Verb was with God, and the Verb was God).

This rendering of *logos* as "Verbo" captures the intended purpose of the early Christian writers, who used the term to speak of Jesus as the personification or living manifestation of the effective power of God in the world. The locution was meant to convey then a sense of God's acting toward and in his creation through the person and ministry of Jesus. English translations do not convey this sense of divine purpose and action, Pedraja believes, because they render the concept of the divine logos simply as "Word." The term "Word" does not remind one of action, animation, and agency, not without prompting or the aid of a theological dictionary at least. It is no wonder then that English speakers find it so hard to break free from the enduring constraints of Greek metaphysics and often end up thinking of God as a distant, immovable, and emotionless or impassive being. Spanish speakers, however, need only to read John 1:1 in Spanish to be reminded of two presuppositions of the Christian faith: first, that God is active, immanent, and relational; and second, that God became actively, lovingly, and redemptively present in the world in the person and ministry of Jesus. Spanish speakers know this because their Spanish translation of John's gospel tells them that God is a Verb (i.e., "el Verbo") and that Jesus is God's incarnate verb (i.e., *"el Verbo hecho carne"*).

The Spanish-language translation of *logos* as "verbo" is significant not only because it captures and conveys the christological intimations of the early Christian writers, Pedraja suggests, but also because it can lead up to suitable representations of God and Jesus in this day and age. It could, for instance, lead us to think of God not as a distant and "passive observer" of world events but as an active and caring "agent of history."[28] This understanding would enable us to look upon God as one who has been active in creation, who was active in a loving and saving way in Jesus of Nazareth, and who continues to be active in history and in our own lives today. The translation of *logos* as "verbo" allows

not only for the elaboration of suitable theological imagery, but also for the
development of sound Christology. Pedraja suggests that it can serve to revo-
lutionize Christology in two important ways. In the first place, thinking about
Jesus as "God's incarnate verb" could prompt us to give prominence to Jesus'
earthly activity. Traditionally, Christology has tended to focus on discussions of
ontology and metaphysical principles in an attempt to explain the nature and
significance of Jesus. This line of reasoning has put Christology in pursuit of
a hyperphysical or transcendent constituent and rationale that could be said to
make Jesus who he is, and has led to its dependence on speculative maneuvers
to explain the distinctive character of Jesus. The problem is that this emphasis on metaphysical reasoning and speculative conjecture has unintentionally
served to divert attention away from the revelatory significance of Jesus' actions
and deeds right here on earth. But this is where our focus needs to be, Pedraja
submits, because Jesus' lifework is ultimately what gives evidence of his true
character and significance. It was Jesus' actions and deeds that led people of his
time to assert that God and God's will for humanity had somehow been met,
encountered, and engaged in the human life of Jesus of Nazareth. Indeed, it was
the memory of the impressiveness of Jesus' actions and deeds that caused the
story of Jesus to be written in the first place, and it was the recollection of these
actions and deeds that inspired talk of his divinity. So, if we truly want to know
who Jesus was and is, and if we truly want to understand why people came to
believe that Jesus reveals the nature and will of God, we need to take into consideration his public activity.

This is what the New Testament writers did, and we stand to learn much
from their example, Pedraja claims. "The writers of the New Testament," he
points out, "do not concern themselves so much with questions about the person of Jesus—that is, his divine nature or substance. Instead, they are concerned
with Jesus' deeds, proclamations, miracles, and salvific actions."[29] In fact, the
New Testament writers seem to assume that Jesus' actions and deeds reveal his
divine character, and that people will come to believe that Jesus is the decisive
revelation of God if they can only hear and learn of them. That's probably why
they mention and call attention to many of Jesus' activities and miracles. For
example, they bring up Jesus' actions of compassion toward those who suffered
from affliction and injustice, Jesus' polemics against the unjust practices of the
political and religious power brokers of his time, Jesus' healing miracles, and
Jesus' call to his disciples and followers to go out and minister to others. The
pages of the New Testament are full of these accounts, suggesting that the early
Christian writers revered Jesus' actions and deeds and were convinced that they
bore witness to his person and divinity.

Theologians who write on and about Christology today must return to this
early Christian focus and conviction, Pedraja claims. And this they must do if
Christology is to be credible and relevant again. Christology, Pedraja suggests,
needs to move beyond its prevailing obsession with ontology and metaphysical speculation to consider the importance of Jesus' actions. Only in this way
will it come to know the person and difference of Jesus, and only thus will it

encounter the paradigmatic and saving value of Jesus' praxis. "Just as liberation theologians have shifted their concern from orthodoxy (right belief) to orthopraxis (right action)," Pedraja asserts, so should interpreters and exponents of Christology shift their christological concerns "from ontology (the structure of being) to ontopraxis (the act of being)."[30] The Spanish language's translation of *logos* as "Verbo" could help to point us in this direction, he suggests, because it compels us to think of Jesus in terms of a verb and, therefore, in relation to action and agency. Consequently, it impels us to think back to and to think better of Jesus' works.

Pedraja is convinced that this particular translation could recondition Christology in a second manner. Because it conveys a sense of agency and enactment, the rendering of *logos* as "Verbo" could encourage us to examine the way we practice our faith today. "When one speaks of Jesus as a Verb," Pedraja writes, "it is difficult to reduce faith to just belief without action." And this is important because faith should neither be reduced to nor confused with the mere acceptance of doctrines or beliefs. Faith incorporates our beliefs, Pedraja assures, but it also "entails a commitment, a risk, a way of being, and a way of living." In short, faith appears as and requires principled and purposeful action. Christian "faithfulness" in particular calls on us to tread in the steps of Jesus of Nazareth. Christians, Pedraja declares, "are called to be God's incarnate presence on earth" in the same way that Jesus was. In the same way that Jesus revealed the creative and redemptive love of God through generous acts of compassion, justice, and sacrifice, so too must Christians bring to light the life-giving and life-affirming love of God today through generosity, self-sacrifice when necessary, and the work of social justice. And this should in fact be the pursuit and purpose of Christology, Pedraja intimates. The ultimate aim of Christology should be to apprise people of Jesus' actions, attitudes, and life choices in the hope that they will be inspired to repeat them in the present. In this sense, then, Christology is less a speculative tradition putting forward abstract theories of divinity and more a practical and moral project that seeks to retrieve and re-create the redeeming praxis of Jesus for the furtherance of liberation today. Christology, Pedraja suggests, is or should be about "the verb"—that is, about the creative and effective agency of God, about the revelatory, exemplary, and saving activity of Jesus, and about the longing for norms and efforts that exemplify the liberating action of God in Jesus and can make a difference today. The Spanish Bible reminds us of this, he believes, because it urges us to think about God, Jesus, and our Christian vocation in terms of "Verbo"—that is, in terms of action, movement, and agency.[31]

These are the christological intimations that we will find in Pedraja's *Jesus Is My Uncle*. That they are enlightening, worthy, and valuable suggestions should already be obvious. But just in case the value of this work is not yet recognizable, I want to touch on some of its important contributions. The book obviously sheds light on the way in which Hispanic expressions, concepts, and experiences serve to clarify christological principles. This cultural enlightenment is valuable in itself. However, Pedraja's book offers more than just cultural edification.

Pedraja's *Jesus Is My Uncle* is an exemplary work in contextual Christology. As such, it offers an example of the conceivability and potentiality of a contextual Christology—that is, of a Christology that makes use of the cultural experiences, customs, expressions, mores, and idiosyncrasies of a social group to put forth fresh and pertinent interpretations of the life, teachings, and relevance of Jesus. It bears mentioning that Pedraja's work on Christology also offers an excellent example of a creative synthesis of intellectual traditions, as it borrows from and deftly weaves together insights gleaned from classical Christology, Wittgensteinian linguistic theory, process philosophy, and Latin-American liberation theology. In this sense, one could say that the book offers a representative illustration of the potentiality of a broad-based and interdisciplinary contemporary Christology. Moreover, Pedraja's work sheds light on the underlying meaning and contemporary relevance of the doctrine of the Incarnation.

The doctrine of the Incarnation looms large in Pedraja's work; in fact *Jesus Is My Uncle* can be read as a commentary on its value. This doctrine, Pedraja suggests, assures us of God's immanence and affirms God's presence in and within the world. It also makes possible the consecration and celebration of human life. God's coming to us in a human being, Pedraja asserts, suggests that God thought highly of human life; so highly in fact that God took up the cause of humanity to make it God's own cause. Furthermore, the doctrine of the Incarnation impels us to take the humanity of Jesus seriously. This is important, of course, because popular Christianity has tended to disregard and to erase the full humanity of Jesus, even if inadvertently. For these reasons Pedraja accentuates the Incarnation in an attempt to get us to take God's immanence and Jesus' human experience seriously.

Pedraja's attempt to promote the doctrine of the Incarnation is commendable, and his reasons for wanting to do so are likewise comprehensible. The only problem is that Pedraja betrays his own calling because he looks right through the particularity of the Incarnation. If one takes the Incarnation seriously then one should take seriously "the time when, place where, and people among whom this event occurred."[32] In other words, emphasis on the doctrine of the Incarnation entails consideration of the first-century Jewish world into which Jesus was born. The particulars of that time and context must be considered because Christianity claims not only that the divine took on human flesh but also that it took on human flesh in Jesus of Nazareth—a first-century Jewish man from the countryside of Galilee. Thus we should reflect upon Jesus' first-century Jewish context and identity. Pedraja pays little attention to these matters of context and identity, however. He thinks nothing of the context of cultural struggle and Roman colonial power within which first-century Jewish life developed. He makes no reference to first-century Jewish thought and practice nor to the symbols and traditions of Judaism. It bears mentioning too that Pedraja consults neither the varied Jewish sources of Jesus' general time period (e.g., the Pseudepigrapha, Dead Sea Scrolls, Josephus, Philo, the Rabbinic texts, and Targumim) nor the historical and archeological evidence of our time to gain insight into the life and times of the "enfleshed divine verb" he speaks of—that is, Jesus of Nazareth. He does mention some of Jesus' reported actions and some biblical passages that refer to Jesus, but he does so in isolation or in a "historical" vacuum and, therefore, without regard to the context within which Jesus lived and acted. As a result, he presents us with a human being in the abstract and leaves us not with a real, historical, concrete, contextually embodied fellow man but with the notion of a man named Jesus. This is ironic, of course, especially because Pedraja claims to want to rescue or to reclaim the full humanity of Jesus. The retrieval of Jesus' humanity requires more than just an allusion to the doctrine of the Incarnation, however, and more than just the citation of some of Jesus' teachings and activities; it also calls for historical study of the Jewish and wider Greco-Roman world of Jesus. Only by knowing the broader historical and cultural setting in which Jesus lived and taught can we fully understand him, his purposeful activity, and the meaning of his life's example.

Deciphering the Christological Inclinations of Our Exemplars

I have offered a summary and analysis of the christological writings of Virgilio Elizondo, Marina Herrera, and Luis Pedraja, making note of their cardinal points, their strong points, and their weak points. And it should be apparent by now that the writings of these three Latino/a theologians are different in style, in purpose, and in substance. But might their writings share some common christological emphases, tendencies, or patterns? I happen to think that they do. Specifically, I submit that the writings of these theologians partake of three christological patterns and directions. In the first place, it is important to note that all three of our authors incline toward a "Christology from below"—all emphasize the humanity or historical life of Jesus, preferring to dwell on the telling features of the historical person and ministry of Jesus rather than on the dogmatic formulations of Jesus' metaphysical and divine status. Elizondo, for instance, calls attention to the historical circumstances of the Galilean provenance and identity of Jesus, leading one to believe that the continuing and liberating significance of Jesus is contingent on his human story of unabashed identity and self-assurance in the face of prejudice and his ability to turn a humble and marginal social status into a virtuous life of good will. Elizondo also gives one to understand that it is through the humanity of Jesus that we discover the nature and will of God and the ultimate potential of human life. As for Marina Herrera and Luis Pedraja, both of them press home the exemplary and saving significance of Jesus' historical praxis as they bring to the fore the impressiveness and paradigmatic value of his actions, his attitudes, and his overall way of life. Like Elizondo, therefore, they too set a high value on Jesus' human story, deeming it the proper starting point for the theological study of the significance of Jesus and the medium of God's liberating and saving action in history.

This does not mean that our three exemplars disavow or belittle Jesus' divinity, however. As a matter of fact, even though they build on and exalt the humanity of Jesus, Elizondo, Herrera, and Pedraja all adopt a rather high view of Jesus with regard to divinity. If one looks into Elizondo's writings attentively one will note that he assumes that Jesus *is* God-with-us—that Jesus is, in other words, the unique revelation or historical manifestation of God. And Marina Herrera? Well, it is telling that she refers to Jesus as the "man-God," a clear sign that she views him as God's self-disclosure in a human life. Luis Pedraja, as we have seen, devotes much of his book to the doctrine of the Incarnation, a doctrine that he interprets literally rather than figuratively. This creedal diligence and literal-mindedness make it known that he looks up to Jesus as God's own spirit reaching out into the world or, in other words, as the very Word or agency of God made flesh. All three of our authors, then, show a penchant for a "high Christology," and give evidence that a Christology from below can still yield a high Christology—that is, a Christology that takes a high view of Jesus' relation to God and/or assumes the divinity of Jesus. They may not flaunt it or express it precisely, but it is unmistakable that our three exemplars anchor on the belief that Jesus is the decisive and tangible revelation of God.

So far I have touched on two patterns of christological thought that I observe in the work of Elizondo, Herrera, and Pedraja, having alluded to their preference for a Christology from below and their predisposition toward a high Christology.[33] There is a third tendency that I detect in their writings, however: all three espouse a liberationist Christology. What I mean is that Elizondo, Herrera, and Pedraja each look to link the historical and theological study of Jesus to the struggle for freedom and justice today. The point of Elizondo's excursion into the particulars of the historical Jesus, for instance, is not only to describe the circumstances of oppression Jesus may have faced as a Galilean peasant and Jewish mestizo, but also to counter conceptions of self and culture that prejudicially privilege the colonizing West and white Anglo-Saxonism and to promote cultural affirmation and achievement of positive self-identity and group identity among Mexican Americans and Latinos/as in the United States. In other words, his Christology unequivocally and unashamedly aims to render assistance to the struggle against cultural imperialism, ethnic prejudice, and racism in this present day. And as for Herrera and Pedraja, they both return to the praxis of the historical Jesus hoping to deliver a criterion of virtue for Christian praxis that can make a difference today. In this sense, it could be said that all three of our exemplars take up the historical and theological study of Jesus not only in the interest of factual discovery and doctrinal erudition but also in the interest of encouraging liberating Christian action by awakening memories of the praxis of the historical Jesus and thus furthering social change for the better in this day and age.

These three patterns of christological thought are noticeable in the writings of Elizondo, Herrera, and Pedraja. I happen to think that they appear in the writings of other Latino/a theologians as well, but that is a claim to be taken up and examined in another place and time perhaps. Here I will simply assert that the christological writings of Elizondo, Herrera, and Pedraja give examples of a Christology from below, a high Christology, and a liberation Christology.

Notes

1. I have chosen these three writers for a number of reasons. To begin with, each one of these thinkers brings to the public either a book-length monograph on the topic of Jesus and Christology or at least a full essay devoted to the general subject matter. Second, the christological writings of these authors extend across a reasonably long span of time within the development of Latino/a Christology, from the early '80s to the late '90s. That being so, they give us a window into the development of Latino/a theological thought, particularly in what I like to call its first and second stage of articulation. Third, Elizondo, Herrera, and Pedraja each represent a different subgroup or nationality within the Latino/a community: Elizondo is Mexican American, Herrera is Dominican American, and Pedraja Cuban American. This offers us representational variety in regard to nationality. Fourth, each of these writers displays both a different depiction of Jesus and a thoroughly different style of writing. This distinguishing literary variety helps to keep things interesting. For these four reasons, then, I deem the choice of Elizondo, Herrera, and Pedraja a good one for the purposes of our christological study. But it is important to note that there are other U.S. Latino/a theologians who have written on the subject of Jesus and/or Christology. Among these are Justo González, Roberto Goizueta, Eliseo Pérez Álvarez, Harold J. Recinos, Miguel de la Torre, and Ada María Isasi-Díaz. See Justo González's chapter on Christology in *Mañana: Christian Theology from a Hispanic Perspective* (Nashville: Abingdon Press, 1990), 139-55; Roberto Goizueta, *Caminemos con Jesús: A Hispanic/Latino Theology of Accompaniment* (Maryknoll, N.Y.: Orbis Books, 1995), esp. 18-76; Eliseo Pérez Álvarez, "In Memory of Me: Hispanic/Latino Christology beyond Borders," in *Teología en Conjunto: A Collaborative Hispanic Protestant Theology*, ed. José David Rodríguez and Loida I. Martell-Otero (Louisville: Westminster John Knox Press, 1997), 33-49; Harold Recinos, *Who Comes in the Name of the Lord? Jesus at the Margins* (Nashville: Abingdon Press, 1997), esp. 37-57; Miguel de la Torre, *The Quest for the Cuban Christ: A Historical Search* (Gainesville: University Press of Florida, 2002); and Ada María Isasi-Díaz, "Christ in *Mujerista* Theology," in *Thinking of Christ: Proclamation, Explanation, Meaning*, ed. Tatha Wiley (New York: Continuum, 2003), 157-76. For a brief but helpful overview of U.S. Latino/a Christologies, see Michelle González-Maldonado's entry on "Jesus" in *Handbook of Latina/o Theologies*, ed. Edwin David Aponte and Miguel A. de la Torre (St. Louis: Chalice Press, 2006), 17-24.

2. See Virgilio Elizondo, *Galilean Journey: The Mexican-American Promise* (Maryknoll, N.Y.: Orbis Books, 1983); *A God of Incredible Surprises: Jesus of Galilee* (Lanham, Md.: Rowman & Littlefield, 2003); and *The Future Is Mestizo: Life Where Cultures Meet* (Bloomington, Ind.: Meyer Stone Books, 1983).

3. Elizondo, *Future Is Mestizo*, 77.

4. Elizondo, *Galilean Journey*, 49.

5. Ibid., 51.

6. Ibid.

7. Ibid.

8. Elizondo, *Future Is Mestizo*, 77.

9. Elizondo, *God of Incredible Surprises*, 8.

10. Elizondo, *Future Is Mestizo,* 77.

11. Elizondo, *Galilean Journey*, 100.

12. Elizondo, *God of Incredible Surprises*, 12-13, 18.

13. For some important recent works that point to the unmistakable Jewish character of Jesus' Galilee, see Sean Freyne, *Galilee from Alexander the Great to Hadrian, 323 BCE to 135 CE: A Study of Second Temple Judaism* (Wilmington, Del.: Michael Glazier, 1980); idem, *Jesus, a Jewish Galilean: A New Reading of the Jesus-Story* (New York: T&T Clark, 2004); and idem, "Archaeology and the Historical Jesus," in *Jesus and Archaeology,* ed. James H. Charlesworth (Grand Rapids: Eerdmans, 2006), 64-83; Jonathan L. Reed, *Archaeology and the Galilean Jesus: A Re-examination of the Evidence* (Harrisburg, Pa.: Trinity, 2000), esp. 23-62; and idem, "Archaeological Contributions to the Study of Jesus and the Gospels," in *The Historical Jesus in Context*, ed. Amy-Jill Levine, Dale Allison, Jr., and John Dominic Crossan (Princeton, N.J.: Princeton University Press, 2006), 40-54; John Dominic Crossan and Jonathan Reed, *Excavating Jesus: Beneath the Stones, Behind the Texts* (New York: HarperOne, 2001), esp. 49-70; Mark A. Chancey, *The Myth of a Gentile Galilee* (Cambridge: Cambridge University Press, 2002); and James D. G. Dunn, "Did Jesus Attend the Synagogue?" in *Jesus and Archaeology,* 206-22. For a concise summary of current research on Galilee, see Mark Rapinchuk, "The Galilee and Jesus in Recent Research," in *Currents in Biblical Research* 2, no. 2 (2004): 197-222.

14. For a helpful analysis of these biblical texts, see Chancey, *Myth of a Gentile Galilee,* esp. 1-27 and 167-74.

15. For some helpful and accessible archaeological studies that shed light on the Jewish world of Jesus, see *The Oxford Encyclopedia of Archaeology in the Near East,* ed. Eric M. Meyers (New York: Oxford University Press, 1997); Reed, *Archaeology and the Galilean Jesus*; Crossan and Reed, *Excavating Jesus*; the excellent essays in *Jesus and Archaeology*; James Tabor, *The Jesus Dynasty: The Hidden History of Jesus, His Royal Family, and the Birth of Christianity* (New York: Simon and Schuster, 2006); and Shimon Gibson, *The Final Days of Jesus: The Archaeological Evidence* (New York: HarperOne, 2009). Mark Chancey's *The Myth of a Gentile Galilee* also contains important information on Galilee's archaeological record. See especially chapter 3 of that work.

16. For noteworthy works that point out the anti-Jewish rhetoric found in the writings of Elizondo, see Jean-Pierre Ruiz, "Good Fences and Good Neighbors? Biblical Scholars and Theologians," in *Journal of Hispanic/Latino Theology* (May 2007); and Jeffrey Siker, "Historicizing a Racialized Jesus: Case Studies in the 'Black Christ,' the 'Mestizo Christ,' and White Critique," *Biblical Interpretation* 15 (2007): 26-53. For signal works that make note of the anti-Jewish attitudes of Christian theologians and even of liberation theologians more generally, see Amy-Jill Levine, *The Misunderstood Jew: The Church and the Scandal of the Jewish Jesus* (New York: HarperCollins, 2006), esp. 167-90; and Mary C. Boys, *Has God Only One Blessing? Judaism as a Source of Christian Self-Understanding* (Mahwah, N.J.: Paulist Press, 2000), esp. 5-14 and 111-37.

17. For a helpful commentary on the marginality of Jesus, and for an informative listing of ways in which Jesus might be considered marginal, see John P. Meier, *A Marginal Jew: Rethinking the Historical Jesus,* vol. 1 (New York: Doubleday, 1991), esp. 1-17.

18. Marina Herrera, "Who Do You Say Jesus Is? Christological Reflections from a Hispanic Woman's Perspective," in *Reconstructing the Christ Symbol: Essays in Feminist Christology,* ed. Maryanne Stevens (New York: Paulist Press, 1993), 72-94.

19. Herrera, "Who Do You Say Jesus Is?" 74.

20. Ibid., 75, 76.

21. Ibid., 89-91.

22. Ibid., 92.

23. Luis G. Pedraja, *Jesus Is My Uncle: Christology from a Hispanic Perspective* (Nashville: Abingdon Press, 1999). This work represents Pedraja's most extended treatment of the topic(s) of Christology. Pedraja also has two chapters on Christology in his book *Teología: An Introduction to Hispanic Theology* (Nashville: Abingdon Press, 2003), 127-64. This later work dwells on some of the themes elaborated in *Jesus Is My Uncle*.

24. Pedraja, *Jesus Is My Uncle*, 15.

25. Ibid., 75.

26. Ibid., 80.

27. Ibid., 93.

28. Ibid., 95.

29. Ibid.

30. Ibid., 106.

31. Ibid., 87, 120.

32. I borrow these choice words from Amy-Jill Levine, *Misunderstood Jew*, 7.

33. For a general discussion of some of the different types of and/or approaches to Christology, see Karl Rahner, "The Two Basic Types of Christology," in *Theological Investigations*, vol. 13 (New York: Seabury Press, 1975), esp. 213-23; John Macquarrie, *Jesus Christ in Modern Thought* (Harrisburg, Pa.: Trinity Press, 1990), esp. 339-47; and Roger Haight, *Jesus Symbol of God* (Maryknoll, N.Y.: Orbis Books, 1999), esp. 27-51; and idem, *The Future of Christology* (New York: Continuum, 2005), esp. 32-54 and 148-79.

6

A Way Forward
for Latino/a Christology

MICHAEL E. LEE

In just over a generation, Latino/a theology has taken up the task of reflecting on the articulated faith and religious symbols and practices of Hispanics in the United States in light of their cultural, economic, and social context/situation. This essay takes up the profound impact Latinos/as have made on Christology by their attention to its aesthetic, cultural, and prophetic dimensions. Whether it be the retrieval and analysis of Hispanic devotions like the *Via Crucis*, or the exploration of the Gospels' portrayal of Jesus from the borderland region of Galilee, Latino/a Christology has served to affirm the complex identity of a people and to critique a dominant U.S. society (and a corresponding dominant theology) that has kept them at the margins.

While this signal achievement of Latino/a Christology deserves further elaboration and continued support, the growing complexity of the U.S. Latino/a population calls for a differentiated rhetorical stance as well. For U.S. Latinos/as, these are ambiguous times. As I write these words, the headlines speak of a Bronx-born Puerto Rican lawyer appointed to the Supreme Court, and a Cuban-born theologian as U.S. ambassador to the Vatican. They are merely two examples of a growing presence of Latinos/as in boardroom positions, political offices, and other places of prominence in U.S. society.[1] At the same time, an economic crisis threatens to worsen those problems that the overwhelming proportion of Latino/a communities continue to struggle with because of their long history of marginalization: poverty, violence, exclusion from educational opportunities and dignified work, inability to access proper health care, and disproportionate rates of incarceration. This growing divide between two stories of Latino/a experience in the United States demands a continual rethinking of theology rooted in that experience.

Therefore, while Latino/a Christology must continue to affirm and empower those Latinos/as who suffer unjustly, it must also assume a stance in relation to those segments of the Latino/a population that have achieved a measure of "suc-

112

cess" within social, political, and economic spheres. If it does not, then what relevance will this theology have for them? Where are these Latinos/as to turn? To a privatistic theology torn from any communal dimensions? To an assimilationist theology that refuses to see the constitutive nature of culture and identity? To a naïve consumerist theology that ignores the suffering of others, and most importantly, the self-implicating reality of "success" in the United States in relation to that suffering? How can the different Latino/a locations be bridged?

This essay will offer Christology as one place that Latino/a theologians can address its "new elite," and by extension, address all elites in the United States. This suggestion is made warily, acknowledging that racial and ethnic discrimination knows no class barriers, and recognizing the penchant of mainstream consumer U.S. society to utilize tokenism in order to commodify culture and to assimilate and domesticate others. Nevertheless, recent developments in theology, exemplified in the insights of the first generation of Latino/a Christology, demonstrate how theology that takes seriously the realities of marginalization and injustice can serve as a voice of transformation both of the wider society and of believers themselves. It is this call to transformation, and particularly one that addresses Latinos/as with the complementary rhetorics of empowerment and kenosis (self-emptying), that signals a way forward for Latino/a Christology.

To give a proper account of Latino/a Christology, its past and its possible future, I will begin with some reflections on the task of Christology itself. Though it would be too ambitious a task to summarize all developments in modern Christology, I will identify three key insights in recent theology that help contextualize, or provide a way to characterize, the emergence of Latino/a Christology.[2] In particular, attention will be paid to how Christology, a real "Christ-word" of believers today needs to be more attentive to the devotions of those believers, to their new insights about Jesus and his ministry, and the account of discipleship that is rooted in these two. Not only will these three insights into Christology help to clarify the key contributions of the first generation of Latino/a work, but those very insights will suggest new paths for exploration in light of the shifting demographics of U.S. Latinos/as, ones that can mean an important role for Latino/a Christology to the wider society as well.

Christology Is a Christ-word: Who Is Saying It? What Is It? How Is It Lived Out?

On the streets of Phoenix, a young man not a year from his arrival in the United States from Guatemala settles down to sleep on a large piece of cardboard in the corner of a quiet alley. He clutches the rosary around his neck, one of his few possessions, and looks at the crucifix on the end. He prays to that crucified Jesus to give him strength for another day.

In Miami, a middle-aged Cuban American couple head off to church on a Tuesday night. Even though there are a million other things to do, they go to their prayer group for a sense of community and to worship Jesus their savior. They give him thanks for the many blessings in their lives.

On the west side of Chicago, thousands line the streets on Good Friday as the *Via Crucis*, the reenactment of Jesus' "Way of the Cross." Women and men dressed as Jews and Romans from the first century walk past homeless shelters and sites of gang violence in an event that simultaneously recalls a past event and protests contemporary social ills.

In the Bronx, an elderly Dominican woman performs her nightly ritual: she lights the candles on her little table and gives thanks to many santos, and of course, to Jesusito, begging them to look over her children and grandchildren.

These are just snapshots, small threads in the vast and complex tapestry of U.S. Hispanic Christian faith. Its expressions may be small and private, or grandiose and public. Yet, all could be considered some form of Christology.

At its root, Christology means "Christ-word." While the Greek suffix often indicates a field of study, such as biology or psychology, one should not overlook that at its basis, Christ-ology is a word uttered by believers about Jesus Christ. It is a spoken word; it is a lived word. To some degree, every believer in Jesus Christ carries out Christology because any attempt to express or reflect on the experience of faith in Christ is a Christ-word.

As the Christ-word of believers gets taken up for reflection, analysis, and critique, then one arrives at a more formal understanding of Christology. As an academic or formally theological discipline, Christology involves, among other things, the study of: Christian scriptures, understandings of Jesus Christ throughout history, doctrinal formulations, ritual and artistic representations, and the often complex interaction between the philosophical language and thought-forms of a particular period of Christian faith. Yet, no matter how complex the material, it cannot be forgotten that Christology at its basis is still the Christ-word spoken and lived out by believers.

The modern period has seen great accomplishments in the area of Christology. The works of figures such as Karl Rahner, Wolfhart Pannenberg, Edward Schillebeeckx, Hans Küng, and Jürgen Moltmann, among others, appear frequently in bibliographies and exam lists that treat twentieth-century theology.[3] Their contributions are well documented and have generated much literature. It would be difficult, if not impossible, to conceive of Latino/a Christology without some of the pioneering work of these figures and their generation. Their handling of the Christian scriptures and ancient christological definitions in light of modern experience and philosophy can at times be powerful in scope and erudition.

However, for all of the great work in the early and middle part of the twentieth century, the limited pool of experience represented in European male academics exploded outward to include many more voices. In the twenty-first century, voices have emerged from around the world, including Latin America, Asia, and Africa.[4] In addition to Latino/a theologians, within the United States those who represent a world of different contexts are making their voices heard. Witness the richness of Christologies from feminist, black/womanist, and others truly begin to make Christology the Christ-word spoken by all believers.[5] Summarizing all of this work would require multiple volumes, but as a way to get a grasp on the importance of these Christologies that have widened the discipline's scope, let us turn now to three important insights that signal key changes in how Christology must be done in the future.

To begin, contemporary Christology is coming to reconsider the transmission of traditional sources. For example, without diminishing the importance of the dogmatic pronouncements made in regard to the heated debates in the fourth and fifth centuries, Christology today cannot merely be the repetition of ancient formulae. At one level, there is the problem of and need for translation: ancient terminology such as *homoousios* and *hypostasis* cannot be understood without employing considerable interpretive apparatus that would attempt to capture the range of meanings that terms from one context might have for another. However, the problem runs deeper than this, and Christology must be more than an exercise in translation.

Exclusive concentration on the interpretation and application of the Bible and ancient creeds, or even subsequent historical reflection (for example, the great Christologies of the Scholastic period), presupposes that meaning comes from only elite educated sources that are then passed on (traditio) to common, uneducated believers, who then "apply" what they have been given. The insight of much contemporary theology has been that the process by which nonelites understand, articulate, and perform the Christian faith has as much to contribute as elite sources do. This retrieval takes many forms. In the area of historical studies, it means eschewing a simplistic "history of ideas" approach in favor of a social history that connects ideas to the complex social realities of a given era. It means the exploration of diaries and oral histories that help illumine the lives of "ordinary" people, and even the investigation of "heretical" movements so that the history that is told is not simply the history of the victors.

The implications that this egalitarian approach to historical sources has for Christology are present in the burgeoning area of spirituality studies. Rather than conceiving of theology and theological figures as disembodied, the area of Christian spirituality places theological research within a wider multidisciplinary approach that seeks a fuller understanding of the Christian experience. As Sandra Schneiders avers, "It seeks to understand it as it actually occurs, as it actually transforms the subject toward fullness of life in Christ, that is, toward self-transcending life-integration within the Christian community of faith."[6] Within this purview, Christology demands much more than simply providing a definition of or describing an understanding of Jesus Christ; rather it requires giving a fuller account that would include ritual practices, artistic representation, and modes of life that constitute the real Christ-word of believers.

If contemporary Christology has experienced a revolution in terms of the believers who utter their Christ-words, it also has shifted how it considers the one about whom the word of believers is uttered—Jesus Christ. So, instead of conceiving of Christology exclusively as a reflection on the so-called christological "mysteries" of incarnation, crucifixion, and resurrection, this trajectory of thought takes seriously the life and ministry of Jesus as it is portrayed in the Second Testament in order to fashion an understanding of Jesus Christ and the vision for discipleship that stems from it. Jesus' teachings, his healings, his fellowship with others, and his conflicts with others all serve to illuminate who exactly the Jesus of Christian belief and worship is and how Christians should conduct their lives in faithful discipleship.[7]

The focus on Jesus' ministry is closely linked to that other exercise that has been called the quest for the historical Jesus.[8] While originally a nineteenth-century attempt to apply "scientific" criteria to a historical reconstruction of Jesus of Nazareth's life that would counter ahistorical dogmatism, this quest's most recent scholarship takes on a rhetorical tone more neutral in character—that is, its expositors claim to seek that which can be said about Jesus using the means of modern historical and archeological research.[9] Of course, the very possibility of neutrality, or of the validity of various modern historical research methods, has come under withering attack as contemporary scholarship has done away with modern assumptions of objectivity.[10]

So, while it may be the case that Albert Schweitzer's claim of a century ago still holds—that scholars of the historical Jesus inevitably find one in their own image—the importance of the turn to the Gospel narrative of Jesus' ministry as an important source for Christology still holds true. For as scholars must grapple with the interpretive inability to access an objective historical Jesus, there can be no doubt that believing communities gravitate to the proclaimer of the kingdom found in the Second Testament Gospels.[11] The focus on this man, this preacher and healer, though not without its own problems, reveals the prophetic nature of Jesus' ministry. Jesus the prophet, drawing on a long tradition within Judaism, calls others to fidelity to a loving God who desires the fullness of life for all people. Thus, like his predecessors in the Hebrew Bible, Isaiah, Amos and others, Jesus as prophet (literally, one who speaks for God) proclaims a good news that elicits not only belief but a change of life. Christology today, by acknowledging the prophetic character of Jesus' ministry, involves articulating how the Christ-word of believers must be expressed as lifestyle.

In our own day, one in which societal ills have been diagnosed not just as the accumulation of a myriad of personal sins but as the expression of sinful societal structures, explicit reflection on how Christians should live out their faith, or proper discipleship, becomes a crucial element of Christology. Christology today cannot be done without asking what sort of discipleship it should inspire in believers, and furthermore, how that discipleship is related to proper social relations in the world. Perhaps the most significant insight in this regard has been the development of the notion now known as the "preferential option for the poor."[12]

Emerging from liberation theologies, the preferential option for the poor is more than just a theological concept among others; rather, it is a new orientation for theology.[13] The reality that the majority of the planet's population lives and prematurely dies in a state of poverty demands theological reflection. It forces an interrogation of all manner of theological issues; but to provide an example in Christology, it allows the experience of the poor to serve as a lens through which we can understand the ministry and death of Jesus. Just glancing at Latin America as one context, a certain proximity of reality obtains for Salvadorans, Chileans, Guatemalans, Argentineans, and others in a Jesus who is taken in the middle of the night, tortured, and executed for proclaiming good news about a reign of justice. The victims of injustice and oppression, then, open up a new understanding of God, of faith, and of the life that is demanded by the gospel.

The preferential option for the poor posits the reality of history's victims as the privileged place to discover God's self-revelation.[14] At its basis, the option is a theocentric option, one that signals the gratuitous nature of God's love, and so is inscribed in any theology (God-word) or Christology (Christ-word). As Gustavo Gutiérrez puts it, "the poor are preferred not because they are necessarily better than others from a moral or religious standpoint, but because God is God."[15]

At its heart, the preferential option for the poor means opting, making a commitment, by and for those who suffer injustice—a commitment that is not optional as one choice among many, which one could or could not select, but part and parcel of being a Christian. To be a disciple means to opt. Christology today requires that one see the self-revelation of God today in the crucified peoples of the world and act so that the good news of the gospel be made incarnate in the world.

Though by no means comprehensive, the three insights related here represent a sea change in how Christology must be done moving forward. Opening to new voices, wrestling with the significance of Jesus' ministry, and linking reflection to discipleship have opened up new vistas in the way Christology is and will be done. These insights will now serve to delineate more clearly the contributions that Latinos/as have made to Christology and to identify ways that it can move forward.

Jesús Nuestro Salvador—The Christ-Word of Latinos/as

Latino/a Christology can be understood as the attempt to utter a Christ-word and to do so drawing explicitly from the well of the U.S. Latino/a experience.[16] I say explicit because while some might pigeonhole U.S. Latino/a theology as a "contextual" theology, it has become clear in our times that the myth of universal or objective perspective has perished and that *every* theology is contextual. When uttering a Christ-word, one cannot but draw on the language, culture, and thought-forms of one's particular context. In this regard, it is almost a truism to point out how much of modern theology's talk about the human "subject" is really talk about a Western, white, male, bourgeois, heterosexual subject. Thus, for all of its universalized talk of human freedom and liberty, this sort of discourse also possesses marginalizing and often oppressive assumptions.

Though Hispanic Christian belief on American soil predates the United States itself, it is only recent decades that have seen an explicit U.S. Latino/a Christology emerge.[17] It has emerged through the method of "teología en con-

junto," a communal process that engages the actual articulated beliefs and practices of Latinos/as and marshals the resources of critical reflection to nurture
Latino/a communities and the wider Christian body.[18] This way of generating theology places a priority on praxis, recognizing that knowledge is more
than merely the abstract-conceptual, but derives from a dynamic and complex
interaction between thought and act. Praxis, then, is a lived conceptuality, an
embodied knowledge profoundly shaped by context. Though Latino/a Christology engages the historical Christian intellectual tradition as well as other philosophical and critical-theoretical streams of thought, this is done ostensibly from
the belief/experience/practice, that is, the praxis of Latino/a Christian faith and
in service to those communities. By exploring the richness of Hispanic symbols,
practices, and talk about Jesus Christ, Latino/a theology has enriched all Christian talk about Jesus Christ.[19]

The great achievement of the first generation of Latino/a Christologies has
been to correlate Hispanic Christian faith and practice in *Jesucristo* with the
experience of marginalization in relation to the larger U.S. society.[20] Though it
is difficult to summarize this achievement, and even then it must be done admit-
tedly in broad strokes, we can use the insights elaborated in the previous section
to illustrate three central characteristics that stand out as contributions made
by Latino/a Christologies.[21] Namely, Latino/a Christology has exemplified the
insights (1) that popular devotion and practices serve as an important well
of christological reflection, (2) that attention to Jesus of Nazareth's ministry
as portrayed in the Gospels should inform christological content, and finally,
(3) that articulating Christology always involves advocating a particular form
of discipleship. Though there may be others, the distinctive manner in which
Latino/a theologians evidence these three insights reveals the great contributions
of this Christology.

The first contribution involves the symbolic/aesthetic dimension of Christology deriving from popular practices.[22] In particular, reflection on devotions
such as the Good Friday Via Crucis has rendered a powerful relational anthropology and vision of salvation rooted in history. Second, Latino/a Christology
has been at the forefront of exploring the cultural significance of Christology.
Particularly under the figure of the Galilean Jesus, Latino/a Christology has
not only prodded contemporary Christians to see the richness of a marginalized peoples' faith in Jesus Christ, but has probed the question of Jesus' own
cultural standing and its significance for contemporary belief and practice.
Finally, Latino/a Christologies have emphasized the prophetic character of Jesus
of Nazareth's ministry, and so, prescriptively have called for a discipleship of
empowerment-seeking-justice for this marginalized population. By bringing out
these dimensions of Christology, Latino/a theologians have been able to render
a vision of Jesus Christ and Christian faith that U.S. Latinos/as can truly call
their own.

Any observer or participant in the life of a Latino/a faith community
recognizes the overwhelming significance of those devotions surrounding the
observance of Good Friday. In cities such as San Antonio, Chicago, New York,

Milwaukee, and many others, Latinos/as enact a public Via Crucis through their city streets, the re-presentation of Jesus' passion and crucifixion. An outsider might evaluate it as overly sentimental, as languishing in Jesus' suffering and death, and might wonder as to the efficacy in promoting active discipleship. Yet a deeper look reveals that instead of understanding Jesus' passion as exclusively a fatalistic "suffering for," Hispanic popular piety expresses Jesus' passion as a "suffering with"—a solidaristic participation in the pain, struggles, and hopes that the people know all too well. Moreover, by linking Jesus' ministry (as confronting the oppressive powers of his time) to his crucifixion, the Christology stemming from the Via Crucis offers a fuller account of hope and salvation than an ahistorical atonement theory of satisfaction. This fuller account provides impetus to an active discipleship.

While some might claim a heritage for Hispanic Good Friday observances in the European passion plays from the Middle Ages, a significant difference exists.[23] While the passion plays, such as Germany's *Oberammergau*, are performances *to* spectators, the Via Crucis involves participation by actors and spectators alike. In fact, there are no spectators because if one walks along the Via one becomes in effect an actor in the play. While I have been struck by the seriousness of participants who have designated roles in the Via Crucis of the Pilsen neighborhood of Chicago (e.g., those who represent the Roman guards, Simon, or Veronica), it is that fuller participation of the community that transforms the city streets into a powerful spectacle.

For many Latino/a theologians, the reenacting of Jesus' passion and crucifixion exists within an inherent anthropology of relationality and produces a theology of accompaniment.[24] For Latinos/as, community is considered preexistent to individual identity and constitutive of it, so that Jesus is defined relationally in Hispanic practice. "Jesus is never just Jesus; he is always also our brother, father, co-sufferer, friend, and, above all, son of Mary."[25] The communal dimension of the devotion undergirds this notion. The strength of familial ties, even giving to children the name Jesus, discloses this anthropological insight. So, as this aesthetic drama is played out, the idea of an individual Christology about an individual Jesus fades from possibility. As present reality mixes with ancient past, ancestors and past members of the community come to mind, and a communal memory has the living and the dead making the walk to Calvary.

This ritual played out on city streets possesses a sacramental character.[26] As the particular is disclosive of (not dichotomous with) the universal, the Jesus of Hispanic popular practices reveals not only who God is but who person and community (also not dichotomous terms) are as well. It is important to remember that the understanding of Jesus' humanity, of his relationality, comes precisely in the very aesthetic physicality of these practices. As Goizueta notices,

> From the ever-present music, to the candlelight, to the aroma of the flowers, to the intermittent gasps heard from the crowd during the crucifixion, to the sound of the soldiers' pounding hammers, to the colorful sights of the market, plaza, and church, the physicality, sensuality,

and particularity of Jesus Christ's presence among us is undeniable and unavoidable.[27]

If Hispanic devotion to Jesus in the Via Crucis reveals the sacramental notion of Christ's presence, it does so through a notion of accompaniment that has deep ramifications on how Latinos/as think about salvation.

While Latino/a Christians would readily accede to the notion that Jesus suffered and died for the sins of the world, this assent goes beyond the acknowledgment of a heroic deed centuries ago to be remembered piously. As we have seen, Hispanic popular spirituality perceives Jesus as a family member, a position that emphasizes accessibility to Jesus and familiarity with him, rather than awe of and distance from him. This familiarity extends to the understanding of redemption wrought by Jesus because the remembrance of Jesus' passion is interlinked with the lives and suffering of people themselves. They see Jesus as identifying with their suffering; and in turn, they identify with Jesus' suffering because they have experienced it themselves. Instead of an abstract "suffering for," there emerges an incarnational "suffering with." As Justo González eloquently notes, "The suffering Christ is important to Hispanics because he is the sign that God suffers with us. An emaciated Christ is the sign that God is with those who hunger. A flagellated Christ is the sign that God is with those who must bear the stripes of an unjust society."[28]

The comprehension of Jesus' passion as a "suffering with" avoids the temptation of a Docetic (Jesus merely appears to be human) or monophysite (Jesus has only a divine nature) understanding of Jesus that is functionally operative in many Christians' understanding of salvation today. The notion of the uniqueness of Jesus' suffering, particularly as Jesus' divine *missio*, seems alien to the Hispanic mind-set of Jesus as one who is also fully human and so truly taking solidarity with their own suffering.[29] This does not imply that Latinos/as do not perceive Jesus as divine, it merely indicates that, as María Pilar Aquino notes, "knowledge and understanding of Jesus Christ has to do with the historical experience of the struggle against oppression and for liberation."[30] The communal knowledge and memory of suffering and structural oppression nourish Hispanic understandings of Jesus, an understanding alien to the individualistic and ahistorical portrait in much modern theology.

Though the Via Crucis focuses on those decisive events in Jerusalem at the end of Jesus' life, the wider familial anthropology of Latinos/as extends the memory of Jesus back to his birth as the son of Mary and Joseph in Galilee. There, in Jesus' Galilean origins, Latino/a theologians have found a deeper sense of the identification and accompaniment with Jesus. This reflection was pioneered in what must be considered the foundational work of Latino/a Christology, Virgilio Elizondo's *Galilean Journey*.[31] In this work, Elizondo takes seriously the gospel narratives concerning Jesus' cultural reality in the borderland area of Galilee from the perspective of those who live in the borderland today. Writing not just from the biblical texts and the work of biblical archeology and history, Elizondo draws from the very experience of marginalization on multiple fronts, which is part of the Mexican American *mestizaje* to develop the notion of Galilee as a symbol of multiple rejection. In a startlingly original work of Christology, Elizondo brings together the Christian confession of Jesus Christ as a fully human being, the biblical account of Jesus' ministry occurring primarily in the marginal area of Galilee, and the Mexican American experience of borderland marginalization in suggesting the provocative image of Jesus the Galilean as a "borderland reject."[32]

For Elizondo, taking Jesus' humanity seriously means taking his cultural reality as a Galilean seriously, and for Elizondo, that cultural reality is marked by the double rejection experienced by Latinos/as. He views the comparison as clear:

> The image of the Galileans to the Jerusalem Jews is comparable to the image of the Mexican-Americans to the Mexicans of Mexico. On the other hand, the image of the Galileans to the Greco-Romans is comparable to the image of the Mexican-American to the Anglo population of the United States. They were part of and despised by both.[33]

This double rejection, this sense of being in-between, this feeling of being part of but rejected by two cultures that is a baseline fact of Latino/a existence in the United States is discovered at the heart of the Gospel portrayal of Jesus. While some have legitimately questioned whether Elizondo's depiction of Jesus strays from what is known in historical Jesus scholarship, or worse, inherits too much from the anti-Jewish tendency to separate Jesus from his own Judaism, it has become clear that the power of Elizondo's work has been in forcing Christology to address the question of culture, and in doing so, naming that rejection experienced by Latinos/as.[34] Theologically, the double rejection of the mestizo serves as a way of understanding the ministry of Jesus in a new light. Jesus' Galilean ministry of preaching, healing, and table fellowship with the marginalized illustrates what Elizondo calls the "Galilean principle," that "what human beings reject, God chooses as God's very own."[35] Thus, reflection on the Galilean Jesus both names the dignity of Latinos/as experience and offers a direction for what their discipleship should look like.

In their attempts to confront injustice and the marginalization they have experienced in the United States, Latinos/as have turned to their faith in Jesus Christ as a source of boldness and consolation in the struggle for justice. In *Galilean Journey*, Elizondo calls this the "Jerusalem principle," as he explains that God calls and empowers the marginalized to resist the powers of exclusion and domination. Elizondo asserts, "God chooses an oppressed people, not to bring them comfort in their oppression, but to enable them to confront, transcend, and transform whatever in the oppressor society diminishes and destroys the fundamental dignity of human nature."[36]

In the mujerista Christology of Ada María Isasi-Díaz, this prophetic principle is tied to the central theme in Jesus of Nazareth's preaching: the *basileia tou theou*, a Greek phrase that has been translated as "kingdom of God" but is now rendered by some as "kin-dom of God."[37] The kin-dom, with its retrieval of the close familial anthropology of Latinos/as, rejects the patriarchal and autocratic connotations of kingdom for a vision more consonant with the egalitarian language of Jesus and the aspirations of Latinos/as for a just place within ecclesial, social, and political communities of which they are a part.

Of course, the nature of prophetic language is such that any positive prophetic vision of the *basileia*, the hopeful aspiration or vision of fullness, stands in opposition to a negative diagnosis, the assessment of the antikingdom, those forces that mean exclusion and oppression. In the case of Latino/a theology, this prophetic dimension of Christology means an indictment of the dominant U.S. society and even of the Christian churches who have marginalized Latinos/as. As we have seen, in the work of Roberto Goizueta, Latino/a understandings of Jesus serve as an antidote to the excesses of modern individualism and rationality. Marina Herrera expands the critique to encompass the entire Western European tradition. "An 'Americanist critique'—done by people of this continent, men and women, young and old, Natives, European, African, and Asian descendents—must be a critique of all things European, including the Westernization of Jesus and his message and the assumption that such Westernization is the only valid interpretation of the salvific event of his life and death."[38]

The prophetic stance makes itself manifest in many of the Via Crucis observances. For example, the Via in Pilsen began after two mothers and ten children perished in a fire. The city's firefighters, unable to speak Spanish, did not realize that there were still people in the building.[39] After years of neglect by the city, organizers planned the Via Crucis not just as a remembrance of Jesus' passion but as the symbolic linking of the community's suffering to that of Christ's. Thus, their Via Crucis paused at the burned-down buildings and other locations in the neighborhood that signify the particular sufferings of the community. As different Vias around the country enact this symbolic linking of Christ's and the community's suffering, the notion of Christ's "suffering with" inspires a discipleship that takes on a palpable, historical makeup.

Theologically, this analogical movement between the sufferings of Christ and that of the community succeeds because sin and its redemption involve the historical lives of the people of God. If salvation were perceived spatially and temporally as exclusively other-worldly, then the action of Christ might remain a remote "suffering for"; however, the solidaristic and historical notion of Jesus' suffering enacted in the Hispanic Via Crucis indicates the fullness of both sin and salvation as permeating history. Moreover, this provides a historical hermeneutic through which Jesus' death can be understood. Rather than separating Jesus' death from his ministry, this view recognizes that Jesus' ministry of proclaiming and manifesting the reign of God put him into conflict with the prevailing powers of his time. His Galilean ministry of solidarity to the marginalized, its preferential option for the poor and not the abstract requirement for satisfaction, spurred the inevitability of his death. As Ignacio Ellacuría suggests, the proper question to ask concerning Jesus' passion is not "Why did Jesus die?" but rather, "Why was Jesus killed?"[40] Latino/a Christology demonstrates a historical

understanding of Jesus' passion and fosters a discipleship of faithful commitment to the just and prayerful transformation of human society.[41]

To be sure, the exact nature of Christian praxis remains a matter of dis-
cernment by particular communities in particular contexts. For example, studies have indicated intense discord over how "political" the symbol system of the
Via should be.[42] Despite these differences, which are often rooted in generational
as well as clerical-lay disputes, it can still be claimed that the solidaristic and historical enactment of the Via indicates a solidaristic and historical discipleship.
A march through the city streets calls for a faith lived on those city streets. This
lived faith involves an understanding of the sufferings of this world, but not a
fatalism in the face of them. Hispanic theologians repeatedly stress this theme in
their works. Luis Pedraja describes Hispanic devotion to Christ crucified as "not
the goriness of death, but the struggle (*la lucha*) of the living God."[43] Isasi-Díaz
reminds us that devotion to Christ crucified is not a glorifying of martyrdom or
suffering because that only justifies the powers who inflict the suffering. Roberto
Goizueta notes that, "If this Jesus bleeds, it is not to sanctify suffering but to
sanctify the flesh; and to sanctify the flesh is to see in it a sacrament, or symbol
of the God of Jesus Christ."[44] Finally, Virgilio Elizondo writes,

> The Mexican-American people celebrates the crucifixion of Jesus
> because his cross makes their cross meaningful and purposeful. It is
> not a fatalism that attracts them to the cross but an awareness of Jesus'
> determination to accept the way ordained by the Father: Jerusalem
> must be confronted. And modern Jerusalems must be confronted if lib-
> eration is to come about today.[45]

From Jerusalem Back to Galilee

Modern Jerusalems do need to be confronted, however the reality of a growing number of U.S. Latinos/as dictates that they do so not from Galilee but as
those raised in Jerusalem itself. Their story of negotiating borders is more like
that of Nicodemus encountering Jesus at night, or standing before Pilate with
Joseph of Arimethea requesting the body of the crucified Jesus. They hear Jesus'
call to meet him in Galilee as a return to the land of their parents, a land they
know perhaps more from lore than from experience. Yet, they are not complete
strangers to the area. They know its dialect and topography enough even to
serve as guides to those who have never been there before. This ambiguous space
between the capital city and the border region that gave birth to Jesus' movement—this is the journey that a new generation of Christology must take up.

The work of the first generation of U.S. Latino/a theology, and thus Christology, has been consistently employed in contradistinction to a "dominant" U.S.
society/culture, and rightfully so. The history of U.S. Latinos/as has been one of
unjust suffering and rejection at personal and social-structural levels because
of ethnic-cultural-racial discrimination, and the power of Latino/a Christology

has been to understand the proclamation of Jesus' good news as affirming Latinos/as' dignity and empowering their efforts to seek justice.[46] This is a crucial task, and it should always remain at the heart of Latino/a Christology.

In confronting the dominant U.S. culture, particularly as the embodiment of an oppressive, liberal-modern discourse characterized by hyper-individualism and the assimilation/rejection of anything that is "other," Latino/a Christologies have proposed sites of resistance in Hispanic culture and (Spanish) language. Yet, more and more these are latent with ambiguity. While many who forged Latino/a Christology were either born in Latin American countries or were raised in tight barrio enclaves, the reality for many younger Latinos/as is quite distinct. Although proficiency, if not fluency, in Spanish can often be presumed of the first generation, this is no longer the case. Though close-knit familial and communal ties could guarantee the passing on of important devotions and practices to an earlier generation, those cannot be presumed now. These facts are noted not in a negative fashion, as in the old assimilationist mode of thinking that views these as purely a loss of culture, because the way that these Latinos/as navigate these relationships indicates their ability to serve as a bridge, a unifying force.[47] These Latinos/as have now witnessed the transformative power of coalitions and solidarity bring an African American to the presidency of a country that they can call their own in a new way.

While much of the analysis in previous Latino/a Christology has been valuable and important, unfortunately, too often the "U.S." dimension of U.S. Latinos/as might be understood exclusively as an oppressive other. Younger Latinos/as, then, not only are left in a position without the same cultural and linguistic resources, but are left in a position of denying a significant part of their own identities. Add to that the ongoing racial and emerging class differences within Latino/a communities themselves and it becomes clear that a theology that attempts to speak from and to the experience of this community has many challenges to face. Second- and third-generation Latinos/as exhibit a biculturalism that is not quite captured in the work of earlier Latino/a Christology and its challenge could help fashion the agenda of the next generation.

The three insights that we have identified and that were used to illustrate the important contributions of earlier Latino/a Christologies can now be employed to ask about and envision new trajectories of work, steps forward for new Latino/a Christologies. For example, how can the turn to popular practices open up Latino/a Christologies to its bicultural, and indeed multicultural, reality? How might a renewed and revised account of Jesus' Galilean ministry address the challenges of the present? Does a new vision of Christian discipleship in relation to a preferential option for the poor emerge?

If Latino/a theology has discovered a rich resource in the popular religious practices of Hispanic communities, then one path for the future may lie in extending and cultivating that project further to better account for the reality of hybridity.[48] It could explore how the religious practices of second- and third-generation Latinos/as assist them in negotiating a real biculturality, particularly as they incorporate elements from the wider U.S. society.[49] Of course, the challenge of investigating and respecting the spiritual eclecticism made possible by the developments in information and communication technology involves a wariness of its commodification and the ever-present danger of consumerism to lived Christian faith.[50] Yet, a Christology born from the ability to negotiate multiple cultural identities without conflating them could illumine a doctrine like the incarnation from the lived experience of believers in ways that rational discourse cannot.[51]

Key to this work would be exploring ways in which Latinos/as serve as a bridge to a U.S. spirituality and Christology that, at the practical level, demonstrates not just a monolithic cultural hegemony, but involves transgressive resources and sites of resistance as well.[52] While U.S. capitalism may encourage a constant reaching for upward mobility, U.S. history also shows a number of Christian movements that espouse a "downward" mobility more consonant with the understandings of the inclusive, egalitarian, and prophetic understandings of Jesus' ministry in current christological thought.[53] As a bridge that links the practices, art, and music of these other Christian movements of resistance to Hispanic practices, Latinos/as may embrace a dimension of their identities without falling into what Homi Bhabha calls "colonial mimicry," which only serves to reinforce subservient colonial relationships.

Certainly, this downward mobility could be substantiated with reference to Jesus of Nazareth's ministry, but perhaps with a perspective different from the first generation of Latino/a Christology. A glance back at Elizondo's seminal work provides an illustration. If Elizondo utilizes the metaphor of "double rejection" to very evocative ends, there is an underlying problem with its application. Elizondo constructs the metaphor out of his Mexican American experience, so therefore the notion of Jesus' rejection by the Romans, by a dominant culture (United States), and by fellow Jews (Mexico) powerfully depicts the in-between space of U.S. Latinos/as, who have a foot in two cultures.

Yet, in order for this metaphor to work fully, the double rejection that Jesus experiences must be from those to whom Jesus feels a sense of belonging. This does not prove to be the case. Nowhere do the Gospels indicate that Jesus feels any sense of "belonging" to the Roman Empire. He is not Roman in any sense. At most, he finds himself to be the subject of an empire that rejects him. This relationship may capture the feeling that not a few immigrants might have as they find themselves in El Norte—subjects of an empire that rejects them. However, this is not the liminal space of U.S.-born Latinos/as, particularly those who possess many of the broader U.S. cultural-linguistic markers as their own. They are "Roman" in a sense that the Gospels never portray Jesus, and that difference underscores what can be a shift in how the Galilean Jesus is considered in Latino/a Christology.

A way to deepen Elizondo's groundbreaking insights regarding the Galilean Jesus would be to take seriously the alternatives to historical Jesus research posed by its critics and to engage in a re-membering of the Galilean Jesus and his ministry in the memory and practices of the Jesus movement.[54] What is important is not so much reconstructing the life of Jesus of Nazareth, but discerning the stance toward history that Jesus' disciples took up in their memory of him. Following the suggestions of Elisabeth Schüssler Fiorenza, rather than treating Jesus as a genius or a great man, an approach that separates Jesus from his context, Latino/a Christology could build on its communal anthropology by viewing Jesus as the "first among equals" in the Jesus movement.[55]

A Jesus richly interwoven in this context would serve as a bridge to a number of others who have found themselves at the margin of Christian thought. This Jesus, firmly rooted in his family's Jewish tradition, would contribute to the hope that the long legacy of anti-Jewish Christology has come to an end. This Jesus would open up dialogue about how the practices of other religious traditions find a resonance in the practices of the *basileia tou theou*.[56] Moreover, the provocative notion of double rejection, then, can be explored through a number of figures portrayed in the Gospels who may be found in "in-between" spaces. For many, the call of Jesus is not just the empowering call to those on the margins in Galilee, but the invitation to the young man to sell all that he had, give it to the poor, and to follow Jesus. It is a call to take up the practices of the Jesus movement even if it means danger in negotiating the tensive power relationships of Jerusalem, and like Nicodemus being scorned and advised that "no prophet is to rise from Galilee."[57] The call of this Jesus to the mighty is to come down from their thrones, particularly in practices, in a lifestyle that imitates Jesus' own kenosis remembered and performed by his followers.[58]

Ultimately, the most important Christ-word of believers is found in the way that they conduct their lives. Christology is enriched by enacting those practices that manifest the *basileia tou theou* that Jesus' own Galilean ministry made manifest as the good news of salvation. In that respect, the future of Latino/a Christology is found at the juncture of empowering those who have been marginalized with the good news of salvation and articulating the role of those who are called to make a commitment to this project as their good news of salvation. The great power of Latin American liberation theologies sprang from their theological reflection on the term that best named the hopes of the overwhelming majority of their people—liberation. By seeking it, by committing to it, by sacrificing for it (often to death), and by praying for it, rich and poor discovered new dimensions to the word salvation.

The United States is a different context and demands a different conceptual framework and expression. Christian discipleship in the most powerful nation on earth requires a confrontation with a notion of power as domination and a witness to the power of solidarity; in this process a deepened understanding of salvation might be discovered. The history and ongoing process of Latinos/as' marginalization gives them a lens for identifying those elements and processes in U.S. society that oppose that vision of Jesus' preaching and those that conform to it. Even though some Latinos/as may be finding themselves on a different side of power relations, by bridging them, they discover something basic about how a discipleship oriented by the option for the poor functions. As Frei Betto put it, "This option for the poor is the bread and butter one chooses for one's life. That is, my life project either goes in the direction of strengthening justice for the poor or in the direction of strengthening the oppressive system for the rich minority."[59]

Conclusion

Second- and third-generation Latinos/as have been called a "gente puente," a bridge people between ongoing Hispanic immigration populations and the wider U.S. society.[60] This bridge role, while filled with possibilities, is also fraught with ambiguities. Though earlier Latino/a liberation movements and Latino/a theologies often intentionally employed a pan-Latin vision of unity out of the need for survival, the growing size and plurality of the Latino/a population in the United States allow for, and even demand, a more rigorous attention to intra-Latino/a differences of class, race, and national ethnic origin.[61]

This essay has focused on how Christology is affected when confronted with questions of culture, class, and power, and specifically how U.S. Latinos/as have been part of significant changes to the understanding of Christology enacted by explicitly contextual theologies. In their attention to Hispanic popular practices, to the cultural identity of Jesus of Nazareth, and to a discipleship of empowerment to a marginalized population, Latino/a Christologies have uttered a powerful "Christ-word" for their generation.

A new generation finds itself taking up this task as both a wonderful inheritance and a difficult challenge. Specifically, a stronger cultural identification with wider U.S. cultural markers along with a measure of greater social, economic, and political power among some Latinos/as calls for a widened rhetoric in relation to the "dominant" U.S. culture. For these Latinos/as, the United States is not exclusively other—it is part of their identity. Yet, because of their history and biculturality, U.S. Latinos/as possess an ear for hearing those voices on the margins, and it is employing that ear, that potential for solidarity that indicates a future for Latino/a Christology. By continued reflection on Hispanic religious practices and their relation to those of others in the United States, by understanding the Galilean Jesus by his impact on all manner of believers, and by complementing the rhetoric of empowerment with one of kenosis, Latino/a Christology can serve as a bridge to the future of all U.S. Christology.

> Jesus Christ was a man who traveled through the land;
> a hard-working man and brave.
> He said to the rich, "Give your goods to the poor."
> So they laid Jesus Christ in His grave . . .
>
> This song was written in New York City,
> of rich man, preacher, and slave.
> If Jesus was to preach what He preached in Galilee,
> they would lay poor Jesus in His grave.

So proceed the opening and closing verses of the 1940 song "Jesus Christ" by Woody Guthrie, one of the great figures in American folk music. The simple lyrics and direct images created by the "Dust Bowl troubadour" render a Christology imbued with the experiences of those who struggled through the Great

Depression and the prophetic call to a more just society. It is an important voice
in the American landscape, and for U.S. Latinos/as it is just as much a part of
their inheritance as any other. By embracing their biculturality fully, and recognizing the dignity and call of Christ in that identity, U.S. Latinos/as will serve as
the bridge from Jerusalem back to Galilee. They can be witnesses who by their
words and lives proclaim, "Go back to Galilee; there you will see him as he told
you" (Mark 16:7).

Notes

1. The *New York Times* describes the 1969 African American and Latino/a recruits
to America's most prestigious universities as a "new elite." "Meet the New Elite, Not
Like the Old," *New York Times*, July 25, 2009.
2. This contextualization does not imply any temporal ordering in which the insight
comes first and then subsequent Latino/a theologies. I wish merely to identify currents
in theology that help frame Latino/a contributions. As we will see, Latino/a theologians
were at the forefront of developing these important ideas.
3. Though Rahner did not write a separate volume strictly on Christology, he wrote
numerous articles, and a good portion of his major synthetic work is focused on the
topic. See Karl Rahner, *Foundations of Christian Faith* (New York: Seabury, 1978), 138-
321; Wolfhart Pannenberg, *Jesus, God and Man* (Philadelphia: Westminster Press, 1968);
Edward Schillebeeckx, *Jesus: An Experiment in Christology* (New York: Seabury, 1979);
idem, *Christ: The Experience of Jesus as Lord* (New York: Seabury, 1980); Hans Küng,
On Being a Christian (Garden City, N.J.: Doubleday, 1976); Jürgen Moltmann, *The Crucified God: The Cross of Christ as the Foundation and Criticism of Christian Theology*
(New York: Harper & Row, 1974).
4. Because of space limitations I will point to only major works or surveys of
major figures. The finest Christology from Latin America is the two-volume work by
Jon Sobrino, *Jesus the Liberator: A Historical-Theological Reading of Jesus of Naza-
reth* (Maryknoll, N.Y.: Orbis Books, 1993); idem, *Christ the Liberator: A View from
the Victims* (Maryknoll, N.Y.: Orbis Books, 2001); see also José Miguez Bonino, ed.,
Faces of Jesus: Latin American Christologies (Maryknoll, N.Y.: Orbis Books, 1983); and
Nelly Ritchie, "Women and Christology," in *Through Her Eyes: Women's Theology from
Latin America*, ed. Elsa Tamez (Maryknoll, N.Y.: Orbis Books, 1989). On Asia, see R.
S. Sugirtharajah, ed., *Asian Faces of Jesus* (Maryknoll, N.Y.: Orbis Books, 1993); and
C. S. Song, *Jesus, the Crucified People* (Minneapolis: Fortress Press, 1996). On Africa,
see Diane B. Stinton, *Jesus of Africa: Voices of Contemporary African Christology*
(Maryknoll, N.Y.: Orbis Books, 2004); and Robert Schreiter, ed., *Faces of Jesus in Africa*
(Maryknoll, N.Y.: Orbis Books, 1991).
5. For feminist, see Elisabeth Schüssler Fiorezna, *Jesus: Miriam's Child, Sophia's
Prophet: Critical Issues in Feminist Christology* (New York: Continuum, 1995); Anne E.
Carr, *Transforming Grace: Christian Tradition and Women's Experience* (San Francisco:
Harper & Row, 1988); and Lisa Isherwood, *Introducing Feminist Christologies* (Cleve-
land: Pilgrim Press, 2002). For black/womanist, see James H. Cone, *God of the Oppressed*
(Maryknoll, N.Y.: Orbis Books, 1997); Kelly Brown Douglas, *The Black Christ* (Mary-
knoll, N.Y.: Orbis Books, 1994); and Jacquelyn Grant, *White Women's Christ and Black
Women's Jesus: Feminist Christology and Womanist Response* (Atlanta: Scholars Press,

1989). One can see a queer Christology emerging in works such as Robert Goss, *Queering Christ* (Cleveland: Pilgrim Press, 2002); and Marcella Althaus-Reid, *Indecent Theology: Theological Perversions in Sex, Gender and Politics* (London: Routledge, 2000).

6. Sandra M. Schneiders, "The Study of Christian Spirituality: Contours and Dynamics of a Discipline," in *Minding the Spirit: The Study of Christian Spirituality*, ed. Elizabeth A. Dreyer and Mark S. Burrows (Baltimore: Johns Hopkins University Press, 2005), 5.

7. In Catholic Christology, Elizabeth A. Johnson describes this as the "second wave of renewal" that occurred subsequent to the pondering of the dogmatic confession of Jesus Christ's identity done in the 1950s and early 1960s. *Consider Jesus: Waves of Renewal in Christology* (New York: Crossroad, 1990), 45.

8. The literature on the quests is vast. Helpful surveys include: Gerd Theissen and Annette Merz, *Historical Jesus: A Comprehensive Guide* (Minneapolis: Fortress Press, 1998); John P. Meier, "The Present State of the 'Third Quest' for the Historical Jesus: Loss and Gain," *Biblica* 80, no. 4 (1999): 459-87.

9. John Meier uses the vivid image of locking up four historians in a library—a Catholic, a Protestant, a Jew, and an agnostic—and forcing them to hammer out a consensus document on who Jesus of Nazareth was (*A Marginal Jew: Rethinking the Historical Jesus*, vol. 1 [New York: Doubleday, 1991], 1). For another representative attempt, see James Dunn, *Jesus Remembered: Christianity in the Making* (Grand Rapids: Eerdmans, 2003).

10. Feminist critique has been particularly valuable in this regard. See, for example, Elisabeth Schüssler Fiorenza, *Jesus and the Politics of Interpretation* (New York: Continuum, 2000).

11. It is the historical dimension of this interest and its implications that differentiate it from earlier Christology, such as European medieval devotion to the human Jesus' suffering.

12. Though the phrase gained recognition with its usage by the Roman Catholic Conference of Latin American Bishops (CELAM) in its 1978 meeting in Puebla, Mexico, the concept was hinted at in the 1968 meeting in Medellín, Colombia, that spoke of "preference to the poorest and neediest, and to those who are segregated for any reason" ("Poverty of the Church," Document on Poverty, no. 9).

13. For a concise elucidation of the preferential option for the poor by one of its great expositors, see Gustavo Gutiérrez, "Option for the Poor," in *Mysterium Liberationis: Fundamental Concepts of Liberation Theology*, ed. Ignacio Ellacuría and Jon Sobrino (Maryknoll, N.Y.: Orbis Books, 1990), 235-50.

14. In this regard, the parable of the Last Judgment (Matt 25:31-46) serves as a classic text of this theological insight.

15. Gutiérrez, "Option for the Poor," 241.

16. The use of the singular, Christology, is used with caution, lest the ruminations of different Latino/a theologians, and more importantly the praxis of different Latino/a communities, be homogenized. Truly there are Latino/a Christologies; however, like other generations or schools of thought, family resemblances and communal working together also allow for the singular.

17. Allan Figueroa Deck notes that though the nineteenth-century Cuban American priest Felix Varela could be considered the first U.S. Hispanic theologian, his is an isolated case without the sense of teología en conjunto of the generation mentioned here. Allan Figueroa Deck, *Frontiers of Hispanic Theology in the United States* (Maryknoll, N.Y.: Orbis Books, 1992), xxv. For more on Varela, see Felipe J. Estévez, *El perfil pastoral de Felix Varela* (Miami: Editorial Universal, 1989).

18. Orlando Espín notes that because of this joint process, "the 'product' ultimately belongs to the community and not to any one individual scholar" (*From the Heart of Our People*, ed. Orlando O. Espín and Miguel H. Díaz [Maryknoll, N.Y.: Orbis Books, 1999], 263).

19. For a brief survey of this work, see Michelle A. Gonzalez, "Jesus," in *Handbook of Latina/o Theologies*, ed. Edwin David Aponte and Miguel A. de la Torre (St. Louis: Chalice, 2006), 17–24. See also her entry, "Jesus Christ," in *Constructive Theology: A Contemporary Approach to Classical Themes*, ed. Serene Jones (Minneapolis: Fortress Press, 2005), 161-200.

20. The term *generation* is used more loosely than simply twenty years. It considers the pioneering work of figures such as Virgilio Elizondo, Justo González, and Orlando Costas coming to fruition in the 1980s in, among other things, the founding of ACHTUS or the journal *Apuntes*. For a history of this emergence and its central figures, see Eduardo Fernandez, *La Cosecha: Harvesting Contemporary United States Hispanic Theology (1972-1988)* (Collegeville, Minn.: Liturgical Press, 2000). For an example of this early writing, see Allan Figueroa Deck, *Frontiers of Hispanic Theology*.

21. Noting again that no causal or temporal relationship between the three previously identified insights and those from Latino/a Christologies is advocated here. On the contrary, for one example, I would suggest that because of the great emphasis in Latino/a theologies on retrieving popular practices, it has served as a primary contributor to the first "insight."

22. No one has contributed more to this area of research than Orlando Espín. A representative work is his *The Faith of the People: Theological Reflections on Popular Catholicism* (Maryknoll, N.Y.: Orbis Books, 1997).

23. Orlando Espín and Sixto García, "The Sources of Hispanic Theology," *CTSA Proceedings* 43 (1988): 122-25.

24. One of the finest examples of these ideas is Roberto S. Goizueta, *Caminemos con Jesús: Toward a Hispanic/Latino Theology of Accompaniment* (Maryknoll, N.Y.: Orbis Books, 1995).

25. Ibid., 66.

26. For a sacramental and eucharistic reading of Christology from a Protestant perspective, see Eliseo Pérez-Álvarez, "In Memory of Me: Hispanic/Latino Christology beyond Borders," in *Teología en Conjunto: A Collaborative Hispanic Protestant Theology*, ed. José David Rodríguez and Loida I. Martell-Otero (Louisville: Westminster John Knox, 1997), 33-49.

27. Goizueta, *Caminemos con Jesús*, 68.

28. Justo González, *Mañana: Christian Theology from a Hispanic Perspective* (Nashville: Abingdon Press, 1990), 148-49.

29. As Orlando Espín and Sixto García put it, "Within the Hispanic faith-experience, Jesus is not God disguised as, or playing the role of a human being." See "'Lilies of the Field': A Hispanic Theology of Providence and Human Responsibility," *CTSA Proceedings* 44 (1989): 84.

30. María Pilar Aquino, *Our Cry for Life: Feminist Theology from Latin America*, trans. Dinah Livingstone (Maryknoll, N.Y.: Orbis Books, 1993), 139-40.

31. Virgilio Elizondo, *Galilean Journey: The Mexican-American Promise*, rev. and expanded ed. (Maryknoll, N.Y.: Orbis Books, 2000).

32. The nomenclature of "Mexican-American" is that used by Elizondo in his text. That this text has been taken up by Latinos/as of other national origins testifies to how he has captured the shared experience of multiple rejection.

33. Elizondo, *Galilean Journey*, 52.

34. For a fuller exploration of and response to the critiques of Elizondo's text, see Michael E. Lee, "*Galilean Journey* Revisited: Mestizaje, Anti-Judaism, and the Dynamics of Exclusion," *Theological Studies* 70 (2009): 377-400.

35. Elizondo, *Galilean Journey*, 91.

36. Ibid., 103.

37. See Ada María Isasi-Díaz, "Christ in *Mujerista* Theology," in *Thinking of Christ: Proclamation, Explanation, Meaning*, ed. Tatha Wiley (New York: Continuum, 2003), 157-76. For an elaboration of this notion within a wider explication of mujerista theology, see her *La Lucha Continues: Mujerista Theology* (Maryknoll, N.Y.: Orbis Books, 2004).

38. Marina Herrera, "Who Do You Say Jesus Is? Christological Reflections from a Hispanic Woman's Perspective," in *Reconstructing the Christ Symbol: Essays in Feminist Christology*, ed. Maryanne Stevens (New York: Paulist Press, 1993), 82.

39. For a detailed analysis of the Pilsen Via, see Karen Mary Davalos, "The Real Way of Praying: The Via Crucis, Mexicano Sacred Space, and the Architecture of Domination," in *Horizons of the Sacred: Mexican Traditions in U.S. Catholicism*, ed. Timothy Matovina and Gary Riebe-Estrella (Ithaca: Cornell University Press, 2002), 41-68.

40. Ignacio Ellacuría, "¿Por qué muere Jesús y por qué le matan?" *Misión Abierta* 2 (1977): 17-26.

41. As Espín and García emphasize, "The solidarity and hope offered by the Cross constitute signs of God's gracious providence, the possibility that prayers for deliverance from oppression and discrimination might be answered. This form of providence is not seen as immediate relief. It is rather a process rooted in history, a Hispanic *Heilsgeschichte* (Espín and García, "Lilies of the Field," 85).

42. See Karen Mary Davalos, "Real Way of Praying"; and Wayne Ashley, "The Stations of the Cross: Christ, Politics, and Processions on New York City's Lower East Side," in *Gods of the City: Religion and the American Urban Landscape*, ed. Robert A. Orsi (Bloomington: Indiana University Press, 1999), 341-66.

43. Luis G. Pedraja, *Jesus Is My Uncle: Christology from a Hispanic Perspective* (Nashville: Abingdon Press, 1999), 68.

44. Goizeuta, *Caminemos con Jesús*, 67, 69.

45. Elizondo, *Galilean Journey*, 114.

46. As an expression of the option for the poor in the United States, see Carmen Marie Nanko, "Justice Crosses the Border: The Preferential Option for the Poor in the United States," in *A Reader in Latina Feminist Theology: Religion and Justice*, ed. María Pilar Aquino, Daisy L. Machado, and Jeanette Rodríguez (Austin: University of Texas Press, 2002), 177-203.

47. One need not presume that the assumption of certain U.S. cultural characteristics is necessarily at the expense or loss of Hispanic culture. For a rethinking on the phenomenon of assimilation and its naming, see Richard Alba and Victor Nee, *Remaking the American Mainstream* (Cambridge, Mass.: Harvard University Press, 2003).

48. Though in danger of losing meaning because of overuse, hybridity (particularly as developed in the work of critic and cultural theorist Homi Bhabha) continues to offer rich possibilities for Christology. See Bhabha's, *Location of Culture* (New York: Routledge, 1994).

49. The resources of transnational and diasporic studies (and their relationship) could be quite useful to this task. See, for example, Michael Peter Smith and Luis Eduardo Garnizo, eds., *Transnationalism from Below* (New Brunswick: Transaction, 1998);

Peggy Levitt and Mary C. Waters, eds., *The Changing Face of Home: Transnational Lives of the Second Generation* (New York: Russell Sage Foundation, 2002).

50. This area of study has a growing literature. Some examples include: Vincent Miller, *Consuming Religion: Christian Faith and Practice in a Consumer Culture* (New York: Continuum, 2005); and Tom Beaudoin, *Consuming Faith: Integrating Who We Are with What We Buy* (New York: Sheed & Ward, 2007).

51. Found in an incipient way in the work of Luis Pedraja, this is developed in the broadening of mestizaje discourse done by Rubén Rosario Rodríguez, *Racism and God-Talk: A Latino/a Perspective* (New York: New York University Press, 2008).

52. A good analog would be the work of Mary McClintock Fulkerson in retrieving the voices of Appalachian women to rethink assumptions of feminist theory in *Changing the Subject: Women's Discourses and Feminist Theology* (Minneapolis: Fortress, 1994).

53. For references to the revolutionary tradition in the North Atlantic and the more recent justice-oriented religious coalitions that could serve this purpose, see Mark Lewis Taylor, "Spirit and Liberation: Achieving Postcolonial Theology in the United States," in *Postcolonial Theologies: Divinity and Empire*, ed. Catherine Keller, Michael Nausner, and Mayra Rivera (St. Louis: Chalice Press, 2004), 50-51.

54. For a summary of these critics and a constructive proposal of his own, see Terrence W. Tilley, *The Disciples' Jesus: Christology as Reconciling Practice* (Maryknoll, N.Y.: Orbis Books, 2008).

55. Elisabeth Schüssler Fiorenza, *Jesus and the Politics of Interpretation* (New York: Continuum, 2000).

56. For an example of the complex and heated arguments regarding Christology and non-Christian religions, see the issues raised in Roger Haight, *Jesus Symbol of God* (Maryknoll, N.Y.: Orbis Books, 1999).

57. John 7:52. As suggested earlier, it would be important when drawing out metaphorical figures, particularly in the Gospel of John, to do so with a sophisticated understanding of John's use of labels such as "Pharisees" and "Jews" so as not to replicate anti-Jewish readings of the Second Testament.

58. Kenosis (self-emptying) is the term that comes from the early Christian hymn found in Phil. 2:7 to describe how Jesus Christ "emptied (*ekenōsen*) himself, taking the form of a slave, being born in human likeness."

59. Frei Betto, as quoted in Mev Puleo, *The Struggle Is One: Voices and Visions of Liberation* (Albany: State University of New York Press, 1994), 96.

60. See, for example, *U.S. Catholic* magazine's aptly entitled "Ni Aquí, Nor There: Latino American Catholics at a Crossroads" (February 2008).

61. I believe that this attention to differences should be done out of a desire for Latino/a unity-in-difference. So, I agree with Orlando Espín's analysis that despite this turn, "There is reason to believe, however, that even today we must still place consensus, unity, and alliance-building among the indispensable goals for all of our communities and theologies" (Orlando O. Espín, "The State of U.S. Latina/o Theology: An Understanding," in *Hispanic Christian Thought at the Dawn of the Twenty-First Century*, ed. Alvin Padilla, Roberto Goizueta, and Eldin Villafañe (Nashville: Abingdon, 2005), 295 n. 6.

7

The Church

A Latino Catholic Perspective

ROBERTO S. GOIZUETA

The practice of the Christian faith is inconceivable without some experience of church. That is, "being church" is an intrinsic, integral dimension of "being Christian." At the same time, the ecclesial character of the Christian faith is among the most difficult to assert convincingly in the context of post-Enlightenment Western cultures, informed as these are by individualistic notions of the person and, therefore, of religious faith. In this historical context, the assertion that religious faith is necessarily ecclesial can seem to represent a threat to individual freedom. Precisely for this reason, however, a critical retrieval of the centrality of church is today more necessary than ever. Indeed, such a retrieval is important not only for preserving an integral understanding of the faith but also for subverting individualistic notions of faith; the very notion of church can itself be among the most subversive, countercultural aspects of our faith.

In this essay, I will suggest that, when undertaken from the perspective of contemporary U.S. Latino/a experience and the theologies emerging from that experience, a critical retrieval of Catholic ecclesiology will highlight particular aspects of the notion of church that can be liberating and countercultural vis-à-vis both the larger church and society. I will examine key models of the church as these have been articulated within the "mainstream" Catholic theological tradition, specifically in the magisterial work of Avery Cardinal Dulles. I will then read those models through the lens of U.S. Latino/a Catholic theologies. I will

Sections of this essay have also appeared in my book *Christ Our Companion: Toward a Theological Aesthetics of Liberation* (Maryknoll, N.Y.: Orbis Books, 2009), my chapter for Orlando Espín, ed., *Building Bridges, Doing Justice: Constructing a Latino/a Ecumenical Theology* (Maryknoll, N.Y.: Orbis Books, 2009), and in my article, "Challenges of/to the U.S. Latino/a Liturgical Community," *Liturgical Ministry* 16 (Summer 2007): 124-31.

argue, finally, that such a contextualized theological reflection will accord—and has accorded—special significance to certain ecclesiological models, or images of the church that, in turn, offer rich resources for future ecclesiological scholarship.

The Christian notion of church finds its roots in the New Testament itself (a series of texts that, as canon, are themselves the product of the church). The seeds of that notion are present in Scripture and are often located, specifically, in the apostles' Pentecost experience. This event gave birth to the community that would embody Christ's presence and perpetuate his mission in history. Nascent forms of that community, however, are already present in the gospels, such as the community formed at the foot of the cross by those who accompany Jesus at his death. And, of course, the apostles themselves are the first community of disciples who will eventually be commissioned to "make disciples of all nations."

From the beginning, certain characteristics were ascribed to the church as a community of disciples. The so-called four marks of the church are referred to throughout the patristic period and were codified at the First Council of Constantinople in 381. These are the four characteristics that, according to long-standing tradition, define what it means to be church: the church is "one, holy, catholic, and apostolic." All of these marks—unity, sanctity, universality, and apostolicity—derive from the headship of Christ, who establishes the church.

One way to understand these various characteristics of the church, and their interrelationship, is to look at various models of the church that have informed Catholic ecclesiology over the centuries. These have been articulated, most famously, by the Jesuit theologian Avery Cardinal Dulles in his classic work *Models of the Church*. In the work's original version, Dulles outlined and assessed five basic ecclesiological models, adding a sixth model in a later, expanded edition of his book. These six models view the church as: institution, mystical communion, sacrament, herald, servant, and community of disciples.

Dulles's Models of the Church

Dulles begins by explaining and defending his approach to ecclesiology through the use of models. Such an approach, he argues, is more sensitive to the fact that, above all, the church is mystery:

> In selecting the term "models" rather than "aspects" or "dimensions," I wish to indicate my conviction that the Church, like other theological realities, is a mystery. Mysteries are realities of which we cannot speak directly. If we wish to talk about them at all we must draw on analogies afforded by our experience of the world. These analogies provide models. By attending to the analogies and utilizing them as models, we can indirectly grow in our understanding of the Church. The peculiarity of models, as contrasted with aspects, is that we cannot integrate them into a single synthetic vision on the level of articulate, categorical thought. In order to do justice to the various aspects of the Church, as

a complex reality, we must work simultaneously with different models. By a kind of mental juggling act, we have to keep several models in the air at once.[1]

It is precisely because of their ability to function analogically, providing multiple images and visions of the church that must be held together simultaneously, in tension, that the use of "models" represents a profoundly "Catholic" approach to ecclesiology; a Catholic ecclesiology refuses to reduce the church to any single entity that can be fully apprehended theologically. "The most distinctive feature of Catholicism, in my opinion," observes Dulles, "is not its insistence on the institutional but rather its wholeness or balance (and here one might indulge in some playing on the etymology of the word 'catholic' as the Greek equivalent for 'universal')."[2]

The first model is the church as institution. This brings to the fore the visible, structural element of the church as a historical society. As institution, the church is able to perpetuate the teachings and carry out the mission of Christ in the world across generations and time periods. The structural character of the church, moreover, makes it possible for the church to stand "over against" other institutions in society and resist assimilation. So, for instance, priests or bishops may have the authority and credibility—precisely as official representatives of the institution—to speak out against political or economic injustices in society. Like all the models, however, the church as institution is susceptible to certain dangers when not viewed in conjunction with the other models. When the church is reduced to nothing but an institution, the result is an institutionalism that can be deadening to the life of the church and oppressive to its members.

The second ecclesiological model is that of the church as "mystical communion." This model emphasizes the communal character of the church, not only as a communion among the living but with the entire "communion of saints." The external, visible character emphasized in the institutional model is here complemented by an attentiveness to the mystical, spiritual, interior character of the church. The church is an organic body with Christ as its head. Here Dulles also introduces the image of the church as the "people of God," which was promulgated especially at Vatican II. Although this latter image is helpful for understanding the inherently interpersonal character of the church, however, it is susceptible to an individualistic interpretation, which would understand the ecclesial community as but one more voluntary association of like-minded individuals, thereby obscuring the organic nature of the ecclesial communion.[3]

A model particularly central to Catholic ecclesiology is Dulles's third model, the church as sacrament. This model expresses the intrinsic unity of the divine and the human in the church. The church is the visible, corporeal mediation of Christ in the world. This model integrates institution and mystical communion, so that the latter is made present in history through the former. Although the church as sacrament makes Christ's grace present, it cannot simply be identified with Christ's presence; the divine is expressed through the human but can never simply be reduced to the human. In ecclesiology, the result would be a "narcissistic self-contemplation" that ignores the outwardly directed mission of the church.[4]

It is precisely that mission that is emphasized in the fourth model, the church as herald. This model expresses the church's identity as a community that has been not only called but also sent out into the world to proclaim the good news and the kingdom of God. Here too is emphasized the distinction between the earthly church and the eschatological kingdom of God. The church announces the kingdom, but it is not itself the kingdom. The danger with this model is precisely that of identifying the kingdom with the church. As opposed to the institutional model, moreover, the herald brings to the fore the local church as not simply a part of the universal church but the mediation of the universal church in a particular time and place, where the good news is announced and preached.[5]

This emphasis on the church's outwardly directed mission is also evident in the fifth ecclesiological model, the church as servant. Here the mission is identified not so much with the Word as with praxis, service in the world. The church must not withdraw, but must engage the world with all its tribulations and struggles, bringing Christ's presence and message not only through word but also through deed. Though the church can never be reduced to merely a service organization, it nevertheless is called to serve as a part of its very identity.[6]

Finally, in the expanded edition of his book, Dulles added a sixth model, which he believed "would harmonize the differences among the five previously described."[7] The church as a "community of disciples" is thus meant as a foundational model that can embrace the other five and harmonize the differences among them. While the term itself was explicitly used by Pope John Paul II, its roots are, of course, in the gospels themselves:

> Together with Jesus, the disciples constituted a contrast society, symbolically representing the new and renewed Israel. The number of the inner group was itself symbolic of the twelve tribes of Israel, headed by the sons of Jacob. The community of the disciples, with its exceptional style of life, was intended to attract attention, like a city set upon a mountaintop or a lantern in a dark place. It had a mission to remind the rest of the people of the transcendent value of the Kingdom of God, to which the disciples bore witness. It was therefore important for them to adopt a manner of life that would make no sense apart from their intense personal faith in God's providence and his fidelity to his promises.[8]

This community, therefore, was identified not only by their internal life (*ad intra*) but by their countercultural mission (*ad extra*). After the resurrection and ascension of Jesus, this community's identity takes on other characteristics. The community's boundaries now extend far beyond those of the original "twelve." Moreover, now that the historical Jesus is no longer physically present, his presence takes on new forms—no less real—through the outpouring of the Spirit in the life and worship of the community. Jesus' ongoing presence was also experienced in the community's life of mutual service, a way of life that, on the one hand, attracted the admiration (and resentment) of the larger society and, on the other hand, set the community apart from the larger society. As a contrast society committed to Christ, the disciples' refusal to participate in political activities that conflicted with that commitment would force them to undergo imprisonment, persecution, and even death. With the increasing assimilation and institutionalization of the church, discipleship also took on increasingly sacramental forms. To be a disciple was to participate in the sacramental life of the community. While each ecclesiological model emphasizes particular dimensions of "being church," all are thus rooted in the lived faith of a community of disciples called out from the world only to be sent back into the world to make present and announce the Good News.[9]

U.S. Latino/a Ecclesiology

All of these ecclesiological models are present, in one or another form, in U.S. Latino/a theology. At the same time, the historical experience and context of U.S. Hispanics make possible a critical retrieval of the above models while generating models more adequate to that experience and context. The result is a further specification of ecclesiological categories such as "communion," "sacrament," and "people."

For instance, Gary Riebe-Estrella has suggested how U.S. Latino/a theology might critique Dulles's second model, mystical communion. Riebe-Estrella would identify that model more closely with the "People of God" ecclesiology of Vatican II. He notes that "one of the great advances in ecclesiology promoted by the Second Vatican Council is its use of 'People of God' as the primary image for its understanding of church."[10] He goes on to argue—quite appropriately and convincingly—for the significance of this image in the articulation of a U.S. Latino/a ecclesiology. A communion ecclesiology identified with the *populus Dei* reflects the sociocentric worldview of U.S. Latino/a culture. At the same time, that worldview becomes a lens through which the "People of God" can be interpreted in a particular context that lends the image greater specificity. Analogously, Latin American theologians have interpreted the image with greater attention to sociohistorical context. For instance, notes Riebe-Estrella:

> Alvaro Quiroz Magaña emphasizes that the socioeconomic categories in Latin America have determined the direction of the reflections these theologians have made on their self-understanding as People of God and on the particular role in church that Latin American Catholics are called upon to play. He posits that there are core facets to the concept of church as the People of God: 1) the priority of Christian existence over the organization; 2) the pilgrim people, sacrament of God's Reign; and 3) church as called to be a permanent historical incarnation.[11]

José Comblin contends that "the concept 'people of God' offered the gateway to a church of the poor . . . The perspective of the people of God helped bring a new appreciation for the historic character of the church's earthly pilgrimage, the fundamental equality of all Christians, the recognition of the value of every human creature, the revaluing of local churches—with some hints of a priority of the poor."[12]

Riebe-Estrella then asks what the specifically U.S. Latino/a experience of cultural oppression might contribute to a further concretization of the people of God. Looking to the Hebrew Bible, he draws on the experience of Israel as a model for understanding the historical experience of Latinos/as as "People of God." The foundation of Israel as people of God is the extended familial relationships that, though circumscribed geographically, radiate outward concentrically through the family's relationships with other families in the community. Likewise, in the Latino/a worldview, "all relationships use family as their paradigm."[13] This is true of not only Latino/a Catholics but Protestants as well: "Although Catholics and Protestants have differing, even at times competing, ecclesiologies, both have a common understanding of the church based on the Hispanic experience of familia. The family is an archetype of the church."[14] As helpful as the paradigm of "la familia" may be, however, the use of such a model must avoid romanticization and remain attentive to the historically ambiguous character of Latino/a familial relationships. Latina scholars, for instance, have examined how, for Latinas, family relationships can be sites of both the liberating development of human agency and the oppressive exploitation of women's labor.[15]

At the same time, when these familial relationships are developed in the context of conflict with a larger, aggressive dominant culture, they are capable of forming the basis for a sense of "peoplehood" that defines itself not only *ad intra*, but also *ad extra*, as "other" in relation to the dominant culture. This sense of otherness "creates a fertile ground for a sense of *latinidad* and for a less biological and more analogous sense of pueblo."[16] Thus, the *Pueblo de Dios* gains a historical concreteness rooted in its socioeconomic and racial-cultural otherness. At the heart of this interpretation of people of God, then, is the insistence that, precisely as a distinct community and "pilgrim people," the Pueblo de Dios always constitutes itself over against a dominant other; for better or worse, confrontation and conflict are at the very heart of the Pueblo de Dios. If the people of God represents the "sacrament of God's Reign," the sacrament of the kingdom, then the moment that sacrament incarnates itself historically, it provokes resistance and confrontation. To paraphrase Jon Sobrino, the people of God as sacrament of the kingdom cannot be understood apart from the counter-image of the anti-kingdom.[17] This emphasis on the historically conflictual character of the people of God as an ecclesiological category points to the inherently countercultural character of the church as communion; the "mystical" must thus not be interpreted as asocial or ahistorical. Precisely as mystical communion or people of God the church stands over against those forces that undermine communion.

Despite these advantages of the Pueblo de Dios ecclesiological model for U.S. Latinos/as, however, Riebe-Estrella notes some latent ambiguities: "The limitations of the sociocentric perspective also have their play, as the sense of church is rather narrowly restricted to the 'Pueblo de Dios en Marcha' (the Latino segment of the church in the United States), or to the local parish, to which there is often a high sense of allegiance, or even more narrowly to the groups of families within the parish to which one is related."[18] To address these limitations, he turns to the central gospel symbol of God's reign: that is, the church as people of God, or even as a Pilgrim Church, cannot be properly understood apart from its intrinsic relationship to the kingdom. In terms of Dulles's models, the model of church as mystical communion, or people of God, is intimately linked to the fourth model, church as herald of the kingdom.

An emphasis on this intrinsic connection is necessary in order to avoid precisely the kind of solipsistic understanding of community to which Riebe-Estrella alludes. To be people of God necessarily implies a practical commitment to the coming of God's reign:

> People of God now becomes the result of personal commitment, yet it is a commitment to a reality that predates the commitment of every individual . . . The way this people lives out with each other the mystery of costly love, embodied in Jesus' death and resurrection, becomes revelatory of the vocation of all humanity to form a single people who live in sisterhood and brotherhood with one another. However, this sisterhood and brotherhood of humanity is neither created nor constituted by the free choice of individuals. Rather, this relationship mirrors how humanity was originally created—not as unrelated individuals but as family (Gn 1:27-28). This relationship constitutes the fundamental identity of each human person. In addition, as family, the creation of humanity images who God is. The peoplehood of humanity, which is signified in the People of God, is revelatory of the communitarian nature of God. In this sense the church as the People of God is an icon of the divine.[19]

The church is not just sacrament (Dulles's third model), and not just the Body of Christ; the church is the sacrament of God's reign. Consequently, membership is never "automatic" (e.g., based on family ties or bloodlines) but demands a practical commitment to *be* what we already *are* by virtue of God's own creative-salvific activity in history. Such a commitment implies, in turn, a "costly love" insofar as the coming of God's reign always provokes violent resistance.

This ethical dimension at the heart of a Christian ecclesiology has been underscored by Latin American theologians, who have also noted certain weaknesses or ambiguities in the image of people of God as a specification of the ecclesial "communio." Sobrino, for instance, observes that the notion of "people" remains abstract so that, while the term may relativize distinctions between clergy and laity, it fails to highlight inequalities among the laity; the term thus historicizes the hierarchical dimensions of the church while retaining an ahistorical understanding of the laity. Moreover, contends Sobrino, while suggesting the possibility of a "church of the poor" (especially given the connotations of the Spanish "pueblo" and "popular"), the people of God fails to integrate a preferential option for the poor as an explicitly ecclesiological—not only ethical—category: "A Church *for* the poor represents an ethical and therefore necessary approach, but it is not necessarily an ecclesiological approach . . . A Church *of* the poor . . . poses a strictly ecclesiological problem; it concerns the very being of the Church."[20] The ambiguity of the term "people" is alluded to as well by European political theologians such as Jürgen Moltmann, who notes that "because not all are 'people' in the same way, . . . the fellowship in which all are to see the glory of God 'together' is created through the choosing of the humble and through judgment on the violent."[21] Unfortunately, moreover, not even within the church itself are "all people in the same way"—witness the exploitation suffered by so many women and children within the walls of the church itself over the centuries. So the term "people" has had an ambiguous history both in society and in the church.

The response Sobrino proposes to this problem is evangelical at its core: "The Spirit of Jesus is in the poor and, with them as his point of departure, he re-creates the entire Church. If this truth is understood in all its depth and in an authentically trinitarian perspective, it means that the history of God advances indefectibly by way of the poor; that the Spirit of Jesus takes historical flesh in the poor; and that the poor show the direction of history that is in accord with God's plan." In no way does the "church of the poor" suggest a "parallel church," rather it specifies the privileged (not exclusive) sociohistorical locus wherein the church *is* church and discovers what it means to *be* church. This understanding does not obviate the need for an official magisterium; rather, it proposes (again, based on the gospel) the way in which the magisterial authority ought to function, namely, in solidarity with the poor. The ecclesiological image of the church of the poor posits not a new church but "a new mode of being the Church."[22]

Inspired by Archbishop Oscar Romero and Ignacio Ellacuría, friends who had shared the common fate of those who identify with the poor, Sobrino would later concretize the ecclesiological image of the people of God even further. If "the Spirit of Jesus takes historical flesh in the poor," if the poor are the privileged mediators of that Spirit not only in the world, but within the church herself (not because they are necessarily morally superior but simply because they are poor), then the very historicity and corporeality of the poor is itself the privileged locus for encountering Jesus' flesh, the Body of Christ in the world today. The sociological category of "the poor" takes on an explicitly theological character. If the people of God remains insufficiently historical until specified sociologically as the church of the poor, this latter remains insufficiently theological until specified as the crucified people, "el Pueblo Crucificado."

The crucified people are the privileged historical mediation of the crucified and risen Christ in the world. As mediators of the crucified and risen Christ not only in the world, but also in the church, the crucified people also remind us that suffering is one of the marks of the church. Ecclesiological reflection undertaken in the context of a preferential option for the poor, for the crucified people, would thus retrieve for contemporary Christians the ancient notion of the "ecclesia crucis" (so central for St. Paul and Luther):

> No other single ecclesiological theme receives the attention that the suffering of the church receives in our textual sources. For centuries theology has maintained that the true marks of the church are the four that are named in the Nicene Creed: "one, holy, catholic, and apostolic church" . . . Each of these notae ecclesia can find some biblical basis, but none of them can claim a fraction of the attention paid to the theme of the church's suffering in these sacred writings . . . The earliest and most prominent manner of discerning the true church and distinguishing it from false claims to Christian identity was to observe the nature and extent of the suffering experienced by a community of faith. Why? Because, of course, as Paul makes clear . . . if you claim to be a disciple of the crucified one you must expect to participate in his sufferings; . . . you will have to become a community of the cross.[23]

To say that suffering is a mark of the church is to privilege the crucified people and to demand solidarity with the victims as the privileged praxis through which we demonstrate ourselves to be church. "Hence," as Shawn Copeland notes, "the community of believers, the *ekklesia*, the church ought to be recognizable in its willingness to stand beside the poor, injured, despised, and excluded sufferers in history, in its willingness to suffer."[24]

This is not to suggest, however, that the crucified people are themselves identical to the crucified and risen Christ. As Gustavo Gutiérrez warns, the poor themselves are called to make a preferential option for the poor; the poor themselves can be accomplices in victimization.[25] (In the U.S. Latino/a context, this imperative becomes especially important as Latinos/as assimilate and achieve "success" in the larger U.S. society.) Rather, again in the words of Copeland, "like Jesus, the church must be willing to risk fortune and future for the sake of those who are abandoned to the scrap heap of history. Above all, these children, women, and men must be loved, for in their suffering they bear the mark of the crucified Jesus, who is no one else than the Resurrected Lord."[26]

Here we have, then, the seeds of a rereading of the ecclesiological image "Body of Christ," which had been appropriately called for by Gary Riebe-Estrella. In this regard, I would suggest that, since the late Middle Ages, the notion of Body of Christ as applied to the community of the faithful has become increasingly spiritualized if not mystified. As Henri de Lubac and other scholars have observed, the term *corpus mysticum*, or "Mystical Body of Christ" was not widely used in reference to the church until the late twelfth

and early thirteenth centuries. The term *Mystical Body of Christ* originally
appeared in the fifth century and referred not to the church but to the Eucharist; the church was the "verum corpus" (true, or real body). The eucharistic
controversies of the eleventh century made it necessary to apply this latter
term to the Eucharist.[27] If, as Joseph Cardinal Ratzinger has posited, the term
mysticum was never intended to mean "mystical" but rather "referring to
the Mystery (of the Eucharist)," it does not stretch the imagination to see
how *corpus mysticum* could have led to a spiritualization of the term *Body*
as applied to the church, even as the same term, as applied to the Eucharist,
became increasingly literalized.[28] De Lubac argues that one result of this shift
was an increasing identification of the eucharistic species with the historical
body of Christ on the cross. The corollary, it would seem, was an increased
gap between the historical body of Christ on the cross and the church. Referring to the Pauline notion of the Body of Christ, Gutiérrez observes: "Readers
often regard this theology of the church as simply a beautiful metaphor. However, we must, shocking though this idea may be, see through to the realism
that characterizes the Pauline approach. He is speaking of the real body of
Christ, which he looks upon as an extension of the incarnation."[29]

What Sobrino and Ellacuría are doing, therefore, is retrieving the original
connection between the people of God and the historical body of Christ on the
cross while, at the same time, concretizing and specifying that intrinsic connection; what unites the two is the cross or, more precisely, the crucified body. In an
analysis of Ellacuría's ecclesiology, Kevin Burke writes that:

> As Jesus' Body becomes the sacramental symbol of the salvation he
> mediates, so too the church's bodiliness enables it to continue making
> that salvation present in history. As Christology needs to approach the
> whole mystery of Jesus Christ by beginning from his historical corpo-
> reality, ecclesiology needs to approach the salvific sacramentality of the
> church from its historical corporeality . . . For the church to be the Body
> of Christ in history, it must be present to history through particular
> historical actions that continue and correspond to the life of Jesus . . . It
> means the church cannot fulfill its vocation with its back turned to the
> crucified peoples of our world. On the contrary, it must seek them out,
> live in solidarity with them, announce God's Good News to them, and
> reflect to them the truth that they are God's beloved ones.[30]

The *ecclesia crucis* identifies itself with the crucified people, seeks their liberation, and in so doing shares in their suffering. The real Body of Christ is thus
mediated by the real bodies of poor persons in history.[31]

Both outside and within the church, the crucified people are the privileged
locus for encountering today the crucified and risen Lord. In so mediating the
wounded and resurrected Body of Christ in the world, the church herself is
called to a cruciform existence in history. This is true not because the cross is
the goal of Christian discipleship but precisely because it isn't. Precisely because

Christian discipleship is *ultimately* not about death but about life. The church thus demonstrates most fully its commitment to life to the extent that it "takes the Crucified People down from the cross" (the phrase is that of Sobrino and Ellacuría). Such solidarity leads to and is rooted in the cross not as an end in itself but as the inevitable consequence of the church's mission as sacrament of the reign of God:

> Consequently, the church fulfills its sacramental vocation to mediate salvation to history when it makes concrete both the critical and constructive demands of the reign of God in each historical situation. The church fulfills the critical demand of God's reign when it prophetically denounces the crucifying powers of the world. It takes up its constructive task when—in deed even more than word—it announces that the reign of God draws near as salvation/liberation of the poor in relation to their terrible situation of captivity and death.[32]

The church becomes a crucified church insofar as it embodies, makes present, and proclaims the reign of God as the continuation in history of Christ's own enactment of that reign. Just as the risen Christ still bears the wounds of crucifixion, so too must the reign of God bear the wounds resulting from its proclamation and enactment in history.

Contemporary consumerist culture likewise fosters a mystification of the body that obfuscates the intrinsic connection between the crucified and risen Christ's body and the church as Body of Christ. For all the dominant U.S. culture's obsession with "the body," our culture is repulsed by any body that is wounded, which is to say, by any "real" body. The Western preoccupation with "the body" as an abstract ideal masks an underlying depreciation of imperfect, scarred, or wounded bodies: the wounded, if glorified, body of Christ as well as the wounded bodies of the poor. Gutiérrez notes that:

> some Christian milieus, usually in affluent countries, have promoted a reevaluation and "celebration" of the human body in cultural expressions—for example, some modern dances and other bodily forms of expression that are used in eucharistic celebrations . . . Whatever the merits of this claim, I want to note here that the concern for the corporeal in Latin American spiritual experiences has come about in quite a different way . . . It is not "my body," but the "body of the poor person"—the weak and languishing body of the poor—that has made the material a part of a spiritual outlook.[33]

The failure to see the Body of Christ as it is, as a crucified and risen body, ultimately prevents us from truly appreciating, truly taking seriously the lived faith of the poor, who do not flee from the wounded bodies in their midst to the illusory security of abstract, ideal bodies; they are not concerned with abstract ideals but with real persons, with the real Christ. The crucified people of God make it possible for us—in Sobrino's words—to be "honest about the real," honest about the real Body of Christ.

The Church of the Borderland

The renewed appreciation of church as "corpus verum," (real Body of Christ), thus demands a retrieval of the intrinsic connection between the body of the historical Christ, as crucified and risen, and the church. I have argued that this is precisely the ecclesiological significance of the notion of the crucified people. At the same time, the notion of crucified people itself demands concretization within the specifically U.S. Latino/a context. To this end, some Latino/a theologians, especially Virgilio Elizondo, have pointed to another aspect of the crucified and risen Christ with ecclesiological implications of special relevance to U.S. Latinos/as, namely, the historical Christ's social location and identity as a Galilean Jew. In the words of Elizondo, "the overwhelming originality of Christianity is the basic belief of our faith that not only did the Son of God become a 'human being,' but he became 'Jesus of Nazareth' . . . Jesus was not simply a Jew, he was a Galilean Jew; throughout his life he and his disciples were identified as Galileans."[34] Consequently, argues Elizondo, any Christology that claims to be rooted in the Gospels—and that takes seriously the Christian doctrine of the incarnation—must take as its starting point the historical-theological particularity of Jesus Christ. That particularity is not merely accidental to the Christian kerygma; it is at the very heart of the kerygma. That identity, moreover, has important implications for a twenty-first-century ecclesiology that speaks to the reality of a global church.

As Christianity becomes increasingly a third world religion, shaped by the worldviews and cultures of those regions where the Christian faith is experiencing its greatest growth, the future of the church will not be determined by ecclesial and theological movements in Europe. For, unlike the "globalization" effected through violence and conquest, this new historical reality is taking root in and being nurtured by local churches and grassroots communities. The face of this global church is marked not so much by colonization as by immigration.

What does a Christian ecclesiology have to say to this reality? I have already suggested how the Body of the crucified and risen Christ can ground an ecclesiology rooted in the historical experience of the "crucified peoples" of our societies. Now I want to suggest that the social location of that figure as a Galilean Jew can further ground an ecclesiology in the experience of those marginalized peoples who today represent the most vital segment of the Christian world. In other words, in the global context as well as in the U.S. context, one way of concretizing and historicizing the notion of "crucified people" is precisely by understanding the theological relationship between crucifixion and Galilee, both with respect to the body of the historical Christ and with respect to the church as *corpus verum.*

Galilee was and is a borderland. In the gospels, this borderland and its inhabitants take on theological significance. It is no mere coincidence that, in the Synoptic accounts, Jesus comes from Nazareth, in Galilee, meets his end in Jerusalem, and, finally, returns to Galilee, where he appears to the apostles after his resurrection (Mark 14:28; Matt 26:32; 28:7, 10, 16).

The theological significance ascribed to the Galilean borderland is rooted in the history, geography, and culture of the region. As Elizondo notes, Galilee "was an outer region, far from the center of Judaism in Jerusalem of Judea and a crossroads of the great caravan routes of the world. It was a region of mixed peoples and languages."[35] Contiguous with non-Jewish territories and geographically distant from Jerusalem, Galilee was often viewed by first-century Jews as "a Jewish enclave in the midst of 'unfriendly' gentile seas."[36] "The area as a whole," writes biblical sociologist Richard Horsley, "was a frontier between the great empires in their historical struggles."[37]

In the Gospels, this geopolitical reality takes on soteriological significance as the place that defines the very character of the Christian revelation, for the good news is incarnated in the person of Jesus Christ, Jesus the Galilean Jew. His ministry and mission, especially, begin and end in Galilee.

In order to understand the Good News, insists Elizondo, we must understand the soteriological value (or, rather, antivalue) of Galilee, especially its villages, such as Nazareth.[38]

The Jewish establishment in Jerusalem could not conceive that God's word could be revealed among the people of the borderland: "Search and you will see that no prophet is to rise from Galilee" (John 7:52). "Galilee did indeed function," observes Sean Freyne, "as a symbol of the newness of Jesus' vision in contrast to the more established circles of Jewish belief for the early Christians, but all the indications are that the symbolic reference was grounded in an actual ministry that was conducted in the real Galilee of the first century CE."[39] It is this "newness" that characterizes Galilee; this is the newness of the borderland—of all borderlands—as, quite literally, marginal to the centers of power.[40]

The crucified and risen Christ returns to the Galilean borderland to reconstitute the community of disciples that had disintegrated when the disciples had abandoned Jesus on the way to Calvary. This renewed gathering, this "ekklesia" will be born not in Jerusalem but in Galilee, not at the center of power but on the margins. Just as the glorified body of the crucified and risen Christ is revealed to the disciples in the Galilean borderland, so is the church as Body of Christ born on that day, on the border—among the crucified people.

A Multi-Discursive Church

If the church is thus an intrinsically borderland church, born alongside multiple cultural and religious influences, these will necessarily influence the church's self-understanding as well as its ritual life and symbolic world. This is true of our own time and it was true of Jesus' time, when Galilean Judaism developed outside the complete control of the religious leadership in Jerusalem and along-side non-Jewish populations. "It is possible, perhaps even likely, . . ." observes Horsley, "that some Jews considered themselves faithful even while they uti-lized what would be classified as pagan or Greco-Roman symbols as a matter of course in their everyday lives."[41] Their religious-cultural diversity, together with their economic wealth, made the Galilean urban centers objects of resentment and opposition throughout the Galilean countryside, where village life among the peasantry was "guided by Israelite customs and traditions."[42]

Yet even the Jewish traditions of the peasants were different from those practiced in Jerusalem:

> Galilee was heir in some form to the traditions of the Northern King-dom . . . Torah was important, as was circumcision in Galilean society, but not the written and oral Torah as interpreted by the Judean and Jerusalem retainer class and enforced where they could by the Temple aristocracy. Rather Galilee was home to popular legal and wisdom tra-ditions . . . Galilee was also ambivalent about Jerusalem, the Temple, the priestly aristocracy, temple dues and tithes.[43]

In short, as Horsley argues, Galilean Jewish practices could be described as a kind of popular religion:

> The distinction anthropologists often make between the "great tradi-tion" and the "little traditions" may be of some help in formulating the issues. A "society" may develop cultural traditions at two levels: the traditions of origin and customary practice continue as a popular tradition cultivated orally in the villages, while specialists codify those same traditions in a standardized and centralized form as an official tradition, which is cultivated orally but perhaps also reduced to writ-ten form. Something like this distinction between official tradition and popular tradition may help explain the situation in Galilee as seen both in sources from the first century C.E. and in early rabbinic literature.[44]

The notion of popular religion—as religious traditions and practices that, though influenced by the larger codified tradition and "official" texts and prac-tices, nevertheless emerge from a borderland people whose lived faith incor-porates influences from both sides of the border—is thus at the very heart of the Christian ekklesia, at the very heart of a Christian ecclesiology. These are the "little stories" that, notes Alejandro García-Rivera, make possible the "Big Story"—or the "demotic discourses" that sociologist Martin Stringer compares with "dominant discourses" in Christian tradition.[45] This is where the Body of Christ is incarnated today.

Latino/a popular Catholicism represents a ressourcement, a retrieval of the borderland church and religiosity that global Christianity itself represents. If we avoid the modern, rationalist temptation to reduce tradition to texts, laws, concepts, or confessions and include within our understanding of tradition the lived traditions of the poor, we can avoid an ecclesiastical revanchism that identifies tradition with only the relatively recent, modern, rationalist understanding of tradition that characterized Trent and Vatican I; and we can avoid a liberalism that assumes the same rationalist understanding of tradition, though in order to reject or deconstruct tradition.

What, in turn, makes possible such a recovery of traditional religious practices and traditional "ways of being religious" is the distinct history of Latin American and, hence, Latino/a Catholicism. That distinct history embodies a premodern understanding of religious practice, faith, and church; the roots of Latin American Catholicism are found in Iberian medieval and baroque Christianity. As historian William Christian has noted, the medieval Christian worldview and faith were not seriously threatened in Spain "until . . . the late eighteenth century." Consequently, Iberian Catholicism was not forced to develop a response to the Protestant reformers' arguments or rebut them point by point—as northern European Catholics and, later, European Catholics in the United States would be forced to do.[46]

In order to defend itself against the Protestant "threat" to orthodoxy, northern European Catholicism would become increasingly rationalist, demanding a clarity, precision, and uniformity in doctrinal formulations that were simply not necessary in areas where "Catholic" and "Christian" continued to be essentially interchangeable terms; in Spain, there was no urgent need to define, clarify, and distinguish Catholic belief, especially in the wake of the reconquista and the expulsion of the Jews in 1492.[47] It would be the more rationalist, northern European Catholicism that would take hold in the English colonies—and it is this understanding of Catholicism that continues to inform the U.S. Catholic establishment to this day, whether conservative or liberal.

The differences between Catholicism in the English and in the Spanish colonies were reinforced by the fact that, like the Iberian colonizers as a whole, Iberian Catholicism interacted—even if often violently—with an Amerindian culture that, in many ways, shared a worldview quite similar to that of medieval Christianity. Conversely, like the English colonizers as a whole, Anglo-American Catholicism in the English colonies generally rejected any such intermingling with the indigenous culture, preferring to expel and exclude rather than subjugate and subdue that culture.

Drawing on his research into the historical origins of Latino/a popular Catholicism, Orlando Espín observes that the Iberian Christianity brought by the Spanish to Latin America "was medieval and pre-Tridentine, and it was planted in the Americas approximately two generations before Trent's opening session."[48] He continues: "While this faith was defined by traditional creedal beliefs as passed down through the Church's magisterium, those beliefs were expressed primarily in and through symbol and rite, through devotions and liturgical practices . . . The teaching of the gospel did not usually occur through the spoken, magisterial word, but through the symbolic, 'performative' word."[49] As yet, in their everyday lives, Christians did not clearly distinguish creedal tra-

ditions from liturgical and devotional traditions; both were assumed to be integral dimensions of the tradition. Espín avers that "until 1546 *traditio* included,
without much reflective distinction *at the everyday level*, both the contents of
Scripture and the dogmatic declarations of the councils of antiquity, as well as
devotional practices (that often had a more ancient history than, for example,
Chalcedon's Christological definitions)."[50] At the grass roots, medieval culture
accepted, and even encouraged, the kind of complexity that would be perceived
as threatening by later generations needing to draw clear and distinct confes-
sional boundaries: "Many of the characteristic features of medieval culture come
from the cultivation of complexity, from the enchantment and the challenge represented by contradictions, from the yes and no as this was expounded by Abe-
lard, the Parisian intellectual and Christian theologian of the 12th Century."[51]
According to Espín, the clear distinction between dogma, that is, the content of
tradition, and worship, that is, the form in which that tradition was embodied in
everyday life, did not become crystallized until the Council of Trent. He goes on
to suggest that, "on this side of the Atlantic the Church was at least in its second
generation, and it took approximately another century for Trent's theology and
decrees to appear and become operative in our ecclesiastical scene."[52]

Its medieval roots also contribute to the peculiarly noninstitutional character of Latin American and Latino/a popular Catholicism. There is no doubt
that popular Catholicism draws heavily from the symbolic, liturgical, and evangelical resources of "institutional" Catholicism and, indeed, contributes to the
development of those broader traditional, "official" resources. Yet the vitality of
popular Catholicism comes primarily from its intimate connection to the everyday life of the people, particularly its deep, intimate connection to domestic
life. Likewise, religious leadership is not primarily male and clerical but female
and lay; traditions are passed down primarily not through official ecclesiastical organs but through educational and catechetical structures that are quite
tangential to the official, sacramental life of the parish. These two dimensions
clearly intersect (especially in the celebration of important life events such as
birth, marriage, and death), but neither are they simply coextensive.

Once again, these characteristics reflect the premodern roots of Latino
popular Catholicism. The exclusive identification of "the church" with the
institution, hierarchy, juridical structure, and clergy became widespread and
entrenched only in the wake of the Protestant Reformation, as a defense against
the challenges it presented. Avery Dulles locates what he calls this "deformation
of the true nature of the Church" in the late Middle Ages:

> Catholic theology in the Patristic period and in the Middle Ages, down
> through the great Scholastic doctors of the thirteenth century, was rela-
> tively free of institutionalism. The strongly institutionalist development
> occurred in the late Middle Ages and the Counter-Reformation, when
> theologians and canonists, responding to attacks on the papacy and
> hierarchy, accented precisely those features that the adversaries were
> denying . . . The institutional outlook reached its culmination in the
> second half of the nineteenth century, and was expressed with singular

clarity in the first schema of the Dogmatic Constitution on the Church prepared for Vatican Council I.[53]

Dulles's point is reinforced by medieval historian Gary Macy: "In the late Middle Ages, in particular, claims for control of ecclesiastical governance became more strident." Prior to that, the precise character of the church and of what constitutes Christian tradition, authority, and belief was broader and less clearly defined. While in the medieval church "there certainly was a quite distinct clerical culture with its own set of laws and rituals," among the forces that helped define medieval Christianity were the laity, religious women, and popular religious practices; these are too often ignored by contemporary historians who read back into that period our contemporary ecclesiological assumptions (for example, that "the church" is identical to what we today might call the "official" or "institutional" church).[54]

The exclusion of the diverse forms of lay, popular religion from our definition of the church in the Middle Ages served the purposes of both the post-Tridentine papacy, which argued that "the one true Church had always and everywhere agreed on the fundamental dogmas proclaimed at Trent . . . thus preserving a unified voice down through the centuries," and the Protestant Reformers, who argued that "the Roman Curia . . . used its totalitarian powers to ruthlessly enforce its heretical will." Moreover, as Macy notes, "this mythology suited equally well the anti-clerical agendas of the Enlightenment and of the nineteenth century. In this scenario, religion—especially institutional religion—presented a unified opposition to science, education, and any form of liberation."[55]

In our contemporary ecclesial context, the identification of the church by the juridical structure and its official representatives has also served the purposes (whether wittingly or unwittingly) of both Catholic neoconservatives and liberals—precisely inasmuch as both are operating within the framework of the fundamentally modern ecclesiology that emerged in the late Middle Ages and gained prominence in the Reformation, Trent, and Vatican I. Whether to promote or reject that ecclesiology, both neoconservatives and liberals are dependent on it. Conservative and liberal Catholics share a common, thoroughly modern institutionalist (to use Dulles's term) identification of church with a monolithic structure, the former to affirm it and the latter to reject it. This is precisely the type of reductionist understanding of his first ecclesiological model that Dulles had rejected.

In the United States, one consequence has been that the important place of popular religion in the life and identity of the church has been either depreciated or ignored altogether; in Latin America, the enduring force of popular Catholicism has prevented its complete marginalization. As post-Enlightenment ecclesiologies gained greater influence in the nineteenth and twentieth centuries, the Latin American Catholic Church has developed on two parallel, if often overlapping levels: the popular Catholic practices that are central to the everyday lives of the vast majority of Latin American Catholics, and what many refer to as "la religión de los curas" (the religion of the priests). Precisely because this complexity retains similarities to medieval Christianity, a better understanding of this latter might contribute to a deeper appreciation of Latino Catholicism as a resource for ecclesiology.

As Catholicism in the United States becomes increasingly Pan-American, the historical argument of scholars such as Dulles, Macy, and Espín becomes increasingly relevant for understanding our ecclesiological context. The church that originally came to Latin America was essentially Iberian and medieval in character; the church that came to the English colonies was northern European and, as Jesuit historian John O'Malley has argued, essentially modern in character.[56] This distinction has important ramifications.

Arguing that the prejudice against medieval Christianity is based on the anachronistic assumption that the medieval church was identical with post-Tridentine Roman Catholicism, Macy has perceptively diagnosed the problem facing Hispanic Catholics in the United States: "If the Church in the Middle Ages was tyrannical, corrupt, and immoral, and the Church in the Middle Ages was (and is) Roman Catholic, then Roman Catholics are immoral, corrupt, and tyrannical. Hispanics, as mostly Roman Catholics, can therefore be expected to be devious, immoral, lazy, technologically underdeveloped, and ignorant."[57]

The point here is not to suggest either that U.S. Latino/a popular Catholicism can simply be equated with medieval Christianity, which it of course cannot, or to suggest that we can or should somehow "return" to some romanticized version of a medieval "way of being church"—which was, after all, also characterized by a great deal of horrific violence, oppression, and corruption. Rather, I simply mean to suggest that an understanding of the historical influences of medieval Christianity on Latino/a popular Catholicism can contribute to a more differentiated understanding of church history, the history of Christian religious practices, and the complex character of Christian ecclesiology. A recovery of that history can be an important resource for ecclesiological reflection in the concrete context of a global church.

Such a reading of church history need not, moreover, be limited to the study of medieval Christianity in its relationship to the contemporary context. So, for instance, if we read early Christian religious practices through such a differentiated optic we would discover a fluid, dynamic panoply of religious practices that include but go beyond the "official" practices of the church. So, for instance, Christian religious practices have always extended beyond the ritual meal that evolved into the central sacrament of the Eucharist:

> The meal has inevitably received most attention because this, in the form of the Eucharist, has become the principal ritual event of the Christian church. However, by focusing on the eucharistic aspects of the meal at the expense of other ritual activity, the impression can be given that there is far more continuity and consistency within the early history of Christian worship than is perhaps the case.[58]

In a fascinating study of the history of Christian worship, Martin Stringer argues that "for much of the first thousand years of Christian history official liturgical worship and lay devotion were largely indistinguishable, each fed off and into the other."[59] The same could be said of the distinction between eucharistic worship and "Spirit-filled" worship. That is, while Christian churches are today divided between those in which eucharistic worship of one form or another predominates ("mainline" and clerical) and those in which Spirit-filled worship predominates (Pentecostal or Charismatic, lay), this has not always been the case.

In its earliest years, the Christian community worshipped in a variety of ways, including the shared meal and ecstatic, Spirit-filled practices that flowed in and out of the meals. So, in the Corinth of Paul's time, "worship was focused around a shared meal and a gathering of the community in which each individual brought hymns, words, songs and various forms of ecstatic gifts." Gradually during the first generations, worship became increasingly formalized and "Paul's ecstatic and disordered gathering in which each person brought a hymn or a psalm or a spiritual experience had no part to play." Though increasingly relegated to the periphery, as worship became focused on formal, highly structured, clerically led worship, such forms of personalized, spontaneous, lay-identified devotion and worship continued into the Middle Ages. In medieval Spain, for instance, while "the dominant discourse was clearly that of the Catholic Church, with its reinforcement in the liturgy," there also proliferated

> local demotic discourses [that] could take many different forms, from the language of saints and devotion to particular images, to those of spiritual powers, local healers, and debates about the role of any number of local sprites, goblins and others . . . Each level of religious discourse clearly interacts, to a greater or lesser extent, with all the others, but need not overlap in terms of perceived contradictions or tensions. Most ordinary people can have dual or even multi-discursive competence and can switch from discourse to discourse depending on circumstances.[60]

Articulating a more concrete notion of church in our contemporary context would also entail, therefore, an openness to the ecumenical character of a borderland church as "multi-discursive." The reality of U.S. Latino/a "pluri-confessionalism" is, by now, almost a commonplace (what Stringer calls above "multi-discursive competence"); for Latinos/as, boundaries are often perceived as much more porous, precisely because of the subordination of those boundaries to multivalent religious practices and symbols as fundamental markers of religious identity (influenced, as noted above, by the diverse, practice-based medieval and baroque religiosity to which Latino/a popular religion traces its roots). Many Latinos and Latinas live on the border between official liturgy and local devotions, the little stories and the Big Story, dominant and demotic discourses. They also live on the border between confessions. As I have tried to suggest above, this is hardly a new reality in the history of Christianity but has defined the Christian community from the very beginning.

Drawing on the wisdom of our lived faith, Latinos/as can begin to articulate how our own "little stories," in the words of Alejandro García-Rivera, make possible—and have always made possible—the Big Story of Christianity. As ekklesia, (as a gathered communion), the church will remain a vital, credible sacrament of the reign of God to the extent that the church identifies itself with those women, children, and men who are the privileged witnesses to the crucified and risen Christ. There can be no authentic communion absent such an identification. The legacy of the borderland as a privileged ecclesial location, a privileged place for being church, is one that Latinos and Latinas have a responsibility to bequeath not only to our adopted country but, especially, to our church, a church born on the border.

The Latino/a experience of church has thus made important contributions to Christian ecclesiological reflection. If "mainstream" ecclesiological models have helped us come to a deeper understanding of the numerous, integrally related dimensions of what it means to "be church," Latino/a and Latin American theologians have brought the preferential option for the poor to bear on those models, thereby retrieving them critically in the context of our contemporary, global reality. In this context, theological notions of sacramentality, mission, "people of God," and Christian discipleship will remain unacceptably abstract unless they are grounded in the lived ecclesiologies of the majority of the world's Christians who live not in Jerusalem but in Galilee, on the margins of society. It is to this task that Latino and Latina theologians continue to dedicate themselves.

Notes

1. Avery Dulles, *Models of the Church*, expanded ed. (New York: Doubleday, 1987), 9-10.
2. Ibid., 10.
3. Ibid., 49, 53-62.
4. Ibid., 63-75, 195.
5. Ibid., 79.
6. Ibid., 89-102.
7. Ibid., 206.
8. Ibid., 209
9. Ibid., 211-17.
10. Gary Riebe-Estrella, "Pueblo and Church," in *From the Heart of Our People: Latino/a Explorations in Catholic Systematic Theology*, ed. Orlando O. Espín and Miguel H. Díaz (Maryknoll, N.Y.: Orbis Books, 1999), 178.
11. Cited in ibid.
12. José Comblin, *People of God* (Maryknoll, N.Y.: Orbis Books, 2004), 41, 45.
13. Riebe-Estrella, "Pueblo and Church," 175.
14. James Empereur and Eduardo Fernández, *La Vida Sacra: Contemporary Hispanic Sacramental Theology* (Lanham, Md.: Rowman & Littlefield, 2006), 68 (referring to the work of Miguel de la Torre and Edwin Aponte).
15. See, for example, Ada María Isasi-Díaz, *Mujerista Theology: A Theology for the Twenty-First Century* (Maryknoll, N.Y.: Orbis Books, 1996), 137-145; Nancy Pineda-Madrid, "Notes toward a Chicana Feminist Epistemology (and Why It Is Important for

Latina Feminist Theologies)," in *A Reader in Latina Feminist Theology*, ed. María Pilar Aquino, Daisy L. Machado and Jeanette Rodríguez (Austin: University of Texas Press, 2002), 241–66.

16. Riebe-Estrella, "Pueblo and Church," 181.

17. See Jon Sobrino, *Jesus the Liberator: A Historical-Theological View* (Maryknoll, N.Y.: Orbis Books, 1993), 67-192.

18. Riebe-Estrella, "Pueblo and Church," 182.

19. Ibid., 182-83.

20. Jon Sobrino, *The True Church and the Poor* (Maryknoll, N.Y.: Orbis Books, 1984), 92; Comblin, *People of God*, 44-45.

21. Jürgen Moltmann, *The Church in the Power of the Spirit: A Contribution to Messianic Ecclesiology* (New York: Harper & Row, 1977), 351.

22. Sobrino, *True Church*, 93, 96.

23. Douglas John Hall, *The Cross in Our Context: Jesus and the Suffering World* (Minneapolis: Fortress, 2003), 140.

24. M. Shawn Copeland, "The Church Is Marked by Suffering," in *The Many Marks of the Church*, ed. William Madges and Michael J. Daley (New London, Conn.: Twenty-Third Publications, 2006), 214.

25. Gustavo Gutiérrez, *A Theology of Liberation* (Maryknoll, N.Y.: Orbis Books, 1988), xxvi.

26. Copeland, "Church Is Marked by Suffering," 216.

27. Henri de Lubac, *Corpus mysticum: l'Eucharistie et l'Église au Moyen Âge. Étude historique* (Paris: Aubier, 1949).

28. Joseph Ratzinger, *The Spirit of the Liturgy* (San Francisco: Ignatius Press, 2000), 88.

29. Gustavo Gutiérrez, *We Drink from Our Own Wells: The Spiritual Journey of a People* (Maryknoll, N.Y.: Orbis Books, 1984), 69.

30. Kevin F. Burke, "Christian Salvation and the Disposition of Transcendence: Ignacio Ellacuría's Historical Soteriology," in *Love That Produces Hope: The Thought of Ignacio Ellacuría*, ed. Kevin F. Burke and Robert Lassalle-Klein (Collegeville, Minn.: Liturgical Press, 2006), 179-80.

31. The significance of corporeality—and of the connection between Christological and anthropological corporeality—for the ongoing struggles of women, especially, has been developed by a number of scholars. For instance, see María Clara Bingemer, "Women in the Future of the Theology of Liberation," in *Feminist Theology from the Third World*, ed. Ursula King (Maryknoll, N.Y.: Orbis Books, 1994); Elisabeth Moltmann-Wendel, *I Am My Body: A Theology of Embodiment* (New York: Continuum, 1995); Sallie McFague, *The Body of God: An Ecological Theology* (Minneapolis: Fortress, 1993).

32. Burke, "Christian Salvation," 178.

33. Gutiérrez, *We Drink from Our Own Wells*, 102-3.

34. Virgilio Elizondo, *Galilean Journey: The Mexican-American Promise* (Maryknoll, N.Y.: Orbis Books, 1983), 49.

35. Virgilio Elizondo, "Elements for a Mexican American Mestizo Christology," *Voices from the Third World* 11 (December 1988): 105.

36. Douglas Edwards, "The Socio-Economic and Cultural Ethos of the Lower Galilee in the First Century: Implications for the Nascent Jesus Movement," in *The Galilee in Late Antiquity*, ed. L. Levine (Cambridge, Mass.: Harvard University Press, 1992), 54.

37. Richard A. Horsley, *Galilee: History, Politics, People* (Valley Forge, Pa.: Trinity, 1995), 241.

38. Elizondo, "Elements for a Mexican American Mestizo Christology," 105.

39. Sean Freyne, "Galilee," in *The Oxford Companion to the Bible*, ed. Bruce M. Metzger and Michael David Coogan (New York: Oxford University Press, 1993). See also Freyne's *Jesus: A Jewish Galilean* (New York: T&T Clark, 2004).

40. As I will discuss in greater detail below with regard to Elizondo's work, it is important to distinguish between a racial-ethnic interpretation and a theological interpretation of Galilee, since the former has a tragic history in Western intellectual and political circles. In other words, I am in no way denying that Galilee was thoroughly Jewish ethnically; what I am suggesting is that its proximity to and history of domination by Roman and Hellenistic cultures (i.e., its character as a borderland) became theologically and soteriologically identified with what Freyne describes as "the newness of Jesus' vision," a newness that—like most newness—was perceived as dangerous and threatening by the centers of power, whether Roman or Jewish.

41. Richard A. Horsley, *Archaeology, History, and Society in Galilee: The Social Context of Jesus and the Rabbis* (Valley Forge, Pa.: Trinity Press International, 1996), 63.

42. Ibid., 122.

43. Jonathan Draper, "Jesus and the Renewal of Local Community in Galilee: Challenge to a Communitarian Christology," *Journal of Theology for Southern Africa* 87 (June 1994): 35-36.

44. Horsley, *Archaeology*, 173.

45. Alejandro García-Rivera, *St. Martín de Porres: The "Little Stories" and the Semiotics of Culture* (Maryknoll, N.Y.: Orbis Books, 1995), 1-3; Martin D. Stringer, *A Sociological History of Christian Worship* (Cambridge: Cambridge University Press, 2005), 150ff.

46. William A. Christian, Jr., "Spain in Latino Religiosity," in *El Cuerpo de Cristo: The Hispanic Presence in the U.S. Catholic Church*, ed. Peter Casarella and Raúl Gómez (New York: Crossroad, 1998), 326-327.

47. Gary Macy, "Demythologizing 'the Church' in the Middle Ages," *Journal of Hispanic/Latino Theology* 3, no. 1 (August 1995): 27.

48. Orlando Espín, *Faith of the People: Theological Reflections on Popular Catholicism* (Maryknoll, N.Y.: Orbis Books, 1997), 117.

49. Ibid., 119.

50. Orlando Espín, "Pentecostalism and Popular Catholicism: The Poor and Traditio," *Journal of Hispanic/Latino Theology* 3, no. 2 (November 1995): 19.

51. María Rosa Menocal, *La joya del mundo: musulmanes, judíos y cristianos, y la cultura de la tolerancia en al-Andalus* (Barcelona: Plaza y Janés, 2004), 24.

52. Espín, "Pentecostalism and Popular Catholicism," 19.

53. Avery Dulles, *Models of the Church* (Garden City, N.Y.: Doubleday, 1987), 36; quoted in Gary Macy, "Demythologizing 'the Church,'" 27.

54. Ibid., 27-32, 38.

55. Ibid., 35.

56. John W. O'Malley, *Trent and All That: Renaming Catholicism in the Early Modern Era* (Cambridge, Mass.: Harvard University Press, 2000).

57. Macy, "Demythologizing 'the Church,'" 40.

58. Stringer, *Sociological History*, 48.

59. Ibid., 150.

60. Ibid., 36, 48, 164-65.

8

Transforming Ecclesiology

Hip-Hop Matters

Harold J. Recinos

The scandal of sin in a violently divided world raises a number of questions for the church's future: Does the church have a future? How will the church interpret its mission in crucified realities? What vision of society will the church serve? Will crucified people have good news delivered to them? Will those dying before their time under oppressive systems of life know life? Will the blind to human suffering learn to see? Will people in the pews hear the cries of the sick and beaten down? The crucified Lord who became flesh in a wretched and excluded neighborhood expects the church to continue his mission among crucified people who yearn for renewal in their lives and communities.

As mainline Protestant churches struggle to understand their identity in the twenty-first century, the ongoing passion of Christ in the world clarifies the meaning and purpose of their ecclesial authority. Jesus' preaching of inclusive community, freedom from dividing hostilities, and relationship with people despised in accordance with the cultural norms of society landed him on the cross. Today, mainline Protestant church leaders are reminded in the barrio that Jesus on the cross dies as one who was rejected by powerful leaders and the institutions governing society. The cross should be at the very center of the mainline Protestant church's Christian identity, which would raise members' awareness of the experience of ultimate exclusion. When the cross is at the center of the church's identity its public witness never turns away from crucified people nor discredits their effort to create peace with justice in the world.

The church is only faithful to the Crucified One when it walks with the forgotten and plundered of the world. The Puerto Rican single mothers who taught me to take seriously the symbol of the cross for my Christian identity raised a generation of children that gave birth to a street style of prophetic witness—hip-hop culture—that offers renewing possibilities for the life of mainline Protestant churches. Although the wider society thinks barrio youth are uniquely lawless, reckless, and threatening, these young people at the edges of society who are systematically disadvantaged by poverty, inadequate education, and discrimination produced a hip-hop culture to give voice to their vision about how to live in a less crucifying world.

In what follows, I will discuss hip-hop culture from its origin on the streets of the South Bronx to the way it offers up the experience of crucified youth and their way of voicing social, political, and cultural criticism in society. I will show how youth feelings of agency and alienation from the wider culture proposes new ways of thinking about the meaning of the mainline Protestant church and alternative thinking that turns out a culture of questioning. I will discuss youth in our wider youth-marginalizing culture, highlighting certain societal functions that negatively impact the activism and identity of youth. I will also argue that mainline Protestant churches can find God in the details of hip-hop culture, which is a public site of learning that provides a voice to voiceless youth—a voice that offers renewal for Christian experience.

Context of Youth Culture

Anthropologist Clifford Geertz notes that one of the most significant aspects about the human condition is that "we all begin with the natural equipment to live a thousand kinds of life but end in having lived only one."[1] As I think about this very basic insight, I cannot help but wonder what it is that shapes the lives of young people and causes them to choose certain paths in life over others. I am concerned that we know too little about what it means for youth to develop their lives in a society that sees basic freedoms abridged, social problems criminalized, the helping functions of society declining, and a government imagined as a protector from crazed terrorists expanding policing functions.[2] I am also concerned with the many ways that youths are denied a hearing within the larger culture of the United States and their voices of dissent against militarism, racism, and economic exploitation are mostly ignored in the church.

We have good reason to worry about how young people are growing up in American society. They are growing up with mass murder and drugs in schools, entertained by violence and crime on television and film, increasingly aware of the lies they inherit from society, impatient with the political deceit and corruption of elected officials, misdirected by a capitalist culture, dying of AIDS, manipulated to back an unnecessary war in Iraq, and misinterpreted by adults who exclude them from conversations about the future and the responsibilities youth will one day have for "society"; indeed, as Henry Giroux noted, "if not represented as a symbol of fashion or hailed as a hot niche, youth are often portrayed as a problem, a danger to adult society or, even worse, irrelevant to the future."[3]

Youth are not a "generation of suspects," who disserve to be silenced, discounted, and prevented from negotiating the uncomfortable truths of their society. Youth are cultural actors whose social and cultural practices need to be taken seriously by adult society. In the 1960s, the racial justice movements and the antiwar movement showed young people playing major roles in the project of renewing the moral outlook of adult society. They challenged social values and practices at home and abroad in light of a vision of shared responsibility for creating a more just world. Youth are today finding ways to make history by telling adult society that life together should not be constructed from a vision of shared fear, but by way of a culture of questioning. But first let's briefly chart the U.S. cultural terrain of young lives, then explore the meaning of youth cultural agency.

The world young people live in is changing in ways that challenge the assumption that modernization and scientific rationality will replace religious worldviews and result in the decline of the role of religion in society and in the mind of individuals.[4] Religion has not been driven out of modern life; instead, religion has established new and various alliances with culture. For those who yet question national and global religious resurgence and insist that religion is in decline, the evidentiary base says: religion matters. In terms of this revised secularist view, some religious sociologists yet argue religious decline varies across Western societies.[5] What we know for certain in the United States is religious beliefs and practices over the last fifty years have changed as reflected by individual concern to reevaluate the meaning of the sacred.[6]

As the church loses its spiritual monopoly over believers, individuals deepen their religious life by visiting new age bookshops, inventing new languages of faith, or picking up clues about spiritual life in films, television, and on the internet.[7] Youth are not only growing up in a world where religion matters, but their religious sensibilities are not limited to any one place or spiritual tradition. Young people are growing up in a society that considers finding God in the details of popular culture important; indeed, the messages they receive is that a way to remain open to the sacred is to pay attention to the complex variety of religious possibilities available in human experience. Lynn Schofield Clark cautions, however, that openness and tolerance to the plurality of religious experience does not necessarily lead young people to desire knowledge and understanding of difference.[8]

Nonetheless, barrio youth who produced hip-hop culture have unfolded a deeper understanding of difference and lofty notions of human community. The hip-hop culture that began with youth of color in post-industrial New York City has become a powerful source of youth identity and social criticism. As an international cultural style now, hip-hop was from the beginning drenched with youth agency and a creative questioning of the commonly held value system of U.S. culture and religion.[9] If baby boomer parents today lament the death of Abbie Hoffman, Allen Ginsberg, Jerry Garcia, Jerry Rubin, William Burroughs, Timothy Leary, and Jimi Hendrix, they should celebrate the new counterculture in the making, which is more multiracial and gender inclusive than was their own. For the ever-evolving and complex constituency of this youth popular culture, hip-hop matters for young people who desire to articulate their theological and political sensibilities in the landscape of prophetic political witness.

Economic and Political Context Faced by Youth

I earlier argued that the new religious climate in U.S. society changes the way young people appropriate religious meaning, but what of the economic and political context of growing up in the United States? Youth are growing up at a time in American society when political leadership celebrates the triumphs of the marketplace, while the economic prospects of most young people grow dimmer. From the moment that the concept of the teenager was socially invented in the first half of the twentieth century until arguably the baby boomer generation, Americans expected that the next generation would do better, but free-market logic produces economic conditions for youth telling a grim story. Among industrialized countries, the United States ranks seventeenth among industrial nations in efforts to lift children and youth out of poverty.[10]

Governmental policies that allow a relative handful of private interests to control most of social life fuels the growing social and economic inequalities that youth experience in their daily lives. For instance, political policies such as lowering taxes on the wealthiest 1 percent of the population, deregulating environmental protections, transferring public funds to the defense industry, and divestment in public education help maximize the personal profits of a small wealthy class. Observing the social conditions of children and youth created by these political policies, a Children's Defense Fund study noted,

> The Bush administration's budget choices before and after September 11th leaves millions of children behind; favor powerful corporate interests and the wealthiest taxpayers over children's urgent needs; widens the gap between rich and poor—already at its largest recorded point in over 30 years; and repeatedly breaks promises and fails to seize opportunities to Leave No Child Behind. While thousands of children, parents, and grandparents stand in unemployment and soup kitchen and homeless shelter lines waiting for food and a stable place to live all across America . . .[11]

Subsequently, economically marginal young people appear to share the assumption that pulling back on hope is the correct thing to do in a society that favors the economic interests of the rich and whose political leaders wrongly say the marketplace will eventually spread the spoils of the good life.

Youth in the United States are growing up in a profit-driven society where millions of individuals who live in the shadow of prosperity experience life as a period between suffering and death. Sadly, the profit-motive logic encourages youth and adults to turn their attention away from schools to malls and the loud message that there is no alternative to the status quo. Because market fundamentalism places a premium on buying and selling and producing citizen consumers, it devalues the democratic culture championed by schools, civic organizations, churches, neighborhood associations, and voluntary associations of various kinds that interact in the public square. As one educator concerned with the dangers of living in a profit-driven society observed, "it is difficult to understand how democratic values are deepened and expanded in a society in which . . . the typical American now works 350 hours more per year than a typical European— almost nine full weeks. Under such conditions, parents are not only working longer, they are also spending less time with their children than they did 40 years ago." One can see why social critiques argue that the cultural transformations facilitated by the current wave of antidemocratic market fundamentalism are felt most greatly by children and youth.[12]

If youth are growing up in a society driven by market relations *über alles,* they are also maturing in a society guided by aggressive global militarism and a blind nationalism defined by uncritical allegiance to government authority. The organized political activism that upheld the deepest values of our democratic tradition and expanded the right to vote, women's rights, civil rights, labor rights, and the rights of racial minorities appears to be, or *is* even, disfavored by the opulent elite of U.S. society. As a context of learning, political society teaches young people today that citizenship or community "demands not courage, dialogue, and responsibility, but silence and complicity";[13] indeed, elite resistance is thrown into high gear whenever popular struggle that takes seriously the political idea of the public good seeks to expand people's claim on public life.

Youth who feel demoralized and powerless under the weight of our society's economic and political culture are, I am glad to say, not entirely silenced. They are not taking a seat beside passive and apathetic adults; instead, they talk back to those in power who are promoting a culture of fear, consumerism, and abdication of public responsibility for government. Drawing on the resources of popular cultural forms such as hip-hop, a growing number of youth across various racial and ethnic communities finds a message that says that the path toward constructing a more livable and humane world can be found beyond the terms set by power and privilege. Young people are today more aware that simplistic formulas for social change do not work; but some nurtured by rap music see themselves as agents of social change capable of holding protests to hold America's global power accountable to itself, to youth, and to the larger world.

In short, the political and economic culture framing the youth experience in U.S. society appears to be in need of theological leadership that can address the belligerent nationalism, financial capitalism, intolerant government authority, and new religious sensibilities. In this regard, I think hip-hop's rap music has the potential to offer a new cultural, political, and religious language of questioning and hope that helps youth to think of themselves and the world in a way that is critical of political arrogance, religious hypocrisy, and market relations. Among the messages carried in rap, one finds a strong voice not only in opposition to the existence of the oppressed and suffering and of economic exploitation, but also in support of a more internationally encompassing vision of freedom and human rights. Let us now more closely examine rap music as a resource of social and theological identity for youth.

A Questioning Culture

I want to hold up rap music as a theological resource for youth and a basis for a reformation of Protestant church life, despite the fierce criticism it receives from many subdivisions of society, including from the U.S. Senate in hearings. Hip-hop is blamed for "allegedly fueling violence, drug abuse and a general devolution of character."[14] Critics such as Bill O'Reilly, William Bennett, or C. Delores Tucker who think rap is morally bankrupt ignore the fact that rap music is not monolithic; rather it includes anything from gangsta rap to gospel rap.[15] The critics of rap music who insist that it only reflects a culture of depravity overlook the social and political contexts from which rap music and hip-hop culture emerged.[16] I think what deserves our attention in hip-hop culture are the existential concerns and material conditions expressed in rap music, which provides a voice of social criticism to young people.[17]

As an expression of hip-hop culture, rap music is a powerful cultural practice that evolved from the experience of Puerto Rican and African American youth in their early teens and twenties.[18] The history of rap reflects a social practice of boundary crossing that produced conversation among different classes of people and functioned as a pedagogical text of youth questioning culture. As a mode of social relations, rap music legitimates the kind of knowledge forming the social experience of young people. Although Puerto Rican and African American rappers began their cultural practice excluded from the white, middle class world, white youth eventually embraced and grew up on rap like "kids grow up on Similac."[19] The interethnic and multiracial bridges shaped by rap have implications for how congregations identify theological resources and raise questions from a youth perspective about the present condition of society.[20]

Rap music has been studied from an African American perspective by Anthony Pinn, Evelyn Parker, Cornel West, and Michael Dyson, among others. For these academics rap music is best understood not as a macho, misogynist, homophobic, violent expression of thug culture. West describes early rap as the expression of black youths' disgust with the "selfishness, capitalist callousness, and xenophobia of the culture of adults, both within the hood and society at large."[21] Dyson's book on rapper Tupac Shakur—*Holler if You Hear Me: Searching for Tupac Shakur*—locates Tupac's music in the wider context of post-civil rights sociopolitical culture and the concern with naming injustice.[22] For Parker, rap is a way for African American youth to embrace a wisdom tradition of hope that humanizes black identity; meanwhile, Pinn argues for finding the theological and spiritual importance in rap as a musical form.[23] These black scholars have largely ignored the rich history of African American and Latino cross-cultural exchange that gave rise to rap, however.[24]

The unexpected history unleashed by rap music was born in a fluid multiracial and multicultural space. As a product of youth cultural practices, rap music issued forth in the slums and barrios of New York where African American and Puerto Rican youth gave expression to their collective historical experiences. In the post-civil rights era, rap music developed as an African American and Puerto Rican popular musical genre responding to the conditions of life created by many factors, including dehumanizing Reaganomics; the crack epidemic in the inner city; capital flight and jobs exportation; the decline of public and low-income housing stock and gentrification passed off as urban renewal; the disintegration of inner-city mainline religious life; and the growth of refugee and immigrant communities from Central America and the Caribbean due to U.S. support of military regimes and economic policy. Early black and Latino rappers were street prophets who angrily contested the U.S. racial, economic, and global order. Their prophetic stance shouted on barrio streets was precisely the vision that was lacking in their neighborhood churches.

In many ways, rap music is a way to challenge more established narratives about youth self-identity and the prevailing system of power and privilege. Rap contributes to listeners critical liberating discourse that "keeps it real" by speaking about racism, sexism, broken families, economic injustice, police brutality, and the search for spiritual meaning. As the gains of the civil rights movement eroded, black political rappers such as Queen Latifah, Public Enemy, and KRS offered messages of cultural resistance. Lawrence Parker, or KRS-One, the Brooklyn-born rapper in "Take It To God" even sang a gospel rap that stated "change is gonna come, where you goin' to run, but to God?"[25] In the 1980s, Afrika Bambaataa and Soul Sonic Force, Run-DMC, and others also rapped about topics like racism, nuclear proliferation, and apartheid.[26]

Although the Latino influence on rap music is largely disregarded by established African American scholarship and mainstream media, rap music or hip-hop culture cannot be limited to the genius of black youth filling public space; rather, it is part of a more extensive multiracial and cross-cultural field of social practice that disallows a biracial reading of it. Juan Flores notes, "Latin rap lends volatile fuel to the cause of multiculturalism in our society, at least in the challenging, inclusionary sense." Early Latino rappers in groups such as Mean Machine, Cold Crush Brothers, Fearless Four, or individuals such as Kid Frost, Fat Joe, Big Pun, and Mellow Man Ace offered "an ensemble of alternative perspectives and an often divergent cultural ethos into the mainstream of U.S. social life." Latino contributions on the origin and development of hip-hop culture oppose the usual analysis advanced by African American scholars whose work suggests that rap music is black cultural property.[27]

Latino rappers assert their genius by enunciating a way of life and thought for youth rendered invisible by society's black-white normative gaze.[28] The first Latino rapper to go platinum was the late Christopher Rios—known to hip-hop audiences as Big Pun—who died of a heart attack at age twenty-eight. As a major hip-hop personally, Big Pun drew between forty and sixty thousand people to the Ortiz Funeral Home on Westchester Avenue in the South Bronx to pay their last respects. Journalist Raquel Rivera reports that those at his funeral included such figures as "Fat Joe, LLCool J, Lil'Kim, Puff Daddy, Exibit, Mack 10 and Members of MOP . . . [and] . . . an impromptu funeral party erupted outside the funeral home, with hundreds of people dancing and singing to Pun's music blaring from a car."[29]

Big Pun was cremated and there is no tombstone to visit, but on a street just a few blocks away from where I grew up you can find a mural of Big Pun on the half block of Rogers Place between 163rd Street and Westchester Avenue.

Standing in front of it you are reminded that graffiti as a part of hip-hop culture
found on other murals in barrios across America are a way to immortalize the
struggles, pains, and hopes of forgotten people. The mural to Big Pun is visited
by many who leave flowers, light candles, and recite prayers. Big Pun overcame
many barriers and acquired material success, but he continued to live in the
South Bronx and produced rap music that refused to accept any kind of marginality in the hip-hop zone.[30] Big Pun makes it plain that without South Bronx
Puerto Ricans hip-hop would not be recognized in its present form.

Unlike African American rappers such as KRS-One, Tupac, or Ice Cube,
Latino rappers do not always consciously engage in a religiously informed critique of social reality; yet, artists like Prince Whipple Whip, Mellow Man Ace,
Kid Frost, Terror Squad, Fat Joe, and Big Pun challenge churches that fail to
address the bad-news situations of the oppressed/suffering and the despair the
Latino/a poor face each day in American society. Big Pun's lyrics may not give
listeners an explicit gospel rap message, but the crucified reality from which he
sings and the ways individuals are portrayed in their struggle to survive raise
theological questions about how to talk of a loving God in a world where street
violence and a thuggish economic system take away life. The Mexican rapper
"El Pecador," however, explicitly sings about forgiveness in a tune called "Confessions (Hell Don't Pay)":

> Oh lord, all I ask is for forgiveness
> though I live the sinful lifestyle
> hopin that you hear me out right now
> You know the truth ever since I was a little kid
> All the sins I committed evil things that I did
> To live it's kinda hard, in this land of temptation
> Takin it day by day but I still pray for my salvation
> or am I facin total darkness I'm guessin
> Stuck between heaven and earth, still stressin progressin
> to live my life around people with fake smiles
> caught up in the midst of lies betrayal denials
> I've been involved in situations that have let you down
> And I know the things I've done is gonna come back around
> I've been affiliated in a few two elevens
> plus one eight sevens damaging my stairway to heaven
> But I know when the moment comes I'll feel it in my soul
> when it's time for me to go it'll be time for me to low
> And I'll be waitin, waitin, waitin . . .

Chorus

> Make it go away, far away, far away . . .
> Because reality shows that hell don't pay[31]

Today, rap music is the cultural construction of the lived experience of young people from various racial and ethnic backgrounds who refuse to hide the violent, dehumanizing, and life-denying conditions in their reality. Mainstream news outlets kept the public from knowing that a hip-hop conference held at York College in Queens, New York, and a West Coast hip-hop summit gathered African American and Latino rappers, grassroots activists, and public leaders to articulate a hip-hop political agenda over the last few years: literacy campaigns in public schools; antidrug and antiviolence campaigns; voter registration projects;[32] and exposing justice issues related to the prison-industrial complex, capital punishment, and music censorship.[33] Before this campaign got underway, a group of Puerto Rican and black activists called the Welfare Poets was formed to promote political culture with the use of poetry and rap combined with Puerto Rican *Plena* and *Bomba*. Ray Ramirez of the Welfare Poets in a piece called "Subliminal" opposes rappers who glorify thug culture and the importance of cultivating a culture of questioning with his rap:

> As most rappers deal with the subliminal
> Wanna be criminals
> For them being unoriginal is habitual
> But our lyrics are clinical
> Can be a vehicle to cleanse the spiritual
> Apprehend the one dimensional
> Cus of oppression
> We spit with so much aggression
> Have intensive sessions
> Where we're pensive and cover extensive lessons
> And come to the conclusion
> That even with all their expensive weapons
> The only solution
> To improve the situation
> Is revolution . . .
> If we try and all die
> It'll be an improvement
> Can you hear the cries?
> From the blood in my eyes?
> We're not stuck on illusions
> Our death is an institution
> Backed by their constitution
> So what we're doing
> The style we're pursuing
> Making sensitive liberals even more apprehensive
> As conservatives find it even more offensive
> But their intentions to censor this is senseless

Slip right under their detections with a stealth projection
This is a form of health protection
for the uninsured from conception to death
too long after their resurrection
shit—we know their transgressions
understand their deceptions
that's why we continue these transmissions to transform our
　　　conditions
and storm with no forgiveness
on the dawn of our resistance
the mourn of their destruction
we scorn at their corruption
telling the world how they were formed from hell's combustion
forcing you to rebel is our function
don't get sucked into suction
where your freedom is auctioned to elections
your thoughts of progression fall short to magicians
don't believe their superstitions
we've had enough of crucifixions
better believe we're coming with an unseen commitment
so we ain't submitting.[34]

Rap music imagines the inclusive reign of God by giving shape to a visibly linguistic, racial, ethnic, and cultural hip-hop community. As a musical genre of importance to young people, it urges church leaders in monolingual and ethnically homogenous congregations to consider the messages rap music contain about interethnic relations as well as possibilities for worship. As the vernacular language of young people, rap music can serve to help churches keep it real with youth on issues of sex, AIDS, violence, poverty, racism, sexism, police brutality, prison life, multiculturalism, war, politics, and spirituality. In its luxurious diversity, rap music as a type of youth cultural production is a way for mainline Protestant congregations to "sing to God a new song . . . with loud shouts" (Ps 33:3).

Surely, not too few Christians who worship on Sunday morning will ask whether or not rap and gospel, noise and the Word go together. Mark Kline Taylor reminds us that "when rappers tell alternative stories while facing police brutality or prison warehousing of the racially stigmatized poor, depicting the struggle, survival and flourishing of oppressed communities, they conjure spiritual practices for these communities."[35] People in the pews are invited by culturally marginalized youth to understand that rappers who keep it real in "da world" help young people evolve a spiritually prophetic stance not afraid to name the idols of death in the structures of society. Rap is something good from the barrio and the slums, stories about life experiences, perspectives with which to renew church ministry.

In the early days of hip-hop, rappers claimed public space by transforming playgrounds, street corners, and neighborhood parks into contexts for building a sense of community and for shaping collective reflection on political, social, and economic life. Today, hip-hoppers are promoting political engagement, antiracism, economic change, and democratic culture by participating in church life with the aim of shaping a dialogue on justice, equality, and engaged spirituality. One cannot overlook the importance of this development in the life of the church, especially when hip-hoppers like the reemerged Public Enemy are taking on the George W. Bush administration on matters of religion and antiterrorism. Their song, "Son of a Bush," strongly critiques the piety and undemocratic policy of the president,

> The Father, the Son
> and the Holy Bush s——t we all in
> Don't look at me
> I ain't callin' for no assassination
> I'm just sayin' sayin' who voted
> For that asshole of the nation
> Déjà Bush
> Crushed by the head rush
> 15 years back
> when I wrote the first bum rush . . .[36]

Nothing Good Comes from Nazareth
(John 1:43-46)

In the early-twentieth century blues was viewed by "good" church folk as "music taken from the devil"; in the 1950s the counter-culture that evolved around rock 'n' roll would also be demonized, while Tipper Gore's *Washington Post* editorial "Hate, Rape and Rap"[37] suggests that few redeeming qualities are now to be found in rap music. In other words, the mainstream cultural discourse consistently tells us that nothing good comes from the barrio! Yet, these indictments of popular culture and the initial refusal to entertain how it may energize spirituality in the church must be challenged by the church seeking renewal of its life. The Word that became flesh in the stench of a stable opposes mainstream culture's demonization of rap. Rap is something good knocking at the church's door, which comes from today's Nazareth (John 14:3-45).

The Galilean region where Nazareth is located was populated largely by a hardworking, exploited class of people with no obvious contribution to make to intellectual and religious centers of power; yet, Jesus comes from this unexpected place that is restless for liberation, and the world has never since been the same. The theologian Virgilio Elizondo puts it like this, "that God had chosen to become a Galilean underscores the paradox of the incarnation, in which God becomes the despised and lowly of the world . . . God becomes the fool of the world for the sake of the world's salvation."[38] I want to suggest that the barrios and inner cities that gave birth to rap music continue revealing to the mainline church the ongoing incarnation of God among rejected and invisible people—listen to the rappers!

Jesus of Nazareth disclosed a God of life on the streets beyond institutional boundaries; he broke laws on behalf of rejected people; he shared a vision of what people should expect and achieve in life; and he grappled with inequality, worsening economic conditions, the illness of others, interethnic alienation, colonial powers, the silencing of the poor, the rejection of foreigners, children, women, and youth. As Karl Barth observed generations ago, "we do not really know Jesus (the Jesus of the New Testament) if we do not know Him as this poor man, as . . . (if we may risk the dangerous word) partisan of the poor."[39] Rappers appreciate Jesus as the "poor, humble, enigmatic, lonely Jewish preacher who fearlessly defended the cause of the hurt of his society."[40] Jesus, who came from a lousy neighborhood, would not be displeased with rappers who use city streets as performance sites to name reality and work for social change.

I find it remarkable that many of the materially deprived and culturally despised youth who come up with rap music share biographical details with Christ. What do I mean? Well, Jesus, like them, was born to a poor teen mother, was raised in a valueless neighborhood, and lacked institutional credentials for speaking about the world and theology. Jesus, who was maligned, falsely charged, arrested, and killed by the politicians and religious leaders of his day, can yet be found on rappers' streets. Christ in the rapper asks the church to listen to the poor, the alien, the sick, and the put down. The church can experience renewal recognizing the One who comes from Nazareth walks the streets of lousy neighborhoods shouting good news through rappers who say that marginal youth need a space to be human.

Church leadership may appreciate that Jesus dropped lyrical bombshells in his day to give shape to a counter-cultural community organized around new social values: (1) Love your enemies (Matt 5:44; Luke 6:27). (2) If struck on one cheek, offer the other (Matt 5:39; Luke 6:29). (3) Give to everyone who begs (Matt 5:42; Luke 6:30). (4) Judge not and you won't be judged (Matt 7:1; Luke 6:37). (5) First remove the stick from your own eye (Matt 7:5; Luke 6:42). (6) Go out as lambs among wolves (Matt 10:16; Luke 10:3). Or (7) say "The reign of God has come near you" (Matt 10:7; Luke 10:9). In other words, Jesus rapped about subverting a sick society and he *kept it real* about situations of suffering and exploitation revealing the coming reign of God.

Rappers who enable youth to articulate their experience of the world would prefer churches to focus less on filling pews and more on bearing witness to the mystery of Jesus of Nazareth through discipleship aimed at transforming societal institutions that are deaf to crucified people. Today, it may well be that the spirituality conjured by rappers at the edges of society reflects God calling the church to the side for those who are most deprived of life and who seek to "build houses and live in them . . . plant vines and eat their fruit" (Isa 65:21-22). Christians will discover with rappers that there is no greater joy than freely confessing Christ in the service of outsiders, beyond the religious and cultural compound, in places lacking money, security, and comfort, in the service of a mission that claims knowledge of God with society's rejects.

Conclusion

Mainline church leaders would do well to remember how the scriptural narrative shows Jesus relating to people dropping lyrical bombshells to shape an alternative perception of society. There is a great deal for the church to rap about once it fully grasps what kind of good news comes out of Jesus' lousy neighborhood and the many found surrounding affluent communities in America.[41] In the church, rappers as producers of cultural and spiritual identity may help more complacent Christians see that the historical Jesus was "not just a thinker with ideas but a rebel with a cause . . . the embodied Galilean who lived a life of divine justice in an unjust world."[42] Once the mainline church takes serious the rap that feeds the souls of young people it will better understand a resource by which youth manage "the painful contradictions of social alienation and [the] prophetic imagination"[43] in them that sings.

Mainline Christians may conclude that hip-hop can save the church and provide a viable means of spreading the gospel. Mainline churches that continue to look away from the barrio and slums as the source of their renewal of a prophetic imagination should not be surprised when rappers show up on their steps saying the words of Isaiah: "You may multiply your prayers, I shall not listen. Your hands are covered with blood" (1:15).[44] All the proper Christians attending church on Sunday morning and fond of the old hymns may benefit from recollecting that the great reformer of the church, Martin Luther, did theology in taverns; hence, hip-hop churches are today a way for young people to evolve a spirituality that engages their experience and addresses the reality defining their lives.

In the first century, a poor Jesus was born in the stench of a stable; today, rappers born and raised at the edges of society and forming part of the church know Christ is crucified with the people in the barrios and slums. When the gospel and hip-hop conjure spirituality, the mainline church can expect renewal to result in: (1) a discipleship that embraces Jesus' option for the poor and crucified people; (2) the development of Christian life according to a prophetic stance that empowers young people to insert themselves in society; (3) a public witness by the church in service to those who lack money, security, and comfort; (4) the discovery of God present in people degraded by power elites; and (5) continuing Jesus' ministry of radically transforming the unjust structures of life in accordance with a new vision for society.

Notes

1. Clifford Geertz, *The Interpretation of Culture* (New York: Basic Books, 1973), 45.

2. Henry A. Giroux, *The Abandoned Generation: Democracy Beyond the Culture of Fear* (New York: Palgrave, 2003).

3. Ibid., xiv.

4. Peter Berger, "The Desecularization of the World," in *The Desecularization of the World: Resurgent Religion and World Politics*, ed. Peter Berger (Grand Rapids, Mich.: Eerdmans, 1999), 2.

5. Stephen Hunt, *Religion in Western Society* (New York: Palgrave, 2002), 23.

6. See especially Robert Wuthnow, *After Heaven: Spirituality in America since the 1950s* (Berkeley: University of California Press, 1998); and Wade Clark Roof, *Spiritual Marketplace: Baby Boomers and the Remaking of American Religion* (Princeton, N.J.: Princeton University Press, 1999).

7. See especially Eric Michael Mazur and Kate McCarthy, eds., *God in the Details: American Religion in Popular Culture* (New York: Routledge, 2001).

8. Lynn Schofield Clark, *From Angels to Aliens: Teenagers, the Media, and the Supernatural* (New York: Oxford University Press, 2003), 228.

9. Mary Bucholtz, "Youth and Cultural Practice," in *Annual Review of Anthropology* 31 (2002): 525-52.

10. Giroux, *Abandoned Generation*, xvii.

11. Children's Defense Fund, *The State of Children in America's Union: A 2002 Action Guide to Leave No Child Behind* (Washington, D.C.: Children's Defense Fund Publication, 2002), v.

12. Henry A. Giroux, "Neo-liberalism and the Disappearance of the Social in Ghost World," *Third Text* 17, no. 2 (2003): 151. See also Cornel West, *Democracy Matters: Winning the Fight against Imperialism* (New York: Penguin, 2004); and Noam Chomsky, *Profit over People: Neoliberalism and Global Order* (New York: Seven Stories Press, 1999).

13. Giroux, *Abandoned Generation*, 4.

14. Heidi A. Hendershott, *"School of Rap: The Politics and Pedagogies of Rap Music"* (Ph.D., diss., Pennsylvania State University, 2004), 22.

15. See Anthony Pinn, ed., *Noise and Spirit: The Religious and Spiritual Sensibilities of Rap Music* (New York: New York University Press, 2003).

16. Ibid., 25.

17. Early rap music provided a commentary on inner-city life, including topics such as growing unemployment, drugs and violence, poverty, and the disintegration of social relationships among the people who daily faced hard conditions of life. The observational rap music that initially came out of the South Bronx in no uncertain terms made it clear that the barrios and slums were nothing less than an "ethnoracial prison" where structural conditions of life in a racist society assured diminished life-chances for making it.

18. Rap music is part of a wider so-called Hip Hop culture, which includes dancing, graffiti, fashion, and stylized speech.

19. Raquel Z. Rivera, *New York Ricans from the Hip Hop Zone* (New York: Palgrave, 2003), 171.

20. Although a great deal of ink has been used to explain rap music as an exclusively black American ethno-musical innovation, not only was it the product of black and Puerto Rican youths, but I think it is best understood as the expression of the "cultural

hybridity" of the postindustrial urban world. In other words, rap is not strictly speaking black music nor Puerto Rican music; rather, it is the sound of a multiracial, multicultural, and multilinguistic world.

21. West, *Democracy Matters*, 179.

22. Michael Eric Dyson, *Holler if You Hear Me: Searching for Tupac Shakur* (New York: Basic Civitas Books, 2001).

23. Evelyn Parker, "Singing Hope in the Key of Wisdom: Wisdom Formation of Youth," in *In Search of Wisdom: Faith Formation in the Black Church*, ed. Anne Streaty Wimberly and Evelyn L. Parker (Nashville: Abingdon, 2002); and Anthony Pinn, *The Black Church in the Post-Civil Rights Era* (Maryknoll, N.Y.: Orbis Books, 2002).

24. See especially Anne Streaty Wimberly and Evelyn L. Parker, eds., *In Search of Wisdom: Faith Formation in the Black Church* (Nashville: Abingdon, 2002); and Pinn, *Noise and Spirit*.

25. KRS-One not only innovates gospel rap but understands that being a Christian also means questioning the Bible, the church, and the system of discourse that legitimates life-denying conditions of life.

26. See Jeff Chang, *"Stakes Is High,"* The Nation 276, no. 2, January 13, 2003.

27. Juan Flores, *From Bomba to Hip-Hop: Puerto Rican Culture and Latino Identity* (New York: Columbia University Press, 2000), 137.

28 Today, rap musicians are not simply Puerto Rican and African American as in the mostly South Bronx-based days; now you will find white middle-class and working-class rappers and rappers in other countries as well.

29. Rivera, *New York Ricans*, 174.

30. See ibid., 175-76.

31. The Mexakins, "Confessions (Hell Don't Pay)" in *The Mexakins* (1996), lyrics found online at http://www.lyricsbox.com/tha-mexakinz-lyrics-confessions-hell-dont-pay-1nd2pd2.html.

32. The 2004 elections inspired the National Hip-Hop Political Convention in Newark, N.J.

33. Manning Marable, "The Politics of Hip-Hop," Worker BRC News, available online at http://www.hartford-hwp.com/archives/45a/594.html.

34. Used by permission from Ray Ramirez, "Subliminal"; member, Welfare Poets.

35. Mark Kline Taylor, "Bringing Noise, Conjuring Spirit," in *Noise and Spirit*, 119.

36. "Son of a Bush," lyrics available at http://www.publicenemy.com.

37. Tipper Gore, "Hate, Rape and Rap," *Washington Post,* January 8, 1990.

38. Virgilio Elizondo, *Galilean Journey* (Maryknoll, N.Y.: Orbis Books, 1990), 53.

39. Karl Barth, *Church Dogmatics,* IV/2 (Edinburgh: T&T Clark, 1958), 180. The German original was published in 1955.

40. Orlando Costas, *Christ Outside the Gate* (Maryknoll, N.Y.: Orbis Books, 1984), 4.

41. Rap services are taking place in various cities and small towns across the country (e.g., Lawndale Community Church in Chicago and Even Redeemer Lutheran Church in Minneapolis, among others; evangelical rap group 3 Shades of Faith is popular with songs such as "Flipside." The group is made up of three Harlem teens: Tykym Stallings, whose stage name is Malakai; Lamar Haney, known as Noah; and Michael Sims, who goes by Mic. 3).

42. John Dominic Crossan, *The Birth of Christianity: Discovering What Happened in the Years Immediately after the Execution of Jesus* (San Francisco: HarperSanFrancisco, 1998), xxx.

43. Tricia Rose, "A Style Nobody Can Deal With," in *Microphone Fiends: Youth Music and Youth Culture*, ed. Andrew Ross and Tricia Rose (New York: Routledge, 1994), 71.

44. At the Brooklyn-based Love Fellowship Tabernacle Church, the Rev. Hezekiah Walker, thirty-five, attracts such worshipers as Sean Combs, Foxy Brown, and hip-hop gospel duo Mary Mary for his hip-hop services.

9

Kin-dom of God

A Mujerista Proposal

ADA MARÍA ISASI-DÍAZ

The implications of calling oneself a Christian are enormous. At the heart of this designation lies the commitment to live one's life according to the Gospel message. What is this message all about? What are the demands the Gospel message makes on us? How can we, living two thousand years after the Gospels were written, use them to set our moral and ethical compass? How can we, living in a vastly different world from the one in which Jesus lived, use the Gospels as a guide in determining our values—what we consider to be right or wrong, good or bad?

Appropriation of the Gospel message is not a simple task as it greatly depends on the intersection of biblical interpretation and ethics. Biblical interpretation, using an ever-growing number of exegetical tools, attempts to bring us as close as possible to the meaning the writers of the Gospels intended and how the original communities for whom they were written understood them. The exegetical task in itself is an interpretative one that necessitates an ideological-theological disclosure or an "ethics of interpretation" that reveals the worldview of the biblical scholar.[1]

Valid appropriation does not stop with the internal ethics that must guide the exegetical task. Bringing the biblical text to bear on present-day reality also demands a conscientious use of ethics. Biblical understandings have to pass through ethics, that is, through a critical evaluation of the values and the

I dedicate this article to my mother on her ninety-seventh birthday. It is from her that I have learned the importance of family and its role in bringing about justice. I want to thank Dr. Melanie Johnson-DeBaufre, my colleague at Drew School of Theology, for conversations about this article and for valuable suggestions of books and articles. My gratitude also to Chung Hwan Kim, a Ph.D. candidate at Drew and my research assistant for the last three years, and to Dr. Ernest Rubinstein, Drew Theological School Librarian.

obligations such understandings endorse. From the Bible we can gather certain principles, values, and ideals, but the application of the Bible to daily life is not direct but proceeds by way of analogy. The ethical turn in this situation is an exercise in analogical thinking, stretching language to fit new situations and circumstances, relying "on imagination and the ability to discern similarities and differences" between the contemporary situation and the biblical one.[2] The question to ask of the Gospels today (and always), is not, What would Jesus do if he were here facing the situation I am facing? Such a question reveals an attempt to "apply" rather than to "appropriate" the Scriptures and bypasses, I believe, taking responsibility for the moral values and norms that guide us in our everyday lives. The question always is, What am I to do, given what I believe to be the central message of the Gospels? This question indicates how each one of us specifically and personally—though not in isolation—is implicated in how we use the Scriptures. Only then can we talk about a responsible appropriation of the Gospels that marks an adult Christian faith, a responsible faith that plays a role in how we live in our present historical reality.

"Kingdom of God"— A Metaphor for "World-Order"

Are there compelling arguments for using different metaphors from those used in the Gospels? Grounded in the generally accepted dictum that all theology and biblical studies follow ethics—that is, that theology and biblical studies cannot assert unethical understandings—this article argues that in the opening decades of the twenty-first century there are important reasons to use a metaphor other than "kingdom of God."[3] "Kingdom of God," though used by the writers of the Gospels and very probably by Jesus himself, needs to be rethought. For a variety of reasons, it does not work today as it seemingly did in first-century Palestine. On the contrary, the use of this metaphor throughout history and to this very day endorses understandings that counter the values that can be ascertained from the Gospels.

Since we have referred to analogical appropriation of the Bible, it is important to understand the difference between using a term or situation analogically and the use of metaphors. Analogical thinking does not necessitate a "latent model." It simply depends "on the recognition that the term employed is of sufficient generality to be appropriate in the new context."[4] However, since metaphors offer figurative usage "that generates new perspectives,"[5] one of the main considerations when working with metaphors is how language fits that to which the metaphor refers. While analogies stretch meaning, metaphors refer to a given model, important for understanding and relevance. My contention is that the analogical thinking that guides the use of the Gospels in our daily life is impeded or made less rich by the use of "kingdom of God," a metaphor that, at best, has little relevancy in our twenty-first century lives.

Metaphors are figures of speech, that is, a mode of language that expands meaning. When using metaphors one is not embracing a literal reference but thinking in terms of the understandings communicated by the metaphor. Metaphors are not deviations or distractions from what is being said. Rather they signal meanings that might not be clear without reference to a predetermined— better known—subject. Metaphors guide us into imagining, into the realm of the psychological, always limited by the similarities they invoke or evoke between what is being talked about and that to which it is being compared. Metaphors use subjects that are well known to explain and to help us grasp what is beyond our own experience. The metaphor "kingdom of God" uses what was common knowledge in the time of Jesus, the dominant world order, to indicate that of which the followers of Jesus had no direct experience: a world order in which justice and peace are central.[6]

"Kingdom" in the Gospels functions as a catachresis, that is, it is a term used for a reality for which there was no term. This reality, "God's world order," was and is out of the realm of human experience. Therefore, the Gospels cannot talk about it directly but have to use imagery—metaphors, similes, and parables—to talk about it. That is what is at play, for example, in the parables of the mustard seed, of the sower, of the yeast, and of the woman sweeping to find a gold coin.

However, "kingdom of God" functions as a "tensive symbol," a symbol having meaning for people in cultural continuity with ancient Israel and its myth of God acting as king, a cultural community in which Jesus certainly stood."[7] But the metaphor "kingdom of God" does not have as a referent the actual kingdoms Jesus and his followers knew from their own history (Egypt, Babylon, Persia, and their own kingdom of Israel), nor does it refer to a governmental set-up, but rather "kingdom of God" refers to the wider social, economic, and political realities that constituted *lo cotidiano*—the everyday of the people of Palestine in the first century C.E.[8] "Kingdom of God" focuses on the values at play in *lo cotidiano* and how those values are to be lived by the followers of Jesus.

A "good metaphor may not simply be an oblique reference to a predetermined subject but a new vision, the birth of a new understanding, a new reference access. A strong metaphor compels new possibilities of vision."[9] Jesus and the New Testament writers used "kingdom of God" to evoke "a complex symbolic vision of an alternative 'order of things' that stands in contrast to and contests with the dehumanizing and oppressive orders of the Roman imperial context."[10] It is, then, in keeping with what Jesus/the Gospels' writers did to communicate a message (use "kingdom" to refer to a world order different from the dominant one) for us today to use other metaphors that better communicate that message. Since the task we have is not to repeat Jesus and/or the Gospels' words but to appropriate them, a different metaphor from "kingdom" would be, I propose, a new reference that enables us today to better understand and value the Gospel message regarding the kind of societal and personal "order" that Jesus envisioned and wanted his followers to have and concretize in their lives.

The metaphor "kingdom of God" is *not*, therefore, the only possible account one can give of the world order Jesus insisted on proclaiming to the point of dying for it. Jesus himself ran into problems regarding how his usage of "the kingdom of God" was understood. His closest followers repeatedly understood "kingdom of God" as a direct reference to a governmental model rather than as a metaphor for a new world order. The author of Acts relates how Jesus' disciples, obviously misinterpreting what he meant by "kingdom of God," asked him, "Lord, is this the time when you will restore the kingdom of Israel?" (Acts 1:6). This misunderstanding is also why his disciples asked whether they should use their swords to defend him at the time of Jesus' arrest (Matt 26:51-53; Mark 14:47; Luke 22:49-51; John 18:10-11). The erroneous understanding of "kingdom of God" is at play in Jesus' exchange with Pilate, the reason given for Jesus' execution, and the mockery of the Roman soldiers (Matt 27:11-31; Mark 15:1-20; Luke 22:63-23:3; John 18:33-38). It also is at play in the request of the mother of the sons of Zebedee for her sons to be given important positions "in your kingdom" (Matt 22:20-28; Luke 10:35-45).[11]

To better grasp what Jesus and the authors of the Gospels had in mind when they used "kingdom," one has to look at the context in which "kingdom" is used, that is, by the overall understandings that emerge from the Gospels as a whole.[12] There is no definition of the "kingdom of God" in the Gospels.[13] What is meant by "kingdom of God" emerges from the teachings of Jesus and the way he lived his life.

In Mark 1:14-15 there is a clear-cut statement of the "kingdom of God," that plainly indicates that it is good news, at least for those who had gathered around John the Baptist, and that Jesus is talking about something that is becoming a reality right there and then. Undoubtedly there is an eschatological tension in this announcement: the "kingdom of God" is here but not yet fully so. However, this tension points more to the Jewish concept of history as "moving forward under God's guidance toward a goal" than delaying the "kingdom" until a later date. This tension also indicates the interplay of God and human beings in bringing about the "kingdom of God." Following what seems to be a general understanding of biblical theology we can indeed say that the "kingdom" is not "directly constructible, much less controllable by men [sic]." Movements, systems, political and social institutions, and personal deeds that make possible and uphold the characteristics of the "kingdom" delineated in the Gospels can be considered "eschatological glimpses" of the "kingdom" but they are not the "kingdom." They might be considered to "hasten the coming of kingdom," "remove obstacles," "to prepare the world for the kingdom," but they are not the "kingdom of God."[14]

One can conclude, therefore, particularly in the texts indicated above that refer to Jesus' arrest and the official reason for his execution, that "kingdom" for him and/or for the writers of the Gospels is not used as a way of describing the world order that existed in Palestine at the time of Jesus and the early communities of Jesus' followers. The "kingdom of God" metaphor in the Gospels refers to a new kind of world order. Jesus used this metaphor in order to make clear the social and political implications of his message. He used a term that was understood by his audience. "Kingdom of God" refers to a world order that can be cogently understood by studying the parables, other forms of preaching Jesus used, and the miracles he worked, rather than by thinking of different actual kingdoms that Jesus and his followers knew from their history (that is, Egypt, Babylon, Persia, their own kingdom of Israel as an independent political unit, or the one they experienced daily, the Roman Empire).

Why Another Metaphor?

One cannot reduce the message of the Gospels concerning Jesus' life-project to the sole metaphor of "kingdom of God." In order to elucidate what Jesus meant, I contend, we have to use other metaphors, other ways of speaking about the world order that he was willing to die for. One might be uneasy, leery, or even wary about offering metaphors other than the ones used in the Gospels. But these metaphors are *not* indispensable or unrevisable.[15] One important reason for introducing other metaphors instead of "kingdom" has to do with the misuse of "kingdom" that has led to negative—immoral—consequences. A second reason from a *mujerista* perspective has to do with its lack of relevancy for Latinas/os and the goal of *mujerista* theology and ethics.[16]

"Kingdom of God" throughout History

The concept of the "kingdom of God" has undergone many transformations since it was first used by the Jewish people. Initially it was a concept based on the kingships that surrounded them. First Samuel indicates this clearly. God explains that Israel is not to be a kingdom like the other ones that existed at the time. It was to be a society held together not by a king but by their beliefs, which signaled a very specific way of life. But the people insisted on asking Samuel for a king so they could be like all those around them: "We are determined to have a king over us, so that we also may be like other nations" (1 Sam 8:19-20). The kingdom of Israel lasted but a hundred years from ca. 1030 to ca. 930 B.C.E. It then divided into Israel in the north and Judah in the south until ca.720 B.C.E. when Israel fell to Assyria. The Jewish people who lived in this northern kingdom never returned as a group to the land they had occupied. Judah fell to the Babylonian Empire in 586 B.C.E. In 538 B.C.E. the Persians conquered Babylonia and allowed the people of the southern kingdom of Judah, who had been exiled to Babylonia, to return to their land while remaining subjects of the Persian Empire. In 331 B.C.E., when Alexander the Great conquered the Persians, Israel, a name that has referred from then on to the people of the kingdom of Judah, became part of his empire. After changing hands several times, Israel fell to the Romans when Pompey conquered Jerusalem.[17] This history is the immediate referent for the term "kingdom of God" founded in the Gospels.

Perhaps influenced by the Assyrians, by the time of Jesus, Israel's under-standing of the "kingdom of God" had begun to have "a transcendent feel." Originally this understanding of transcendence "did not mean that the expec-tations of the kingdom became any less rooted in this earth and the present time."[18] An earthly rooted understanding of the "kingdom of God" is what many scholars consider the main one found in the message of Jesus as recorded in the Gospels.[19] This message was influenced not only by the history of the Jew-ish people, but, perhaps much more directly, by the actual political situation of Galilee and Judea in the time of Jesus.

As a "client state" of the Roman Empire, Israel maintained its own kings but they had little political power. By the time Jesus started his itinerant preaching, Herod the Great had died and Palestine had been divided among his sons. Galilee was ruled until 39 C.E. by Herod Antipas as a client king of the Roman Empire. Judea was ruled by another of the sons of Herod the Great, Archelaus for only nine years; and then he was deposed by Emperor Augustus because of his inability to establish order in the area. Judea became a subprovince of the Roman province of Syria and its prefect, who at the time of Jesus' public life was Pontius Pilate. Pilate worked though the high-priestly houses that controlled the Temple in Jerusalem, depending on them to collect taxes and maintain order.[20] The priestly class made a living by adding to the taxes imposed on the people so they could skim off the top and still send to Rome what was demanded. They focused mainly on the economy of Jerusa-lem, where they lived, increasing the divide between rich and poor—between Jerusalem and the countryside of Judea.

The Gospels give ample evidence of Jesus' struggle against the world order established by the Roman Empire, which its own Jewish strands proposed and upheld by the priestly class and Herod Antipas. Therefore, it seems logical to conclude that what he meant by "kingdom of God" was *not* modeled on either the form of government or on any of the societal—political and/or religious—institutions operating during his lifetime.[21] On the contrary, Jesus' preaching about the "kingdom of God" was a critique of the government and of the ruling classes. It is very possible that the experience Jesus and his followers had of them acted as a foil for the understanding of "kingdom of God" Jesus promoted and not as a referent. In other words, "kingdom of God," as already mentioned, meant precisely the opposite of what Jesus and his followers experienced during their lifetime and referred to a world order that was being made present in the life and teachings of Jesus.

By the end of the first century C.E., however, a clear distinction emerged between this world, its end, and the setting in place of a new world order. In other words, a split was created between this-world reality and the "kingdom of God."

The psychic landscape changed significantly from a circle of hope, committed action, change and back to hope, to divine intervention and unchanging absolutes . . . From that point, engagement with the world became replaced by moral paralysis within it and a desire to flee from it. Instead of being empowering archetypes, the ideas of Messiah and the kingdom of God became theological and political crutches. They were political excuses for nonengagement with the real stuff of life.[22]

The ethical implications of the "kingdom of God" for the Christian life in this world lost relevance for the followers of Jesus with the passing of time. In a way we can say that the "kingdom of God" was kidnapped from this world and taken to a world yet to come. Originally, this move might very well have responded to the need of the Christian communities to protect themselves against the world order of the Roman Empire. They had to emphasize that the "kingdom of God" was not a political threat to the world order of the Roman Empire. The fact is that the "kingdom of God" became heavenly, other-worldly, or eschatological. When in 313 c.e. the Edict of Milan legalized Christianity, the earthly dimensions of the "kingdom of God" began to be correlated with the Roman Empire. Eventually the church became the only access to the "kingdom of God," which was thoroughly entrenched in the world to come.[23]

The church became the most powerful symbol of the "kingdom of God" in this world, a church that placed itself above the reality of this world and insulated itself against the vast majority of its members. The church became identified with the "kingdom of God." Unfortunately the church often has linked its life with the life of the established order, which it grew to resemble more and more. Though it repeatedly claimed that its role was only religious, the church throughout its history has legitimized and supported those with social, economic, and political power. Historically the church has become more and more a tool in the hands of the dominant groups in society, at the service of its world order, instead of proclaiming the "kingdom of God" as a different world order.[24]

In the Catholic Church it was only with the Second Vatican Council in the second half of the twentieth century that one finds meaningful movement in redrawing the meaning of the church and the "kingdom of God." The most relevant statement from the Second Vatican Council concerning the relationship between the natural order and the supernatural order where the "kingdom of God" had been ensconced is found in *Gaudium et Spes* no. 39. The text does not go far enough in relating the growth of the "kingdom of God" to temporal progress, but at least the conciliar document affirms "a close relationship between temporal progress and the growth of the Kingdom . . . Those engaged in the latter not only cannot be indifferent to the former; they must show a genuine interest in and value it." This step taken by Vatican II opened the door for considering theologically "temporal progress as a continuation of the work of creation," and, therefore, for seeing temporal progress as linked to the redemptive act of the life and mission of Jesus of Nazareth.[25]

The theological understanding that "the human work, the transformation of nature, continues creation only if it is a human act, that is to say, if it is not alienated by unjust socioeconomic structures,"[26] developed by Latin American liberation theology, opened the possibility for rescuing the "kingdom of

God" from the supernatural order. Various liberation theologies elaborated in the second half of the twentieth century make it clear that the "kingdom of God" was the expression that Jesus used as the central metaphor for talking about his mission, for which he died on the cross. Every aspect of the life of Jesus related by the Gospels, every word ascribed to Jesus by the Gospels gyrates around the "kingdom of God": "the ultimate for Jesus is God in relationship, rendered explicitly as kingdom." In this Jesus showed himself to be heir of the religious tradition of his people in which "God is never God *in se,* but is always in relationship with history."[27] In what he did and in what he said, Jesus always announced the "kingdom of God" or denounced the antikingdom—that is to say, the actual socioeconomic conditions not only that could not be present in the "kingdom of God" but that make the realization or coming of the "kingdom of God" impossible.

Mujerista *Hermeneutics*

Mujerista hermeneutics is anchored in the goal of *mujerista* theology and eth-ics: fullness of life for Latinas and our communities, that is, liberation for our-selves and our families and friends, which we understand cannot be attained at the expense of others or while others are oppressed. *Mujeristas,* therefore, read Scriptures in an attempt to discern the central Gospel message so as to bet-ter struggle against systems and institutions that are oppressive, that allow the few to live at the expense of the many, of which Latinas form a part. *Mujerista* hermeneutics attempts to contribute to a valid appropriation of the Gospel mes-sage by using the many resources that biblical scholarship has developed and by being clear and forthright about our goal in reading and appropriating the Scriptures. Our use of Scripture has as its goal providing much-needed resources to Latinas and those who stand in solidarity with us for our struggle against oppression and for liberation. Giving authority in our lives to the Gospels is a clear indication that in them we find understandings and values that help us to ever more clearly grasp the most profound meaning of liberation and how we must live to contribute to make fullness of life available to an ever-increasing number of persons in our communities and beyond.[28]

One of the elements of *mujerista* hermeneutics is our preferred future— *proyecto histórico*—which we link to the unfolding of what is called "the kingdom of God." Our preferred future as *mujeristas* is a rejection of present oppressive systems and institutions. Our goal as third world people living in a first world context demands a choice not to partake of the privileges to which we might have access, since they are at the expense of third world people. The centrality of a preferred future in which liberation can flourish shapes *mujerista* hermeneutics in four concrete ways. First, for us all theology, biblical studies, and Christian ethics are a praxis. Our work in all of these fields is a "doing," a way of claiming our right to think, to know critically.[29] This "doing" is a com-munal task not an individual task. It is one that has to be fed and in turn feeds our communities of accountability. Second, for us the theological, biblical, and ethical enterprise is embedded in a "grassroots ecumenism" that skirts traditional doctrinal purity and embraces diversity. Third, part of our struggle in living into our *proyecto histórico* is a systemic one, particularly dealing with the hierarchical, elitist, and authoritarian structures that make it impossible for our preferred future to become a reality. Fourth, we aim to influence the social, political, and economic reality in which we live by rejecting a split between the personal and the political because persons are not individuals but social beings. We look to the day when power will be about enabling instead of about controlling and dominating, and when the most important thing will be for societies to provide what everyone needs to develop fully one's human capabilities.

We began to struggle with *hē basileia tou theou*, most of the time translated as "kingdom of God," less often as "reign of God," over two decades ago. Given the lack of resonance of this metaphor in the lives of Latinas, "kingdom of God" is often spiritualized or is not seen as a reality rooted in history. We have proposed "kin-dom of God" because the Gospel's teachings will be taken into consideration insofar as they resonate with the people.[30] For *mujerista* theologians, therefore, it is of great consequence to present the message of the Gospels using images and languages that find echo in Latina/o lives. Language and images that do not resonate with our community alienate members from what is being communicated and make the Gospel message seem foreign and irrelevant. The opposite is also true. Finding no resonance with *basileia tou theou* can make us feel like outsiders to the Gospel message. The second reason for working to change a metaphor that is irrelevant to our reality has to do with participating in "the ongoing struggle to define Christianity and to shape Christian identity in a changing world."[31] Our attempt to find a metaphor that has resonance with our Latina reality and cultural values, then, is a way for Latinas to take an active role in making relevant the central message of the Gospel and defining its meaning in today's world.

Kin-dom of God

In the late 1970s feminist ethicists, theologians, biblical scholars, and church historians began to grapple with the patriarchal and elitist implications of "kingdom of God." It was within this framework that I first proposed "kin-dom of God," a term I did not create.[32] "Kin-dom" struck a chord with me given the centrality of family in Latina/o culture. Since then I have used the term and have examined the epistemological, hermeneutical, and praxical implications of using *la familia de Dios*—kin-dom of God—instead of "kingdom of God."[33]

To understand kin-dom of God, one has to examine the meaning and importance of family in Latina culture. The exposition that follows is an exercise in an "ethics of interpretation" that discloses the ideological-theological underpinnings of *mujerista* ethics and theology. A study of the understanding of family that can be drawn from the Gospels, reading such an understanding within the socioeconomic and political dynamics of the times of Jesus and his early followers, follows. My attempt is simply to ground the metaphor kin-dom of God in the understandings presented in the Gospels, with the understanding and importance of family in Latina/o communities as its referent, and in view of its importance for living the gospel message, and because of its importance to the *mujerista proyecto histórico*—Latinas' hopes and dreams: our life-project.

Familia *in Latina/o Cultures*

Family is very important in Latina/o culture, so much so, that in our communities we bring into our families all those who are important to us. And those we bring into the family are as much family as those born into the family. Hardly any Latina/o family is without non-blood relatives who have the same duties and privileges as blood relatives. The institution of *compadrazgo* and *comadrazgo* is a system of relationships established between godparents, their godchildren, and the parents of the godchildren. This system reaches beyond religious occasions such as baptisms and confirmations to secular activities and enterprises. Sponsors of dances, businesses, and sports teams are called *madrinas* (godmothers) and/or *padrinos* (godfathers), for they not only provide monetary support but also supply vital connections that protect and promote the well-being of those with whom they are identified. The *compadrazgo* and *comadrazgo* institution creates and sustains an effective infrastructure of interdependence that has the family at the center and extends family values such as unity, welfare, and honor in all directions into the community.

Besides *compadres* and *comadres,* the inclusion of non-blood relatives among Latina/o families is quite common. Only accidentally might one come to know that a child is not a biological daughter or son. If one asks why the silence about this fact, one will be told that it is irrelevant that this child was not born to the family. She or he is family just the same!

One of the difficulties Latinas/os have in the workplace in the United States is that we cannot get time off to take care of emergencies of aunts, uncles, or cousins, because in this country they are not considered immediate family. The Cuban community living in the United States, for example, was incensed when in 2004 the administration of George W. Bush decided to limit visits to Cuba only to those who had parents or children there. The indignation had nothing to do with political ideology. It simply seemed ridiculous to the Cuban community that aunts, uncles, and cousins were not considered by the U.S. government to be immediate family.

The Latina/o understanding of family also plays an important role in political struggles against oppression. In the Zapatista struggle in southern Mexico, for example, when the army was firing on *campesino* communities, the women began to shout, telling the soldiers not to shoot because "*somos de la misma sangre*—we are the same blood." They were appealing to the soldiers to consider that they were family and that being of the same blood trumped any orders the army officers gave them. A similar situation happened in El Salvador. The immediate reason for the assassination of Bishop Oscar Romero in El Salvador in 1980 by the right-wing faction of Roberto D'Aubuisson, was the appeal the bishop made to the soldiers, shortly before being shot while celebrating Mass, not to obey orders to kill other Salvadorans. It is important to notice that before arguing that no soldier is obliged to obey an order against the law of God, Romero appealed to the value of family held by his people, "I would like to make an appeal in a special way to the men of the army, to the police, to those in the barracks. Brothers, you are part of our own people. You kill your own *campesino* brothers and sisters."

The goal of *familia* in Latina/o culture is to be a true home—*hogar*—where one belongs and is safe to be and become fully oneself. *Familia* for Latinas/os "is the central and most important institution in life."[34] Whether *familia* is a life-giving structure for us or, unfortunately, sometimes a source of repression and oppression, *familia* is a key marker of Latina communities. *Familia* is a duty but also, for most of us, it is a never-failing support system. From a very young age, Latinas begin to understand that because of our families we do not have to face the world alone. We are taught that precisely because the *familia* stands with us, we have a moral responsibility to each of its members who have invested so much in us by claiming us as their own. Who we are personally and what we do have repercussions for everyone in the *familia*. It is in the midst of *familia* and because of *familia* that at a very young age we are introduced to the ethical world of responsibilities and obligations, a world where one *is* because one is in relationship to others. In our *familias* we learn that persons are more important than ideas and that, therefore, we have to take time and care to cultivate family relationships.

For Latinas/os our honor—our value as persons—is intrinsically linked to the honor of our *familias*. We do not conceptualize ourselves as individuals but as persons in relationship with our families and friends. Our self-identity is not at all individualistic but rather is tied to our families, to the members of our extended families, many of whom, for those of us not born in the USA, are miles away in our countries of origin.[35] *Familia* relies on interdependence, not subsuming the person but making one realize that the members of our families enable us to be who we are. *Familia* provides the security needed to extend ourselves into the community and form the kind of personal relationships that are vital to us without losing our sense of self. In our families we learn that "as in a prism, reflection is also a refraction . . . [and that] the identity of the 'we' does not extinguish the 'I'; the Spanish word for 'we' is '*nosotros*,' which literally means 'we others,' a community of *otros* [and *otras*], or others."[36]

From a *mujerista* perspective the critique of the Latina/o understanding of family centers on the patriarchal aspects that are at the root of the sexism and homophobia of society. *Mujeristas* do not endorse the patriarchal family with its authoritarian and hierarchical structures. Neither does it endorse understanding family as being only those constituted by heterosexual couples. As a matter of fact, *familias* not centered in a heterosexual couple are plentiful in our

communities: *familias* headed by single mothers, by the mother and the grand-
mother or aunt, by a mother and a neighbor, and, more recently, by fathers and
the grandmothers, aunts, or sisters. Furthermore, we aim to support at all cost
the intrinsic value of each and every member of the family and denounce vehe-
mently any idea of the mother or any member of the family having to sacrifice
herself for the sake of other members of the family.

This *mujerista* critique of Latina families makes it clear that we are not proposing them as the referent or model for kin-dom of God. What we claim is that
familia denotes important values that must be part of a new world order and
that the importance of *familia* for our culture makes kin-dom of God have great
resonance in our communities.[37] The deep *nosotras/nosotros* made possible by
the ties of *familia*, the mutuality and reciprocity it entails, is at the heart of the
new world order that is intrinsic in the Gospel proclamation, which is precisely
why we believe kin-dom of God—*familia de Dios*—can function as a metaphor
for what Jesus referred to as the "kingdom of God."

"Family" in the Message of Jesus

Metaphors occur within a context and when the context changes, as it has from
the time of Jesus, the metaphors may/should change.

> . . . a change in preferred metaphor or notation is always a theoretical
> possibility, and indeed, Christian religious language like that of any
> other religious tradition is a mobile thing, responsive to the needs and
> perceptions of religious adherents . . . Talk of the Christian as "slave
> of Christ" or "slave of God" which enjoyed some popularity in the
> Pauline Epistles and the early Church is now scarcely used, despite its
> biblical warrant, by contemporary Christians, who have little under-
> standing for or sympathy with the institution of slavery and the figures
> of speech it generates.[38]

The fact that "kingdom of God" has remained the governing metaphor for
Jesus' vision of a world order centered on justice and peace, speaks more to the
interests of those who exercise power in the churches—institutionalized Christianity—than to the relevance it has in the lives of the common people, of the
people of God. The claim that "kingdom of God" is a metaphor that cannot
be changed indicates a literalist understanding of the Scriptures that "equates
religious truth with historical facts," that is, with what Jesus said.[39]

A metaphor almost always introduces or discloses new elements.[40] The
analogous metaphor we are proposing—kin-dom of God—contributes a new
understanding of the gospel message not by adding alien elements to the Gospels but by looking at them through a different lens. Kin-dom of God as a metaphor includes the meaning that "kingdom" had for Jesus and his community
while neither endorsing nor sustaining the oppressive understandings that have

been added to it throughout history. "Kingdom of God" in the time of Jesus and the early Christian communities and kin-dom of God today are religious metaphors and as such they evoke "an emotional, moral, or spiritual response," and also perform an explanatory function. They are "action guiding" metaphors because they are "reality depicting."[41] It is precisely because "kingdom of God" is not any longer "reality depicting" in the twenty-first century, and because it has been used to endorse understandings that are anti-Gospel, that we instead propose kin-dom of God.

Can kin-dom of God be rooted in the Scriptures? It is true that in the Old Testament there are few instances of a kinship title being used to refer to God. It does happen, for example, in the Song of Moses in Deut 32:6: "Is he not your father, who created you, who made you and established you?" A few verses later the mothering and mother images are also used, "You were unmindful of the Rock that begot you, and you forgot the God who gave you birth" (Deut 32:11, 18). In contrast with the sparse number of Old Testament texts that use kinship imagery when referring to God are the 170 times that God is addressed or described as "father" by Jesus, and God "is never invoked in prayer by any other title."[42] For the Old Testament writers, the idea that we should be kin to God seemed preposterous. Yet in the New Testament, the idea of humans being kin to God is considered quite usual. This use of kin metaphors to talk about the relationship between humans and God has been quite common in Christianity from the beginning. Perhaps it became so common that the deep meaning of the metaphor, the mutuality between humans and God that is intrinsic to being kin, was lost or diminished. It seems to have been feminist attempts to speak about God as mother that reawakened the true meaning of kin metaphors and highlighted the fact that "the principal reason why the biblical writings are so dependent on gendered imagery (a dependency which increases as we move from the Old to the New Testament) is not because its writers were so very interested in sex, or even hierarchy and subordination, but because they were interested in kinship."[43]

Q, the compilation of sayings of Jesus written in Greek that has not survived as a separate document, includes eleven references to "kingdom of God." Since there is no explanation of this expression, one can conclude that it was a common term in the communities from which Q emerged. Though this has not been the central scholarly debate concerning Q, contemporary biblical scholars, particularly feminist biblical scholars, are interested in Q uses of "kingdom of God" "to seek out ideological kinship."[44] "Kingdom of God" is used by Q to refer to a different world order from the one imposed by the Roman Empire on Palestine in the first century C.E.: "the Q people endeavored to imagine and construct an alternate reality to the dominant social institutions of their immediate context and moral values."[45] The metaphor "kingdom of God" associates an alternative or new world order, "a particular ethos (or emerging social formation)," with the history of Israel.[46] This alternative world order is imaged as human kinship with God, thus introducing the family unit as the frame of reference for understanding what "kingdom of God" refers to or connotes. The kinship of humans with God found in Q is not to be read having the modern atomized family as the point of reference but rather having the family of Jesus' time, as "a socio-political frame of reference." Furthermore, the sense of family behind the kinship between God and humans clearly did not resemble the Roman *paterfamilias,* which replicated and sustained the world order of the empire. This kin of God that Q offers has justice as a central value. It is a family in which "the sick are healed and the poor receive good news . . . [and] those who have no justice receive justice."[47] What motivates those who are God's kin is inclusion, not exclusion.

How could Jesus and his followers "make a difference in the world of 1st century Palestine? If peasants were no longer bound to the temple system with the incessant demands for tithes and offerings, they were better able to maintain the kinship networks on which their survival depended." But the link to the Temple through tithes and offerings of the peasants was their way of keeping the covenant. Perhaps Jesus is trying to offer another way of keeping the covenant when he summarizes the Torah in the love of God and love of neighbor commandment (Mark 12:28-34). His listener includes the following phrase in summarizing what he has just heard from Jesus, "This is much more important than all whole burnt-offerings and sacrifices" (v. 33b). Here

> love of neighbor trumps the demands of the temple . . . How then is love of neighbor to be shown? In offering forgiveness and cancellation of debts. The chief danger caused by Herodian control was that villagers would be tempted to mimic the behavior of their rulers. This meant using debt to gain control over others and, in pursuing this course of action, breaking down the kinship ties of the village and the commitment of neighbors to each other.[48]

Villagers needed to love one another instead of seeking to control by indebtedness. They needed to develop a sense of "open sharing based on generosity or need."[49] This necessitates the kind of reciprocity found in "kinship groups, or fictive kinship groups, where members regard each other as family." Since the clan or extended family had disappeared from Palestine, the village could replace it, but for this to happen, "peasants had to forge new ties and regard each other in a new light. Jesus models this possibility when he redefines the meaning of kinship in his own family."[50]

Jesus' sentiments in Mark 3:31-34 and in Matthew 8:21-22 are not to be read as antifamily sentiments. Instead, these passages could be understood as a way of imbuing in his disciples a sense of kin among themselves. These texts can be read as Jesus focusing on the importance of family and expanding who is included in his family rather than as an attempt to weaken or discard family. To constitute his disciples as kin, with God as Father, can be read also as a way for Jesus to counter the Roman Empire's societal organization that had the emperor as father. This could well have been Jesus' way of challenging the power of the empire.[51]

The fact is that ties to one's family were intrinsic to one's personal identity (Mark 6:3). Then, we might ask, why do the Gospels give us so little information about the family of Jesus? It could very well be that when the Gospels were written knowledge about Jesus' birth family was common and there was no need to write about it.[52] Perhaps, the lack of information about his birth family points to Jesus' "undoing-redoing" of family, because, if it is true that the Gospels give little information about his birth kin, they give us ample information about his newly constituted kin—giving us specifics about many of his disciples and particularly about the worldview he preached to them and which he lived.

Consider the answer of Jesus to Mark 6:3, "Is not this the carpenter, the son of Mary and brother of James and Joses and Judas and Simon, and are not his sisters here with us?" This query centers his identity in his birth family, but the answer (Mark 6:4) extends what he understands as family: "Prophets are not without honor, except in their home town, and among their own kin, and in their own house." Here Jesus roots himself not only in his household (immediate family) but also in kin and village.[53] Can this not be read as part of his "redoing" family and recapturing the importance of kin and village in order to distance the people and himself from the Roman Empire? Is this not also what is at play in the repeated use of household or family and village in Jesus parables? Of course their use was because of the familiarity his audiences had with them. However, if family and village had lost or were losing importance because of the way empire/Temple worked to diminish their centrality in people's lives, was the repeated use by Jesus of images of family and village a way of recapturing the importance of family while redefining its characteristics?

In some texts in the Gospels Jesus seems to be by himself, without any place to rest his head (Matthew 8:20; Luke 9:58). In these texts, "the images used of the foxes and the birds and the terminology used of their dwellings indicate that they have permanent dwellings, something that was the sign of human society, a mark of civilization."[54] Can this be read not merely as a statement of fact but as an attempt by Jesus to signal that he was moving outside the world order of the empire/Temple?

In constituting the community of his followers as family, as a fictive kin, Jesus is confronting the established world order of first-century Palestine.[55] The key texts from which we draw this understanding are Mark 3:31-35 (Matthew 12:46-50; Luke 8:19-21) and Mark 10:29-30. These texts invite people to leave their households or families in order to become part of a new kin. Mark 3:31-35 pictures Jesus' blood relatives outside the household and his new kin inside with him. His brothers and his sisters are the ones who are surrounding him inside the house, people not related to him by blood. What constitutes them as kin is doing the will of God. In Mark 10:29-30 the hundredfold that is a sign of the "kingdom" includes mothers, brothers, sisters, and children—an increment in the new kin gathered around Jesus.[56] This new kin is the one that will live according to the teachings of Jesus, according to the values that are constitutive of a new world order.

Given that he makes no mention of fathers when he proclaims that those
who do the will of God are ones that are his kin or when he promises new
members for his kin, Jesus' concept of kin is a critique of the organization and
practices of family in Palestine during his lifetime. Jesus used the imagery of
family and the relatedness embedded in family to portray the new world order.
He imbued his kin with new values: to forgive and to love one another as a sign
of their relationship with the Covenant. To establish a new kin was central to
Jesus' mission: bringing about a new world order that begins to make present
the kin-dom of God.

Conclusion

Kin-dom of God very much hinges on the way Jesus molded his disciples
into his new kin. Kin-dom as metaphor can be valuable in helping to create a
contemporary understanding of the world order that Jesus worked and died
for. It values kinship without canonizing the patriarchal family. It moves away
from the elitist and authoritarian characteristics of kingdoms and empires and
focuses instead on relationality and mutuality. It highlights forgiveness and
love as values characteristic of the new world order. Being a fictive kinship, it
rejects exclusion and instead endorses inclusion of new members as a blessing, that is, as part of the hundredfold. The proposal of using kin-dom as a
metaphor for the new world order that Jesus brought to the world opens new
perspectives, new vistas as to how to live the Gospel message of justice and
peace in our world in the twenty-first century. Kin-dom resonates with today's
societies where families continue to be a central institution. Kin-dom of God
also provides an impetus for reconstituting families not as an authoritarian
and patriarchal institution but one that protects each member and provides
a warm space for constituting lasting relationships. Kin-dom of God brings
new understandings that strengthen the sense of mutuality, justice, and peace
to Christian communities and to society at large.

Notes

1. Elisabeth Schüssler Fiorenza, *Rhetoric and Ethics: The Politics of Biblical Interpretation* (Minneapolis: Fortress, 1999), 17-30._
2. William C. Spohn, *What Are They Saying about Scripture and Ethics?* (New
York: Paulist Press, 1995), 7.
3. My use of metaphor in this article is parallel to Norman Perrin's use of "tensive
symbol." See his book, *Jesus and the Language of the Kingdom: Symbol and Metaphor
in New Testament Interpretation* (Philadelphia: Fortress Press, 1976).
4. Janet Martin Soskice, *Metaphor and Religious Language* (Oxford: Clarendon
Press, 1985), 66.
5. Ibid.

6. My understanding of metaphors and how they operate is based on Soskice's very complete discussion in the book cited above.

7. Perrin, *Jesus and the Language of the Kingdom*, 197.

8. For an elaboration of the meaning and use of *lo cotidiano*, see Ada María Isasi-Díaz, "Lo Cotidiano—Everyday Struggles in Hispanas/Latinas' Lives," in *La Lucha Continues: Mujerista Theology* (Maryknoll, N.Y.: Orbis Books, 2004), 92-106.

9. Soskice, *Metaphor*, 57-58.

10. Melanie Johnson-DeBaufre, *Jesus among Her Children—Q, Eschatology, and the Construction of Christian Origins*, Theological Studies 55 (Cambridge, Mass.: Harvard University Press, 2005), 24.

11. The difficulties of understanding what God wanted Israel's political organization to be, as indicated in 1 Samuel 8, serves as an important background for the disciples' lack of appreciation of what Jesus meant by "kingdom of God." Contrary to the views expressed in this text are pro-monarchical texts like the one immediately following the anti-monarchical text, 1 Sam 9-10:2.

12. Soskice, *Metaphor*, 85-86.

13. Romans 14:17 can be considered the closest to a definition: "For the kingdom of God is not food and drink but righteousness and peace and joy in the Holy Spirit." Benedict T. Viviano, OP, *The Kingdom of God in History* (Wilmington, Del.: Michael Glazier, 1988), 18. Viviano presents a quite complete history of how kingdom of God has been used and interpreted. See also Norman Perrin, *The Kingdom of God in the Teaching of Jesus* (Philadelphia: Westminster Press, 1963); and idem, *Jesus and the Language of the Kingdom*.

14 Viviano, *Kingdom of God in History*, 14-15, 21-22.

15. Soskice, *Metaphor*, 116.

16. I believe "kingdom of God" is irrelevant to and carries erroneous connotations for the vast majority of Christians. I limit myself here to a *mujerista* perspective, but it is my hope that other communities will come to recognize the need to change this metaphor.

17. I use as a guide for the history of Israel, John Bright, *A History of Israel*, 4th ed. (Louisville: Westminster John Knox, 2000).

18. Lisa Isherwood, *Liberating Christ* (Cleveland: Pilgrim Press, 1999), 133.

19. I follow here the way that Herzog deals with the Scriptures. My intent is to draw as close as possible to Jesus' and the Gospel writers' understanding of kingdom. Of course this study is very much influenced by *mujerista* hermeneutics (explained below), which serve as a lens through which I read the data I gather. I do not consider *mujerista* hermeneutics to be a closed system but rather understand it as being open to corrections, deletions, and additions, particularly those suggested by a careful study of the biblical texts. See William R. Herzog II, *Jesus, Justice, and the Reign of God: A Ministry of Liberation* (Louisville: Westminster John Knox, 2000), 34-46.

20. Herzog, *Jesus, Justice, and the Reign of God*, especially 103-5.

21. The Gospels have many "conflict stories" indicating these struggles of Jesus. See Herzog, *Jesus, Justice, and the Reign of God*, 123-43, 168-90.

22. Isherwood, *Liberating Christ*, 133. This is not the place to engage the rich and never-ending discussion regarding the eschatological/beyond this world "feel," to use Isherwood's term, and its predominance at the time of Jesus. From an ethical and theological perspective I take the view that in Jesus' teaching as reported by the New Testament writers, there is an eschatological tension—the kingdom here but not yet fully here.

23. Dennis C. Duling, "The Kingdom of God in the Teaching of Jesus," *Word and World—Theology for Christian Ministry*, 2, no. 2 (Spring 1982): 117-18.

24. Ibid.

25. Gustavo Gutiérrez, *A Theology of Liberation*, 2nd ed. (Maryknoll, N.Y.: Orbis Books, 1988), 99, 100-101.

26. Ibid., 101.

27. Jon Sobrino, *Jesus in Latin America* (Maryknoll, N.Y.: Orbis Books, 1987), 83. For a thorough analysis of the "kingdom of God" from a Latin American liberation theology perspective, see Juan Luis Segundo, *The Historical Jesus in the Synoptics* (Maryknoll, N.Y.: Orbis Books, 1985), particularly part 2.

28. For a fuller analysis of *mujerista* hermeneutics, see Ada María Isasi-Díaz, "*La Palabra de Dios En Nosotras*—The Word of God in Us," in *Searching the Scriptures: A Feminist Introduction*, ed. Elisabeth Schüssler Fiorenza (New York: Crossroads, 1993), 86-97.

29. Leonardo Boff makes clear that critical thinking must trump the dogmatic. See Leonardo Boff, *Jesus Christ Liberator: A Critical Christology for Our Time*, trans. Patrick Hughes (Maryknoll, N.Y.: Orbis Books, 1994), 45.

30. Richard A. Horsley, *Jesus in Context: Power, People, and Performance* (Minneapolis: Fortress, 2008), 14.

31. Johnson-DeBaufre, *Jesus among Her Children*, 4.

32. I first heard kin-dom from Georgenne Wilson, a Franciscan nun from Wheaton, Illinois, in the second half of the 1970s.

33. For an earlier exploration of kin-dom of God, see Ada María Isasi-Díaz, "*Identificate con Nosotras: A Mujerista* Christological Understanding," in *La Lucha Continues*, 243-51.

34. Roberto R. Álvarez, Jr., "The Family," in *The Hispanic American Almanac*, ed. Nicolas Kanellas (Washington, D.C.: Gale Research, 1993), 155.

35. Judge Sonia Sotomayor's remarks when President Barack Obama announced he was nominating her to be a Justice of the Supreme Court make this point so poignantly: "The president has said to you that I bring my family. In the audience is my brother, Juan Sotomayor—he's a physician in Syracuse, New York; my sister-in-law, Tracey; my niece, Kylie—she looks like me. My twin nephews, Conner and Corey. I stand on the shoulders of countless people, yet there is one extraordinary person who is my life aspiration. That person is my mother, Celina Sotomayor. My mother has devoted her life to my brother and me. And as the president mentioned, she worked often two jobs to help support us after dad died. I have often said that I am all I am because of her, and I am only half the woman she is. Sitting next to her is Omar Lopez, my mom's husband and a man whom I have grown to adore. I thank you for all that you have given me and continue to give me. I love you." http://www.whitehouse.gov/the-press-office/remarks-president-nominating-judge-sonia-sotomayor-united-states-supreme-court; accessed, April 15, 2010.

36. Roberto Goizueta, "*Nosotros*: Toward a U.S. Hispanic Anthropology," *Listening—Journal of Religion and Culture* 27, no. 1 (Winter 1992): 57.

37. In no way am I implicating that this is not true for other cultures.

38. Janet Martin Soskice, *The Kindness of God: Metaphors, Gender, and Religious Language* (Oxford: Oxford University Press, 2007), 68.

39. Soskice, *Metaphor*, 160.

40. Ibid., 90. This is a catachrestical function, as explained in the first part of this article. Today we would refer to what the Gospels call "kingdom of God," as world order. The use of "kingdom" to refer to something other than a political reign is a cata-

chresis; it supplies "a term where one is lacking in the vocabulary" (Soskice, *Metaphor*, 61). However, naming a reality always carries implications and affects the way the reality is understood. So the catachrestical function always uncovers or ascribes new insights.

41. Soskice, *Metaphor*, 109-12.

42. Robert Hamerton-Kelly, "God, the Father in the Bible and in the Experience of Jesus: The State of the Question," in *God as Father?*, ed. J. B. Metz, E. Schillebeeckx, and M. Lefébure (Edinburgh: T&T Clark, 1981), 96-98.

43. Soskice, *Kindness of God*, 4. Of course *mujerista* theology has problems with the exclusive use of "Father" when referring to God. My point here is to consider the kin relationship that the use of such a term signals. I am also aware that "the evidence that Jesus applied the title 'Father' to God is slight." Also, "the use of the Aramaic *abba* does not support a specialized meaning conveying the intimacy between father and child," does not mean that *abba* is disconnected from the structure of kinship. See Kathleen E. Corley, "Gender and Class in the Teaching of Jesus: A Profile," in *Profiles of Jesus*, ed. Roy W. Hoover (Santa Rosa, Calif.: Polebridge, 2002), 153-59. See also Mary Rose D'Angelo, "Theology in Mark and Q: 'Abba' and 'Father' in Context," *Harvard Theological Review* 85 (1992): 149-74; and eadem, "'Abba' and 'Father': Imperial Theology and the Jesus Traditions," *Journal of Biblical Literature* 111 (1992): 611-30.

44. Johnson-DeBaufre, *Jesus among Her Children*, 23.

45. Leif E. Vaage, *Galilean Upstarts: Jesus' First Followers according to Q* (Valley Gorge, Pa.: Trinity, 1994), as cited in Johnson-DeBaufre, *Jesus among Her Children*, 23.

46. Michael L. Humphries, *Christian Origins and the Language of the Kingdom of God* (Carbondale: Southern Illinois University Press, 1999), 45.

47. Johnson-DeBaufre, *Jesus among Her Children*, 67.

48. Herzog, *Jesus, Justice, and the Reign of God*, 213.

49. Bruce Malina and Richard Rohrbaugh, *Social Science Commentary on the Synoptic Gospels* (Minneapolis: Fortress, 1992), 246, cited in Herzog, *Jesus, Justice, and the Reign of God*, 213.

50. Herzog, *Jesus, Justice, and the Reign of God*, 213.

51. Halvor Moxnes, *Putting Jesus in His Place: A Radical Vision of Household and Kingdom* (Louisville: Westminster John Knox, 2003), 3. Moxnes's work has proven to be key for the arguments in this article but I do not always draw the same conclusions he does.

52. Ibid., 30.

53. Ibid., 33.

54. Ibid., 51. Moxnes uses Q12:24 and Gospel of Thomas 86 as the source for these texts; instead I have used the Gospel sources. My conclusion about Jesus not buying into the world order of his day is in line with what Moxnes proposes but pushes in a somewhat different direction. Moxnes also considers Mark 6:4 along these same lines of Jesus not acting as someone from Nazareth usually acts to indicate that Jesus "breaks out of the mold and will not be limited by the place defined by his lineage and household. He opts to stay outside of it" (ibid., 53). I would read this as Jesus opting to go beyond the constituted world order of his time.

55. Ibid., 114.

56. Ibid., 61.

Index